Search for the Lost Trail of CRAZY HORSE

ISBN 1-886225-50-8

Thomas Hart Benton painting on the cover. Museum of Nebraska Art, Kearney, Nebraska;
        Sunflower and Buffalo,
Julie Walstrom, Lincoln, Nebraska,
        artwork on the back of the cover: *The Spirit Riders in the Sky.*
David Hammett, Marysville, Kansas, made maps and symbols.
Marilyn Janovec, Niobrara, Nebraska,
        art teacher to the Sioux, White, and Ponca people, made symbols.

Editor in Chief: Jacquelyn Carter
Editors: Rosemary Walstrom, Sheila Reiter, Jeff Morris, Barbara Sladky, Linda Dageforde,
        and Meghan Sittler
Cover design: Rebecca Johnson

Library of Congress Cataloging-in-Publication Data
Walstrom, Cleve, 1952-
    Search for the lost trail of Crazy Horse / Cleve Walstrom.
        p. cm.
Includes bibliographical references (p.   ) and index.
    ISBN 1-886225-50-8 (alk. paper)
    1. Crazy Horse, ca. 1842-1877--Death and burial. 2. Oglala
Indians--History. 3. Teton Indians--History. 4. Teton
Indians--Interviews. I. Title.
    E99.O3C729446 2003
    978.004'975--dc21

                                                                20030115

Dageforde Publishing, Inc.
128 East 13th Street
Crete, Nebraska 68333
1-800-216-8794
www.dageforde.com

Printed in the United States of America
10 9 8 7 6 5 4 3 2 1

Dedicated to those who have lost a son
and to those who have a son.
May you both have feeling for the spirit.

Contents

Crazy Horse's Genealogy Tree viii

Introduction 1

Part One: The Death of Crazy Horse 9

1 KILI and the Green Highway Sign 11

2 Search for the Burial Sites of Sioux Nation Chiefs 17

3 Conquering Bear and the Sandoz Girls 19

4 Visions of a Hard Road 23

5 Ambrose Red Owl on the Santee 26

6 The Black Elks of Wounded Knee Valley 28

7 Close Calls and the Conflict Within 33

8 Beckoned to the Battle Site at the Little Bighorn and Dowsing for Gravesites 39

9 Crazy Horse and the Battle of Little Bighorn—Was He Late? 47

10 The Aftermath of Little Bighorn: Another New Treaty
and the March to Camp Robinson 53

11 The Conspiracy against Crazy Horse as Reported
by Indian Scouts Frank Grouard and A.G. Shaw 58

12 The Final Days 62

13 Who Wielded the Bayonet? 68

14 Dr. McGillycuddy's Account of the Death of Crazy Horse 74

15 Final Reflections 77

16 In Crazy Horse's Territory and the Story of an Olympic Athlete 79

17 Mourning a Lost Son 84

18 The Crazy Horse Legend: Larger than a Mountain 87

19 We Pause to Look Back at the Setting Sun 89

20 In the Area of the Burial Grounds 94

Part Two: The Burial of Crazy Horse 97

21   The Feather of a Hawk 99

22   Bradley's Opinion—Wounded Knee is the Crazy Horse Burial Site 104

23   The Green Highway Sign: Four Possible Burial Sites 106

24   The Beaver Creek Theory 120

25   At Camp Sheridan on Beaver Creek 128

26   In the Pine Ridge Area 138

27   The Rosebud Reservation 162

28   The Missouri River 177

29   Basketball on the Rez and the Chicken Coop Diaries 207

30   South Central South Dakota 215

31   The Circle of Life: From Birth to Death 227

32   Where the Spirit Rests 237

References 248

Personal Contacts 254

Index 261

And to Dr. V.A. Walstrom...
The spirit of your guiding eagle circled on clear days
and showed me the way on partly cloudy crescent moon nights.
I simply followed.

CRAZY HORSE'S GENEALOGY

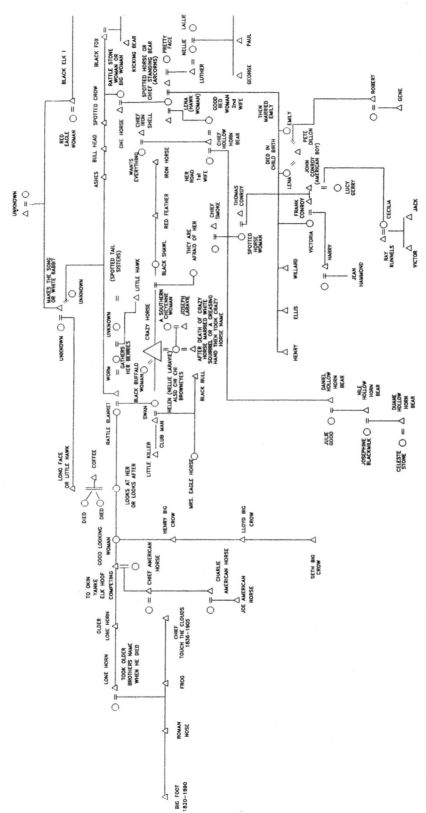

OTHER NAMES OF CRAZY HORSE

1) COLT TAIL
2) CURLY
3) YELLOW FUZZY HAIR
4) LIGHT HAIR
5) HORSE STANDS IN SIGHT
6) HIS HORSE IS CRAZY (REAL NAME AFTER 1861)
7) BUYS A BAD WOMAN (1861 TEMPORARY NAME AFTER AFFAIR WITH BLACK BUFFALO WOMAN)
8) HIS HORSE IS CRAZY (IS TRUE NAME OF CRAZY HORSE)

Crazy Horse's Genealogy CONTINUED

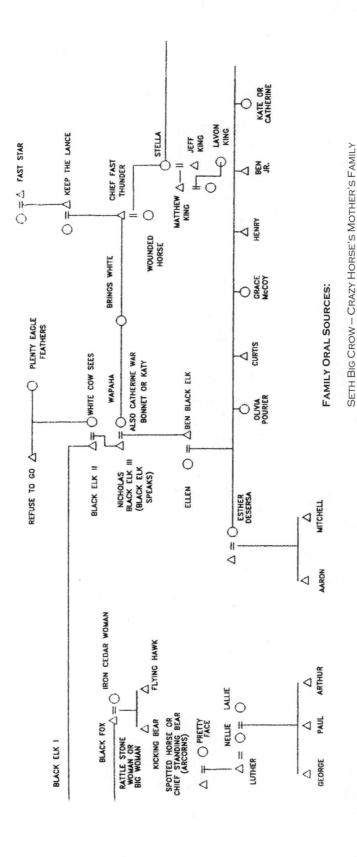

FAMILY ORAL SOURCES:

SETH BIG CROW – CRAZY HORSE'S MOTHER'S FAMILY
GENE DILLON – STANDING BEAR FAMILY
LILLIAN FIRETHUNDER – FASTER THUNDER
ESTHER DESERSA – BLACK ELK FAMILY
JACK RUNNELS – CONROY FAMILY
BARBARA ADAMS – FAST THUNDER
JEAN HAMMOND – CONROY AND BIG WOMAN FAMILY
DUANE HOLLOW HORN BEAR – IRON SHELL FAMILY
DARLENE ROSANE – AMERICAN HORSE FAMILY
MARTY FROG – TOUCH THE CLOUDS FAMILY

CRAZY HORSE'S GENEALOGY CONTINUED

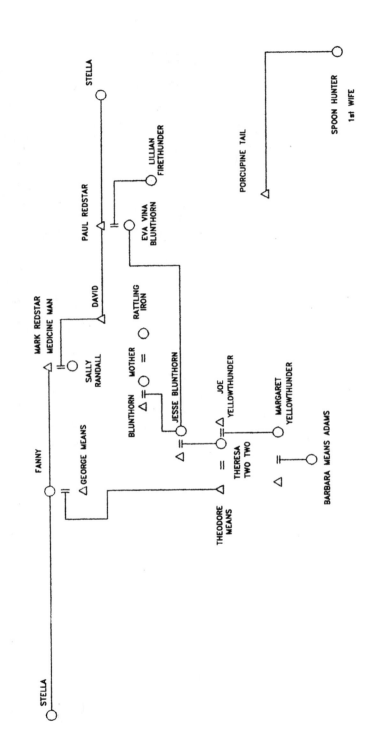

WRITTEN SOURCES

LUTHER STANDING BEAR — STANDING BEAR
ELMARIA LITTLE SPOTTED HORSE (INDIAN COUNTRY TODAY)
RICHARD HARDORFF — DEATH OF CRAZY HORSE — LONE HORN FAMILY
FOOLS CROW — FOOLS CROW
NATIVE AMERICAN TESTIMONY — HOLLOW HORN BEAR
MARI SANDOZ — NOTES
BLACK ELK SPEAKS — BLACK ELK
HE DOG AND HINMAN — INTERVIEWS

CRAZY HORSE'S GENEALOGY CONTINUED

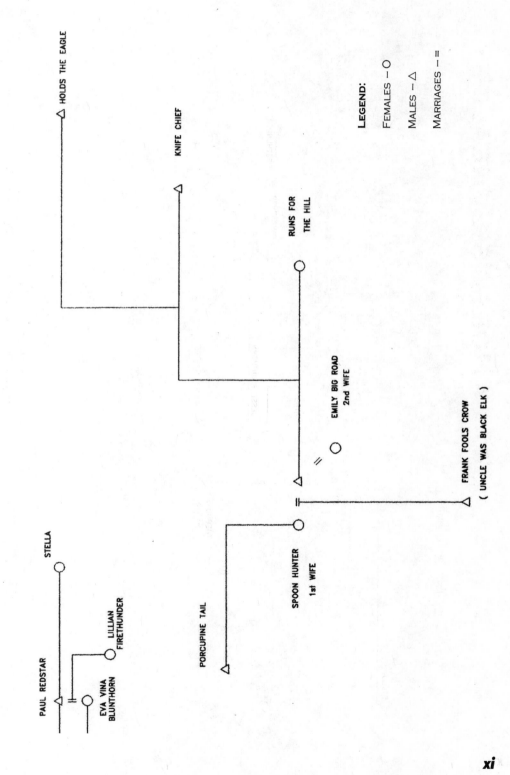

LEGEND:

FEMALES — ○

MALES — △

MARRIAGES — =

HOLDS THE EAGLE

KNIFE CHIEF

RUNS FOR THE HILL

EMILY BIG ROAD
2nd WIFE

FRANK FOOLS CROW
(UNCLE WAS BLACK ELK)

STELLA

PAUL REDSTAR

LILLIAN FIRETHUNDER

EVA VINA BLUNTHORN

PORCUPINE TAIL

SPOON HUNTER
1st WIFE

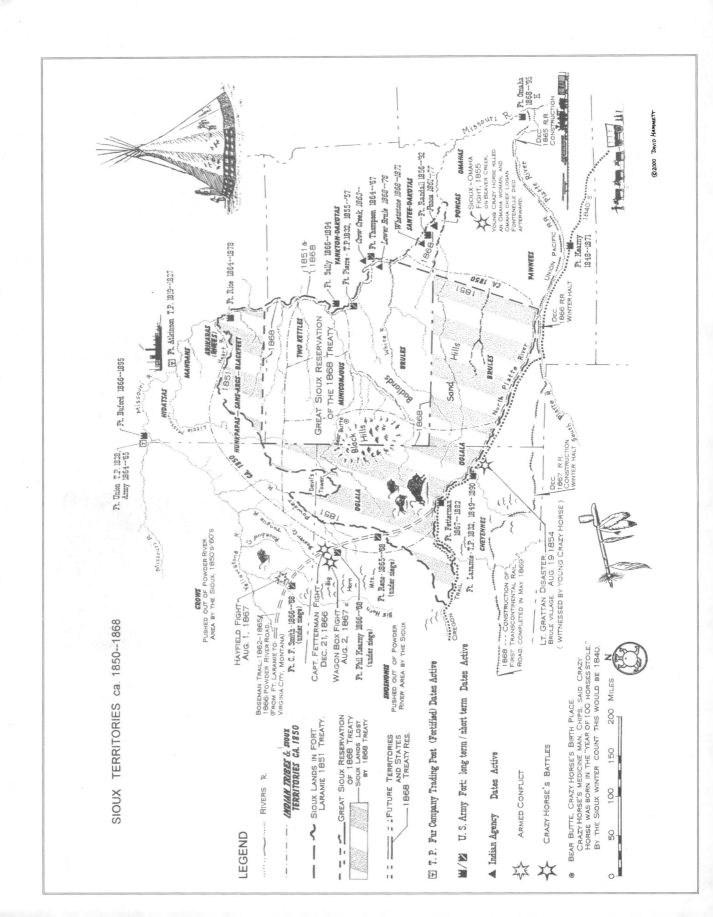

SIOUX TERRITORIES ca. 1850–1868

LEGEND

...... RIVERS R.

INDIAN TRIBES & SIOUX TERRITORIES CA. 1850

— — — SIOUX LANDS IN FORT LARAMIE 1851 TREATY

GREAT SIOUX RESERVATION OF 1868 TREATY

SIOUX LANDS LOST BY 1868 TREATY

= = = : FUTURE TERRITORIES AND STATES 1868 TREATY RES.

T.P. Fur Company Trading Post (Fortified) Dates Active

U.S. Army Fort: long term / short term   Dates Active

▲ Indian Agency   Dates Active

✶ Armed Conflict

✶ Crazy Horse's Battles

◉ BEAR BUTTE, CRAZY HORSE'S BIRTH PLACE.
CRAZY HORSE'S MEDICINE MAN, CHIPS, SAID CRAZY
HORSE WAS BORN IN THE "YEAR OF 100 HORSES STOLE."
BY THE SIOUX WINTER COUNT THIS WOULD BE 1840.

| SCALE |
| 0 50 100 150 200 MILES |

©2000 DAVID HUMMETT

Introduction

I'm not sure why the spirit of Crazy Horse would seek out and touch a white man. Crazy Horse did not like white men because they encroached upon his beloved wide-open prairie. He detested their developments that chased away the buffalo his people depended on for food and clothing. The moccasins the great warrior wore when he rode to protect his land, the sinew used for sewing, the bones for tools, needles, shovels and hoes, all came from the buffalo. When the cold came roaring down on the Plains, the buffalo faced those raging winds with its head into the white storm as if it were cleansing itself from hardship and discomfort. Those were the same winds blowing against Crazy Horse's face as the footprints of white men more and more stamped across the land.

Plenty has been written about Crazy Horse—most of it about the time of his killing at Camp Robinson, Nebraska. Many have speculated about what happened to him after his death. A green South Dakota state highway sign near

Pristine look in the Sandhills. Cleve Walstrom stands in the Dismal River land where Crazy Horse went to escape the soldiers who found it difficult to follow his trail through shifting sand.

Wounded Knee, South Dakota, lists the four possible burial sites of Crazy Horse. After hours of reading fragile army archive reports and many other published accounts, and from Lakota oral history and families' stories, I have found many more than those four.

Crazy Horse lived under the generous western sky. He was a Lakota Sioux and a member of the Hunkpatilia Crescent Moon band. His people set their camp up in the shape of that moon, and Crazy Horse would camp at the end of that crescent.

There are six other tribes, or campfires, of the Lakota Sioux: the Oglala (Scattering of the Ashes), of which Crazy Horse's father was a member; his mother's tribe, the Sichangu, or Brulé (Burned Thighs); the Itazichipo (Without Bows); the Minneconjou (Plant Beside the Stream); the Sihasapa (Black Feet); and the Ooenunpa (Two Boiling Kettles). At different times, Crazy Horse hunted with many of these bands. The Lakota Sioux were those who camped west of the Missouri River, and the Dakota Sioux were those located on the eastern side.

I was touched by the spirit of Crazy Horse as a young man. As a youth I observed the image of Crazy Horse being carved on a mountain in South Dakota, such a huge memorial to a great warrior. Yet I was told that no one knew where he was buried, or at least that it was a closely guarded secret of a few of his people. Why? I wondered. It did not really haunt me; that is, it did not haunt me until I helped my father write a book about Sioux chiefs and we found several locations where he might possibly be buried. Where was he, or was that something I shouldn't know?

The information I'd gathered, and kept gathering, on Crazy Horse was more than we could—or should have—put in my dad's book. We kept finding stories of where Crazy Horse "was buried," or "might be buried." And since my dad's death in March 1997, connections to the stories keep finding me. It's time now to tell about my travels and the wonderful people I have met along the way. I have come across more than twenty different locations where Crazy Horse might have been buried or is buried. The mystery to all of us is which of those areas is the most likely burial ground—or is there even more to it than that? One thing I have learned is that once I began to solicit stories with the intention of publishing them, the stories got better, I listened to them more closely, and the conversations—with inevitable connections to other stories and other tellers—became much more interesting.

I grew up traveling across the Santee and Yankton Sioux Reservations helping my father tend to his veterinary calls. I suppose it was when I helped my father catch and vaccinate the dogs and animals that belonged to the Sioux that I began to understand his appreciation for their culture, their spirituality and search for the circle of life. In my quest, if I have not come face to face with the spirit of Crazy Horse, then surely I have been given a special feeling from many people who are in the Crazy Horse *tiyospaye* (family). It is here that I began to understand the care the parents had for a son who came to the end of his earthly trail. These people have taken me on a journey beyond where Crazy Horse was killed at Camp Robinson, to the rising sun, to where the wind blows, to the source of water, and then to where the cleansing winds are. Let me take you to the Plains where the spirits have spoken.

The Start of the Journey

In 1970, when I was a still a student at a small high school in northern Nebraska near the border of the Santee Sioux Reservation, I applied for a job at a mortuary in Lincoln, two hundred miles from home. I was visiting colleges I thought I might want to attend. I'd been out almost all night on a Thursday, and was driving by Roper's Mortuary when it occurred to me that I was going to need a job for the summer. At 7:30 A.M. there was activity around the mortuary, so I just walked in. A guy named Glen told me the fellow who did the hiring would be there in about an hour. At a friend's house, I got a quick shower and some fresh clothes and was back at Roper's at 9:00 A.M. I visited with Max Roper for about fifteen minutes and he asked if I had any teachers who would give me references. "I'm not sure," I replied. "My girlfriend's father is the school superintendent and sometimes I don't get her home before his nine o'clock curfew on Saturday night. My art teacher is my mom; she would give me a good reference, but you wouldn't want to hear about it. But I do get along with my principal, Mr. Glen Moon, pretty well." Max quickly said, "Glen Moon and I were best buddies in college. We played football at Nebraska Wesleyan; he was fast on foot and one of the most brilliant men I ever met. If you hit it off with Glen Moon, that's all I need to know. We have an opening for a student resident this summer; you're hired."

This was the first of many critical connections—some of them almost mystical—that would lead me through my life in the funeral business and my journey in pursuit of the trails left by the legendary Lakota Sioux warrior, Crazy Horse. Max Roper was a good guiding light, and I appreciate the times he had to adjust the light to show this young man the way of understanding people and funerals.

After my internship at Roper's, I was invited to work in a mortuary in Marysville, Kansas, by a college classmate. Jon Padden and I have been in partnership for almost twenty-seven years now, and I'm grateful to him for keeping that light burning, and for taking up the slack while I have been following Crazy Horse's afterlife.

People enter the funeral business to help others, as well as themselves, understand the loss of a loved one. I have spent thirty years trying to find ways to help folks who are grieving ask for guidance. Part of my search is about the grieving and coping process a Lakota mother and father had for their son when he met his death.

My own father was a veterinarian in general practice for more than fifty years. He liked to take time off from ranch calls to stop and wander through country cemeteries. As a kid, I'd explore them with him. Somewhere in our wanderings, my dad observed that there was no published record of the burial sites of Sioux chiefs. It was my mom who suggested that he research and write that record; he had already gathered plenty of stories about Indian burials and interesting gravesites. Her suggestion was also motivated by the thought that it would act as therapy to keep his mind off his ailments. I often accompanied him through South Dakota and western Nebraska with its wide-open and untouched miles of beauty, clean air, and friendly Native American people who shared so much with him. I always felt humbled by their kindness and regard for my father. He wrote that the Dakotas had called him and he could not stay away.

Time after time, he was mysteriously rescued from adversity—almost as though unseen spirits protectively surrounded him. On his journey, he heard stories of great courageous people and their triumphs and tragedies; some of them were the victims of the white man's greed and treachery.

As my father's health declined, it was time to stop researching and to publish his book, *My Search for the Burial Sites of Sioux Nation Chiefs*. Dad encouraged me to write some of the stories we'd accumulated about Crazy Horse that, to our knowledge, had never been heard by the public. He didn't have to tell me twice; I was off and running, researching and writing. After I decided to continue his research, the stories about Crazy Horse often seemed to flow to me. Around every corner, it seemed, I would run into someone who had information or a story to share, many of which I had never heard or read anywhere else.

This book is divided into two parts: Part I, which deals with understanding what Crazy Horse stood and died for; and Part II, which tells of the burial stories of Crazy Horse and the mystery of what happened to him after his death at Camp Robinson in northwestern Nebraska. There has never been a problem having enough to write about; I have found that the problem has been sorting out and trying to order the stories of the events that occurred after the death of Crazy Horse. This is the result.

Search for Burial Sites

In April 1999, I was invited to speak at Sinte Gleska University in Mission, South Dakota, about my father's book on Sioux chiefs. The instructor, Victor Douville, asked me to explain how my father had researched his information about the chiefs. Victor has been consulted by film producers and novelists inquiring about Lakota heritage, so he knew plenty about research himself. The class was three and a half hours long, and Victor asked me to include some of my own discoveries about Crazy Horse. His students, he informed me, regarded Crazy Horse as a hero, much as Christians regard Jesus Christ. That led me to consider that there were probably other parallels: neither man took tributes for himself; both loved to teach children; both fought to free their people from oppression; both died at a young age; and both men were killed by their own people. Like many who died for what they believed in, their mysteries live on.

Because I wanted to tell these students, most of whom were Lakota, about my father's work as a veterinarian in the region of the Santee Sioux, and about his affinity for tribal stories and traditions, I talked for forty-five minutes about my father. I explained that, although he was an educated man, he did not enjoy reading nearly so much as he enjoyed gathering information from the people sitting in the Indian casinos. When he was researching the Sioux chiefs, four or five times he had to resort to directional dowsing to locate burial sites, when he could not locate a site in other ways. I explained that dowsing was the same process used to locate underground sources of water. I described my father's appreciation for Native Americans' spirituality, and for their ways with animals and nature. I wanted them to know that my father had valued the Lakota unending circle of life and the search for it, and that I, too, respected that life view. I was concerned about the students' possible negative opinions of a white guy writing about Native Americans. I wanted them to know that my father had written his book with his heart.

Suddenly, one student stood, raised his notebook above his head, and slammed it down on his desk forcefully. "I came here to hear about Crazy Horse," he demanded. The room was dead silent for a minute. Later, that student and his professor laughed about his dramatic outburst, but I understood it then, and understand it still, as testimony to what Crazy Horse means to Lakota people.

I moved on to draw them into the stories of the search for Crazy Horse's burial site, and the histories of the possible places that have been identified. While no one may ever be sure of the actual location, I explained how important it is for those who are left to have a place to go to grieve, to remember. As a dramatic example, I offered the story of a tragic airliner crash that killed 132 passengers; the families of the survivors may each have buried their own dead, but, collectively, they chose to purchase the seven-acre site of the crash, making it a place where all could come to mourn both privately and as a community of those remaining.

Thus it was that I began to relate the stories of the search for the burial site of Crazy Horse, knowing that many continue to search for that place to seek understanding and acceptance of his life and death. But, through all the stories, which are as alive today as they were a century ago, Crazy Horse has chosen to remain a mystery. This collection of stories about my search examines some of the mysteries surrounding his death, his burial, and his parents remarkable compassion for their slain son. That the research of others continues, and continues to be published, speaks to the power of this warrior for many people.

As I concluded my presentation to that class of young Native Americans, I shared the story of my father's discovery of a monument to White Ghost, another Lakota chief. The inscription on the back of the formidable tombstone reads:

> White Ghost always wished the welfare of the Whites and Indians. During his last illness he said: Let all the people follow the right path, and let us have peace and friendship. I want the Dakotas to give up fighting and have friendly feelings among themselves and for the whites.

Thirty-seven years before White Ghost's death in 1905, Custer led an expedition into the Black Hills after gold was discovered. "You have driven away our game and our means of livelihood," White Ghost is reported to have said. "We have nothing left that is valuable except the hills that you ask us to give up. The hills are full of minerals and the ground covered with heavy pine. When we give these up we know that we give the last thing that is valuable either to us or the white people." In his remaining years, White Ghost would see treaties broken again and again and still he promoted peace between his people and the whites.

Class was over. Students came forward to extend their hands and to share their stories. Friendship had begun and peace was being made. The spirit of White Ghost had brought us together.

Short Buffalo or Short Bull was a member of Crazy Horse's Last Child Society. It was a military lodge whose members were selected from the last born males of Lakota families. Crazy Horse offered this group of 40 people an opportunity to reach esteem. Many of these members were his body guards at the time of his death.

This photo was originally from the A.G. Shaw collection. It was found in my brother-in-law Larry Shaw's shoe box. A.G. Shaw was his grandfather.

Crazy Horse's Appearance

There are no known photographs of Crazy Horse. In E.A. Brininstool's *Chief Crazy Horse: His Career and Death*, Crazy Horse reportedly told one photographer who requested a photo, "My friend, why should you wish to shorten my life by taking from me my shadow?" Dr. Valentine McGillycuddy, the Camp Robinson medical doctor in 1877, affirms that Crazy Horse adamantly refused to have his photo taken.

I don't recall consciously embarking on a search for a photo of him, but I soon became curious about the many reports I heard about photographs of Crazy Horse. The first time I recall hearing such a story was one summer when my children were headed to the University of Kansas in Lawrence to pole vault camp. Our business accountant, Delmar Falen, told me that a picture of Comanche, one of the few army horses to survive the Battle of the Little Bighorn, was in the natural history museum on the university campus. He also mentioned that there were photos of several Sioux chiefs on display. When we checked it out, there was one photo labeled Crazy Horse in the exhibit. A former librarian from Marysville, Sally Hayden, worked on the KU campus and checked out the authenticity of the Crazy Horse photo. Within hours of my request, Sally called back to inform me that the photo was not, in fact, Crazy Horse but a Native American called Crazy Lodge. Sally reported that the photograph had been donated by a Lawrence attorney as representing Crazy Horse. It was disappointing, but I had suspected all along that the photograph was not of Crazy Horse.

Eleanor Hinman, who traveled the Pine Ridge and Rosebud Reservations gathering information about Crazy Horse, interviewed Short Buffalo, younger brother to He Dog, in 1930. He Dog was a member of the Shirt Wearers' Society with Crazy Horse. Shirt Wearers were appointed by the chief and entrusted with the welfare of the Oglala tribe. In Hinman's interview, Short Buffalo referenced a photograph of Crazy Horse. He said, "I have seen two photographs of Crazy Horse that I think were really he [sic], both showing him on horseback. One showed him on a buckskin horse he owned and one on a roan. I have seen a third photograph that I am sure was him because it showed him on the pinto horse he rode in the Custer fight. I could not possibly make a mistake about the horse, and nobody rode it but Crazy Horse. The man who owns the pictures got them from soldiers who used to be at Fort Robinson. He has quite a collection of pictures of chiefs. I think he lives out in California now, near the national park. I do not know his name." Short Buffalo, like his brother He Dog, was said to have a remarkable memory and carried much tribal history within him.

Several supposed photographs of Crazy Horse have surfaced, but none can be proven to be authentic. Lakota people have told me the eyes of Crazy Horse looked far away and that he always seemed to be listening to a voice that no one else could hear. Older people always spoke of him as someone special, something special. Since there are no verifiable photographs of Crazy Horse known to exist, it's natural to assume that the physical descriptions of him are often romanticized. Crazy Horse's brother-in-law, Red Feather, described him as being a handsome man, "He was a nice looking man, with brown hair, not black, a sharp nose and a narrow face. Nobody on the reservation nowadays looks like him. His nose was straight and thin. His hair was very long, straight and fine textured. His parents buried him; not even his wife knew where he was buried. And his wife, Black Shawl, was my sister" (Paul, 180-216).

What Drove Crazy Horse?

Mario Gonzalez is the tribal attorney for the Kickapoo Nation. He lives in northeast Kansas, not far from Marysville. Mario is the Sioux tribal attorney who fought for the Black Hills and won a one hundred million-dollar lawsuit. The money was never accepted, and it sits in a bank drawing interest. The tribe wants the land, not the money. Mario explained, "One must understand the attitude of white people towards the Lakota to understand why Crazy Horse fought with such a vengeance." I understood what he was saying. Fourteen years after Custer's defeat at Little Bighorn, the Seventh Cavalry was reconstituted and went on to wipe out about 180 Sioux, predominantly older men, but including women and children at Wounded Knee. A newspaper editorialist from Aberdeen, South Dakota, wrote in support of the mass extermination of "these untamed and untamable creatures from the face of the earth." That proponent of total extermination of the Indians was L. Frank Baum, author of *The Wizard of Oz*. With the heart of a lion, the high pitched squeak of a tin man in need of oil, and the rage of a burning straw scarecrow, that insidious attitude stormed over the Plains.

The evil deeds of the whites drove Crazy Horse, but he may also have been affected by the loss of his blood mother, Rattle Blanket Woman, who died a tragic death at a young age. At dinner one night, I asked Mario Gonzalez what he knew about the death of Crazy Horse's blood mother. He related a story from tribal oral history that he'd heard from Elaine Quick Bear Quiver, a descendant of Rattle Blanket Woman's sister, Good Looking Woman. The story passed down tells of Rattle Blanket Woman running away with her brother-in-law, her husband Worm's brother. In shame, Rattle Blanket Woman hanged herself, thereby ceasing to exist in tribal genealogies. Such unforgivable acts, running off with a brother-in-law, and suicide, bring great dishonor to one's memory. She was forever excluded from the history of the tribe.

Mario had heard another version of that story from Ellen in the Woods, a woman also related to Rattle Blanket Woman. The family history told that Rattle Blanket Woman also went by the name She-na-sna-wi, a quiet woman. Ellen told that Rattle Blanket Woman caught her husband Worm with another woman, and it was then that she hanged herself. This version, Mario explained, made her suicide an honorable act for a dishonored woman, and if this story was true, she would have been remembered and revered for her courage.

Joe Swift Bird had told Mario that Rattle Blanket Woman hanged herself just south of Wolf Creek in Nebraska where she had been living with her husband Worm. This is south of Pine Ridge, South Dakota, not far from Beaver Creek where Crazy Horse was taken after he was killed. She had hanged herself from a tree at the foot of a hill. Ellen Quick Bear Quiver told Mario that Crazy Horse grew up with his father and moved back and forth between his father's and mother's relatives, but he was never happy. Worm was later married to the two sisters of Chief Spotted Tail. I told Mario that I'd heard about Crazy Horse's mother hanging herself, and I'd also heard, in whispers, that his blood father was white and that his mother had been violated.

Part One
The Death of Crazy Horse

When engaged in war, Crazy Horse's battle plans were so cunning you could stick a tail on them and call it a weasel. Even today, West Point cadets study his battle tactics. He was determined to hold onto the country that was his own. He was—he is—the most revered of all Sioux warriors. Crazy Horse was dedicated to the freedom of his people and their nomadic way of life. The first part of this book contains some of the stories I have collected over the years, both about his life and death and what he believed in, and about the many wonderful people I have met on this journey.

Thinking over the memories of the past: From stories that I have been told, this is how Crazy Horse's father may have reflected over his son's death at a sweat lodge ceremony.
Photo courtesy Nebraska State Historical Society.

1

KILI and the Green Highway Sign

It was a gray fall day with mist in the air as I was driving on the Pine Ridge Reservation toward the site of the Wounded Knee Massacre. Pine Ridge is an area in northern Nebraska and southern South Dakota that is about twenty miles wide (north and south) and running east and west for about two hundred miles. Ponderosa pines grow on the limestone buttes that overlook the buffalo grass lined valleys below. There hadn't been another vehicle on the road for miles. Driving my father's Grand Prix with my left hand, I was videotaping him with the other. We were talking about collecting and writing stories about Sioux chiefs. He was telling about his shock at seeing the mass gravesite at Wounded Knee on a previous visit. He described it as a desolate place, one where you cannot help but think about what occurred there over a hundred years ago.

The green highway sign seven miles south of Wounded Knee, South Dakota.

"It is a sad and shameful story," he told me, "perhaps the most tragic of all injustices to the Sioux. At Wounded Knee, at least 180 unarmed Indians were slaughtered by the US Cavalry troops. Colonel Forsythe was in command of the US troops during the massacre. Some say the total death count was as high as 300, and that the majority were women and children. Many died later of their wounds and exposure."

I was moved by my father's feeling for this injustice. As he was retelling this story, I gradually became aware of the Indian drum music that was playing on the car radio. A filmmaker could not have documented the scene any more dramatically. The mist dotted our windshield like the goose bumps on my arms.

My father continued, describing how the frozen bodies were gathered up by the white people and dumped into a common ditch that served as a mass grave. He mentioned a monument erected by surviving relatives and other Oglala and Cheyenne River Sioux in memory of the massacre of Big Foot and his people at Wounded Knee. The drum music on the radio became more insistent until I interrupted taping my dad to ask, "Where are those Indian drums being broadcast from?" He told me it was a radio station just around the bend on Porcupine Butte—KILI. I thought to myself, KILI at Wounded Knee? The Sioux are still looking for retribution; they have not forgotten.

This trip was intended to add to the stories my father had been putting together for his book on burial sites of Sioux chiefs. I resumed videotaping as my father told more about Big Foot, a Minneconjou chief. "His warriors fought in the battle of the Little Bighorn; then he moved the band to the Cheyenne River Reservation. Worried by the turn of events when Sitting Bull was assassinated, Big Foot and about 350 men, women, and children started out hoping to find safety with Red Cloud at the Pine Ridge Agency 150 miles away. They walked day and night in snow and sub-zero weather. Their clothes and moccasins were thin and worn out. They were sick and starving. Some had frozen hands and feet. They were apprehended by US Cavalry contingents and marched to Wounded Knee Creek.

My father related this historical event:

Troop reinforcements arrived, along with four Hotchkiss cannons for the soldiers who were celebrating the capture of Big Foot. The Indians were surrounded. The cannons were placed on a hill above them. Big Foot admonished his people to be humble. He had pneumonia, had hemorrhaged, and could no longer walk. There was a large number of women, children, and elderly. It was bitterly cold.

The following morning, December 29, 1890, the Minneconjou Sioux were forced to give up their weapons. This meant they would not be able to hunt for food. After they were lined up and searched, a gunshot—some say it was an accident—rang out, and the terrible massacre began.

Most of the men, including Big Foot, were killed during the first part of the shooting. The cannons opened up on the women, children, and the elderly. Those who tried to run away were chased down by soldiers on horseback. Bodies were found two or three miles away.

The Seventh Cavalry was probably happy to get revenge for the defeat of Custer. A great blizzard and twenty degree-below-zero weather hit the Dakota Plains. The frozen bodies were not gathered up for burial until January 3. A few were said to have been buried alive. One of the babies found nursing from its dead mother was taken away and adopted by a soldier. She died in California at the age of twenty-nine, and was later reinterred near the Wounded Knee mass grave in July 1991 at a ceremony that I attended. She had been given the name Lost Bird.

Each year after 1990, Big Foot Riders have journeyed to Wounded Knee to commemorate the lives of Native Americans killed there. During the last week of December 1994, forty-five riders in period dress completed the memorial journey which began at Sitting Bull's homesite west of Mobridge, South Dakota, and finished at the 1890 massacre site.

We came around the bend in the highway and the KILI radio station came into view. We stopped in just to say hello and to tell the D. J. how well the drum music he was broadcasting fit our journey. In his office, he was playing other music on his personal CD player. He smiled and waved to the beat of his American hard rock music.

The drum music was still playing as we came down the hill to where the road flattened out and brought us to a green historical marker on federal Highway 18, seven miles south of Wounded Knee. I pulled over to read the large sign which had writing on both sides:

Oglala Sioux
1840—War Chief Crazy Horse—1877
Taskunke Witko

This sign is dedicated to the greatest of Sioux Warriors Chief Crazy Horse, light haired, fair-skinned, gray-eyed, he was modest, courteous, generous, of great physique, and known for his self-denial. His success and influence were his personality and bravery in battle. He was never involved in any of the numerous massacres on the trail, but was a fine leader in practically every open fight. "Listen now," Crazy Horse said, "you cannot sell the ground you walk on." He never signed a peace treaty. His loyalty to his people caused the army to trick him to his death. Crazy Horse represented the fighting Sioux from 1870 to 1877. He never was photographed.

Somewhere in the buttes fourteen miles northwest of this sign, between the forks of White Horse Creek and Wounded Knee Creek, is the unmarked grave of this famous war chief, says Batiste Pourier and Jake Russell. Ben Black Elk says Crazy Horse was buried on the bluffs (S5 T37 R43W) east of Wounded Knee Creek by his mother. Later, when she was living with Felix Bald Eagle, she continued to leave food at the grave to nourish the soul of Crazy Horse. Ben Irving says that, in 1905, Sleeping Bear, then eighty years old, showed him the burial spot of Crazy Horse on a bluff on White Horse Creek four miles south of Manderson.

An army report dated 1877 says:

The body of Chief Crazy Horse was taken from the hostiles at Red Cloud Camp near the mouth of the Wounded Knee Creek given to his parents who disappeared with the body on a travois into the Badlands—they were gone all night returning to camp the next noon. This one-day journey establishes the burial area. Chief Crazy Horse in boyhood was called "Curly" or "The Light Haired One." Born on Rock Creek—Blackhills, South Dakota, about 1840. His unsurpassed skill as a horseman—His fearless riding of a horse alone into enemy bullet and arrow fire to the enemy lines, killing opposing warriors and returning in his own fighting band unharmed earned him the name Crazy Horse. War Chief Crazy Horse was an Oglala Sioux—His family had long been holy men—His father, also named Crazy Horse, was Oglala Sioux. He became known as "Worm." His mother, a sister of Chief Spotted Tail, was a Brulé Sioux.

Crazy Horse from boyhood had two inseparable warrior friends: Lone Bear, killed in the Fetterman Massacre in 1866; and Hump, teacher and bodyguard of Crazy Horse, killed in an Oglala raid on the Shoshones in 1873. In desperation, Crazy Horse ran among the Shoshones and with his quirt put them to flight. From that hour, said his nearest friends, Crazy Horse sought death. He had a superstitious belief he'd never be killed by bullet. He carried a small blue stone in the back of one ear and was a member of Strong Hearts and Tokala Lodges.

Crazy Horse fought in all of Red Cloud's major battles in 1866, known as, "The bloody year on the Plains." He was included in many raiding parties and war ventures. His presence brought success because of his complete control of the wildest warriors under his command.

Fort Phil Kearny had been attacked fifty-five times when on December 21, 1866, in the Fetterman Massacre, Crazy Horse carried out the strategy of decoy and ambush killing Captain Fetterman's eighty men. There were no survivors.

Aug. 2, 1867—Wagon Box fought Crazy Horse and Hump attacked Captain Powell's Wood Cutters, losing 400 warriors to the new Springfield Breech loading rifles use [*sic*] for the first time against the Sioux. [There were not nearly this many warriors (Buecker).]

Nov. 6, 1868—Sioux Treaty at Fort Laramie—Chief Crazy Horse, Sitting Bull, Gall, Black Moon refused to sign.

1874—Custer reported gold in the Black Hills—Unquestionable Territory of the Sioux—Paha Sapa was part of the country ceded the Sioux by the treaty of 1868 at Fort Laramie.

June 17, 1876—Battle of Rosebud Creek—General Crook was attacked by Chief Crazy Horse's Warriors crying "Hoka He" in relayed formation—They fought all day—General Crook was forced to retire and awaited reinforcements.

June 25, 1876—Battle of Little Bighorn—General Custer and 225 men were killed by Oglala and Cheyenne Warriors led by the fanatical Crazy Horse in a flanking movement cutting off Custer's retreat—No survivors.

May 6, 1877—Crazy Horse voluntarily surrendered his hostile band—145 lodges—889 people—117 guns—170 ponies—They marched into Fort Robinson. Crazy Horse was the idol of the young fighting Sioux, but suffered from the jealousy of an older chief at Fort Robinson.

Sept. 3, 1877—General Crook counseled Crazy Horse at Fort Robinson—Frank Grouard—was interpreter—Crook asked Crazy Horse's aid in fighting the Nez Perces—Crazy Horse told Crook, "We will fight with you until not a Nez Perces is left." Frank Grouard erroneously interpreted, "We will go north and fight until not a white man is left." Crook left the council—Dr. McGillycuddy in Crook's quarters that evening advised him of Grouard's false interpretation. That night Crazy Horse's band moved to Camp Sheridan.

Sept. 4, 1877—Chief Spotted Tail—Lt. Lee—Big Bat Pourier persuaded Crazy Horse to return to Fort Robinson. Crazy Horse agreed to return—he wished to explain the misunderstanding—That he wanted peace not trouble. Col. L.P. Bradley in the meantime had received orders from Lt. General Sheridan's Chicago office—"Imprison Crazy Horse—Send him to Dry Tortugas, Florida."

Sept. 5, 1877—upon Crazy Horse's arrival at Fort Robinson, Col. Bradley refused to see him. He was tricked to the door of the guard house—whirling, knifing, he fought. Crazy Horse died near midnight in the Adjutant's office attended by Dr. McGillycuddy, Crazy Horse's father and Chief Touch the Clouds. He was bayoneted by William Gentles of the 14th Infantry. Next day the body was hauled by pony travois NE forty miles to the Spotted Tail Agency (1874-1877) Camp Sheridan (1874-1881) on Beaver Creek.

Sept 8, 1877—the body of Crazy Horse wrapped in a blanket was given a Sioux Scaffold burial on a hill east of Camp Sheridan. His parents squatted beside their son for three unbroken days and nights—without food and water within sight of Lt. Lee's quarters.

Sept. 13, 1877—Black Shawl, Crazy Horse's wife died and was placed by Lt. Lee on the scaffold beside the body of Crazy Horse.

Oct. 25, 1877—Red Cloud's Band escorted by army troops left Fort Robinson, moved NE down the White River toward the Missouri River.

Oct. 28, 1877—Spotted Tail's Brulé Band and hostiles from the Crazy Horse Camp moved from Beaver Creek, Camp Sheridan, eastward toward the Missouri River. From a Spotted Tail Camp near this sign about a thousand Oglala "Crazy Horse Hostile," led by Big Road and Little Hawk broke away, carrying the body of Crazy Horse, headed north—meeting the Red Cloud Band near the mouth of Wounded Knee Creek—then proceeding to Canada. The army took the body from the hostile and turned it over to Crazy Horse's parents who disappeared into the Badlands.

Delineator of the Green Highway sign—Guy White Thunder
by Stanley S. Walker, Sup. High Engineer

2

Search for the Burial Sites of Sioux Nation Chiefs

As we drove from the historical highway sign that day, the sun started to burn through the damp haze. My dad and I talked about his book on Sioux Chiefs and the mystery of where Crazy Horse is buried. That was the day he said to me, "You know, that is something you might want to write about someday." And I said, "You know, considering my occupation as a mortician, it might be interesting work."

At that time, my father had recently been diagnosed with an illness that the doctor explained as a slow-moving bone cancer. Dad's doctor thought Dad might have three good years, followed by some tough ones. While we traveled around gathering stories on the burial sites of Sioux chiefs, it was clear that Dad was looking in on the spiritual world, searching out the hereafter, coming to terms with his earthly adventure.

I once asked Steve Warner, a clinical psychologist and a longtime family friend (who, incidentally, had grown up on an island in the Platte River between Chimney Rock and Scottsbluff, Nebraska), why my father might pick such a topic to research and write on. Steve Warner replied, "Because he is a chief. He likes to hold council and tell stories."

Those next few years, my father and I would travel together three or four times a year gathering information for his book. I would drive 270 miles north from my home in Marysville, Kansas, to where my father practiced veterinary medicine in Verdigre, Ne-

Doc and Cleve Walstrom in search of burial sites of Sioux Chiefs. We were 15 miles south of Fort Thompson. We paused for road construction and a worker told us it was just discovered that the hill in the background was believed to have 600 burials of the Arikara Tribe. These Indians also used the steep cliff to direct buffalo to stampede over. Many bones were found at the base.

braska. We would then drive another 300 or so miles to the reservations in South Dakota to visit with Native Americans.

My father called me one day in August a few years later to say that he did not think he would be able to finish his book and get it published. My mother was being too particular about sentence structure, and documenting and referencing quotes. My father was not patient on these matters. He did not think he would ever get his project off the ground—or out from under the ground, as it were. My mother was an English and art teacher, who had managed to graduate from Kansas State University in less than two years by taking a double load. My dad respected her, and she probably intimidated him, so the process of developing his writing was slow.

I found a publisher and worked with an editor who knew time was critical. My father was losing weight and wanted to see his work in print. Three weeks before Christmas 1995, his book, *My Search for the Burial Sites of Sioux Nation Chiefs*, was printed. He put his shirt and tie and stocking cap on and we drove in my pickup truck to the publisher, Pine Hill Press, in Freeman, South Dakota, to pick up several large boxes of his books. I have never seen him happier or more distinguished looking even though his sun was setting. Although the battle with the cancer was lost, there were life-affirming victories throughout the many good stories from two cultural backgrounds: the Native American chiefs' and the author's. In many ways, the stories paralleled one another, both were about journeys to an afterlife where eagles fly.

As we drove south to his office in Verdigre with the books, we were just about at the Nebraska border when my dad said, "I bet my eighth grade English teacher never thought I would be an author." I thought to myself, I bet your wife didn't either. What I said aloud was, "You are looking good, Dad," and he said with a big grin, 'Looking Good'; that's my Indian name."

3

Conquering Bear and the Sandoz Girls

One of the first things I had to do as I prepared to tackle this project was to review and organize the information my father and I had already gathered. This would be my road map, so to speak, of my journey to finding the burial site for Crazy Horse. All of these stories have served as educational guides and inspiration. I have been amazed at people's willingness to share stories with my father and me. This is one such story.

My father and I had originally traveled to the home of Caroline Sandoz Pfeifer in 1995 to ask questions about a chief named Conquering Bear, on whose gravesite my father had no information. Caroline's sister, Mari Sandoz, had written a book, *Crazy Horse Strange Man of the Oglala*, in which she stated that Conquering Bear was buried on her family ranch. We drove to Gordon, Nebraska, and met with Caroline.

Caroline was in her mid-eighties and a bundle of energy and enthusiasm. She ran her ten thousand acre ranch by herself and had no plans of ever slowing down. She was a wealth of knowledge, and quite by chance, I heard for the first time an interesting story about Crazy Horse that I would never forget. I will never forget Caroline, either.

She drove us to where the scaffold had stood, marking Conquering Bear's final resting site, which was located near a home the Sandoz family had built a few years after the Chief's death.

It was a wintry February day; the kind locals say is so cold the coyotes have to jump start the jackrabbits before giving chase. She wanted to warm up her pick-up truck in a hurry, I guess, because we traveled over the Sandhill trail at over seventy miles per hour. When we arrived at the location of the scaffold, after my heart rate returned to normal, the story of how Conquering Bear died came to mind, paraphrased here from Mari Sandoz's book.

It was a tense time for both the army soldiers and the Sioux in 1853. People were nervous and itching for a fight on both sides. It was all Conquering Bear could do to keep his braves in line. People on both sides were openly talking about how they could whip the other in battle. It was a conflict waiting to happen.

This was the Sandoz ranch overlooking the Niobrara River where Conquering Bear's death scaffold was. Picture courtesy Caroline Pfeifer.

At Fort Laramie one summer afternoon, a Sioux warrior asked a soldier for a ride across the Platte River on a small boat being used as a ferry. The soldier refused, and to show his anger at the decision, the warrior fired an arrow at the skiff as it crossed the river. It was like throwing kerosene on a fire.

The next day, twenty soldiers rode out to arrest the warrior. There was confusion on both sides, and in the turmoil, a gun discharged. Both sides fired their weapons, and the result was six dead Sioux. The soldiers were outnumbered and returned to the fort, with no prisoner and an alarming story. Emigrants traveling along the Oregon Trail heard the story, and were panicky, thinking that the Sioux were going to retaliate against them. The Sioux did just that, attacking an emigrant camp near the fort, killing four.

Soldiers from the fort marched and opened fire on the first Indians they saw, killing one and wounding another. Things were spiraling out of control and Conquering Bear, being committed to peace, didn't want this to escalate any further. He managed to regain control of his warriors and by autumn had smoothed things over with the army.

Conquering Bear led his braves north for the annual fall hunt, but when they returned in the spring, trouble re-surfaced thanks to a small band of Sioux known as the Loafers. The Loafers were camped near Fort Laramie, waiting for the distribution of food and supplies from the army. A large number of warriors were impatient, and they rode to a nearby emigrant encampment, hoping to scare the settlers into parting with sugar and coffee.

A cow bolted from the emigrant's wagon train, and the cow's owner gave chase to the edge of the Sioux's Big Brulé Village. When he saw the Indians, he retreated. A warrior named High Forehead shot the cow and butchered it.

When the wagon train reached Fort Laramie, the settler complained that the Indians had stolen his property. He demanded that the army take action, so the fort's commander sent for Conquering Bear, who had been designated as the head of all Sioux by the army. To try to keep peace, Conquering Bear offered to pay for the cow. The Chief pointed out that the cow was old and lame. He said it never would have survived the journey anyway. He offered to pay ten dollars but the settler wanted twenty-five dollars.

Stuck between a rock and a hard place, the Fort Commander ordered that the cow killer, High Forehead, be turned over to the army. Conquering Bear said that wouldn't be possible; High Forehead was a guest at his village so the army would have to arrest him themselves.

The next morning, a unit was dispatched to arrest High Forehead. John L. Gratten, a brash young lieutenant fresh from the academy at West Point, led the soldiers. He had no experience with the Sioux, but was sure that they were no match for him and his troops. He was eager for battle and had been known to strut around the fort saying so.

Gratten was accompanied by an attachment of twenty-nine soldiers, two small cannons, and an interpreter named Auguste Lucien, who had been drinking heavily. The Sioux disliked Lucien because of his drunken antics in the past, such as proclaiming that he would kill the Sioux and eat their hearts. Having him along was not a good thing.

Conquering Bear and tribal leaders met the soldiers as they approached the Sioux camp. The intoxicated Lucien immediately began hurling insults at the Sioux, demanding they turn over High Forehead or face the consequences. The Sioux were shocked and angered by his threats.

Crazy Horse was a boy known as Curly at the time this took place. He was at the Big Brulé Village camp visiting his relatives. He was watching with hundreds of other young Indians from the bluff above the village. He watched as Conquering Bear traveled back and forth from the village to the soldiers. High Forehead refused to surrender. The soldiers fired on the camp. Conquering Bear was seriously wounded, but alive.

Young Crazy Horse watched enraged warriors pour out of tepees and ride down from the bluff, slaughtering the soldiers in revenge. Gratten's body was riddled with twenty-four arrows. Lucien tried to hide in a tepee from the warriors. When he was found, he was beaten to death with clubs.

Young Crazy Horse was distraught over what he had witnessed, and rode off seeking guidance from the spirits. Alone on a hill, the young warrior had a vision, one he would not share for three years. He saw a lake, and from the depths of the lake emerged a young warrior riding a horse like his own, but the horse in his vision floated, danced and changed colors. Bullets and arrows flew all around the warrior on horseback, but he was unharmed. The warrior wore blue leggings and a buckskin shirt. His face was not painted, and his long brown hair was adorned with a single hawk feather, which waved in the wind. There was a small brown stone behind his ear, but he carried no scalps or war trophies.

In this vision, a storm swirled behind the warrior, forcing him to ride through the arrows and bullets. People gathered around the warrior, attempting to stop him. Still riding the floating horse, he broke their grasp and seemed to become one with the storm. A lightning bolt struck down his cheek, and white spots resembling hail formed on his body. There was a red-tail hawk circling and screaming above the warrior. The vision faded to black, and when he woke, young Crazy Horse saw his father and his close friend, Hump. They were relieved to have found him, but were angry that he had ridden off alone during such turbulence. Crazy Horse knew from that moment on that the spirits were with him and would guide him as he became a great Sioux leader.

In the meantime, a badly wounded Conquering Bear was taken by travois to a medicine spring in the Nebraska Sandhills. The Sioux believed that the spring could heal him. He didn't survive the trip, dying along the Niobrara River, where his body was placed on a scaffold in keeping with tribal ritual.

It was to this location, where the scaffold stood, that Caroline had led us. This was a fascinating journey through time, and it seemed fitting to visit that area on a dark and windy, bitterly cold February day.

Caroline also told us a ghost story about Crazy Horse that would fuel my imagination and haunt me in my own work. Little Bat Pourier had told her father the story.

According to Little Bat, there was an Indian ghost dressed in a buffalo robe, with a knife hidden in his hand, stalking the guardhouse at Fort Robinson. With his head down, his one line feather pointing straight up into the sky, it was said to be the ghost of Crazy Horse. Crazy Horse was tricked into going to that guardhouse the day he was stabbed in the back and killed. Little Bat explained there are two theories as to why the ghost of Crazy Horse walked. One explanation is that he was looking for the man who killed him to get revenge. The other is that his spirit was doomed to walk in front of the guardhouse until all of the warriors he led into battle against Custer had died.

I wished that I had the chance to speak to Little Bat as I researched this book, but he had died many years before. I didn't realize just how closely the spirits were listening…

4

Visions of a Hard Road

A few months after visiting with Caroline Sandoz, I was sitting in a Holiday Inn not far from the campus of the University of Kansas where my sons, Woody and Wally, were at a track and field pole vault camp one summer week. I was having breakfast and a man walked by my table wearing a baseball cap with the words "Crazy Horse" embroidered on it. My first thoughts were to let the man be, but I had an overwhelming feeling that I should introduce myself. (As I said earlier, some of the connections that have carried me forward in this journey seemed like strange fate.) Not only would this chance meeting prove to be yet another ironic story for this book, but it served a greater purpose in opening my eyes to the struggles of the modern day Native American. I introduced myself to the gentleman, and explained that I was researching a book about Crazy Horse.

His name was Bat Pourier—the great-grandson of Little Bat, the man Caroline Sandoz had spoken about. Bat's great-grandfather had accompanied the funeral procession for Crazy Horse on the forty-mile trip from Fort Robinson to Beaver Creek. The death of Crazy Horse caused our paths to cross, but it was life today on the reservation that would bring the past full circle to the present, and give me a deeper understanding of history.

Bat was down in Kansas enrolling his son at the Haskell Indian College. Bat owns a gas station on the Pine Ridge in South Dakota. I'd stopped there many times for a Sunny Delight and a roast beef sandwich, but neither of us remembered the other. His gas station was the center of activity on the reservation. Unemployment in this area is high and native people spend a lot of time just driving around the town. They gas up and go driving to somewhere…anywhere…nowhere. They're pretty dependent on Bat's gas pumps.

Meeting Bat Pourier reminded me of my friends on the Santee Reservation close to where I grew up. And that reminded me of an article I'd read in my son's *Sport's Illustrated* in a 1991 issue. It was the February 18 issue with the Dream Team that was slated to play in the 1992 Olympics on the cover. After reading about the USA's prospects of trouncing the rest of the world at basketball, there was another interesting story about basketball players from Hardin, Montana, traveling to a state high school basketball tournament some years earlier. The article, titled "Shadow of a Nation" by Gary Smith, told about the realities of modern day reservation life. A photograph in *Sport's Illustrated* showed Hardin High's starting guard, Everette Walks, with his nose pressed against the window of the bus, a boy with huge hands who had never known his father. In a few weeks, he would drop out of school, and then cirrhosis would begin to lay waste to his mother. He would wind up pushing a mop late at night in a restaurant on the Crow Reservation.

In another seat was the other starting guard, Jo Jo Pretty Paint, a brilliant long-range shooter and a dedicated kid who, just a few minutes before a game at Miles City, was discovered by his coach, alone, crouched, shuffling, and strangely covering an invisible opponent in the locker room shower. In two years, Pretty Paint would go out drinking one evening, get into a car, and careen over an embankment. He would go to his grave with a photograph of himself clutching a basketball.

Hunched near the others, all knees and elbows and shoulders, sat Darren Big Medicine, the easygoing team center. Sixteen months after Pretty Paint's death, he would leave a party after a night of drinking, fall asleep as he sped along a reservation road, drive into a ditch, and die there.

According to Gary Smith's article "Shadow of a Nation" there is weeping in the land for those missing from that caravan headed to the state tournament. Weeping for those decaying in the reservation dust, for Dale Spotted, and Star Not Afraid, and Tim Falls Down; Crow stars of the past, dead of cirrhosis and suicide and knife-stabbing and a liquor-logged car wreck. There are tears for the slow deaths occurring every night a mile from the school, where an entire squad of other jump shooters, dunkers, and power forwards from past years can be found huddled against the chill and sprawled upon the sidewalks outside the bars on the south part of Hardin. "Good Lord!" cries the computer science teacher and past basketball scorekeeper at Hardin High, "How many have we lost? How many?"

The answer is too many. The deeper question is why? Could it be that when the white man took the land away from the Indians, he also took away their sense of identity? Could this be why Crazy Horse and other chiefs fought so desperately? Could they possibly have known that incrementally, the white man was replacing freedom and self-sufficiency with a life of dependency and feelings of inadequacy? They were forced to live on government handouts, when for centuries they'd been quite adept at providing for themselves. Their sense of self-worth was shaken to the core, and the foundation of their livelihood remains cracked and decaying to this day. No sense of direction and purpose survives, only hopelessness, frustration and anger.

The article continued on, rhapsodizing about the Indians' fluid shooting touch and their great endurance. I knew this was true. It was one of the best articles I have ever read dealing with Native American basketball players' successes, their many state championships...and their plight with alcohol. I knew personally that there were problems over at the Santee Reservation near where I grew up. I wondered how similar things might be at Pine Ridge.

How many Native American parents have mourned the untimely deaths of their warrior/athletes? And how different is their mourning from that of Crazy Horse's parents in the time of the blue coats and single shot firearms?

Today, when I ponder the consequences of the conflicts between the Indians and the white man over a century ago, I think of Ambrose Red Owl; he ran like a man trying to catch the spirit lost.

5

Ambrose Red Owl on the Santee

Those Native American athletes and the reservation problems reminded me of a high school friend, Ambrose Red Owl, who had been one of Nebraska's best two-milers. Ambrose had a big barrel chest and skinny legs. He was all lungs and he had a smile that would send a morning reflection off the Missouri River bright enough to even make the catfish jump for surface bugs. Our high school track teams competed against each other. I was a sprinter of short distances and Ambrose was made for endurance. Although we never competed directly against each other, we had a mutual respect for each other's abilities.

Ambrose qualified for the state meet as a sophomore. During the week before the state meet, he was thrown in jail for drunk driving. As a junior, Ambrose qualified again. He cele-

brated with beer and was put in the county jail again. His senior year, Ambrose was dedicated to his sport and had the best two mile time in the area and was among the statewide leaders in that event. He qualified for the state track and field championships at Kearney, Nebraska. He did not neglect or abuse his body. Ambrose rode with his coaches the two hundred miles to the meet. But the car they were riding in had engine trouble and broke down. The car was repaired and they were on their way again. When Ambrose arrived at the meet, he walked into the games and found the starting gun had already gone off for his event without him. He was crushed, and spent the next few years in and out of the county jail.

After reading the article about the Hardin, Montana, Native Americans, I thought of Ambrose and sent the article to my father and asked him to deliver it to Ambrose in person. My father jumped in his car and drove twenty-five miles to Santee to look for Ambrose.

Ambrose Red Owl.

At his home, Ambrose's wife said he was in the county jail. My father drove another twenty-five miles, winding through the hills of Knox County on a road cut beside the Bazile Mills Creek. He arrived at the county jail at Center, Nebraska, with a brown envelope in his hand. My father, Dr. V.A. Walstrom, told the jailer he would like to give Ambrose Red Owl a *Sport's Illustrated* article. The jailer looked in the envelope, gave my dad a funny look, and then led him to Ambrose's cell. Ambrose was not there. They looked in the exercise yard and found Ambrose shooting hoops. The ball bounced over the fence and one of the skinny inmates was lifted up over the fence to retrieve it back into the county jail exercise yard. Ambrose told my dad later that they retrieve the ball themselves without asking the guard for help. If they pushed the buzzer to signal the guard for help, they would have to go back to their cells and their game would be cut short. My dad gave Ambrose the brown envelope with the story.

A week later, in March 1991, I received a letter from Center, Nebraska. The writing was very fluid; large letters with nice round swirls. It was from Ambrose. He started out by saying he was surprised to hear from me. He wrote that he liked the story of the basketball players and reading about the tough things they had encountered in Montana. He went on to say that the problems those players faced with alcohol were a lot like what happened to him:

> Too many government checks and not enough purpose. Our problems are the same on our reservations; idle time is filled with alcohol. We need to do something and I am working on it to make myself better. It would be better if the government left us alone and then we would be forced to fix economic woes. But Cleve I want you to know those Indians up there are Crows and the Crows were hired scouts for Custer. They rode with him at the Little Bighorn and we don't want anything to do with them. I am a Sioux, like Crazy Horse.

Six years later, Ambrose came to my father's funeral in Verdigre. In Marysville, at funerals, I see people give memorials, send cards, and stop by our mortuary to pay their respects to folks in the community. Those gestures help the ones who grieve. When I saw Ambrose walk into my father's funeral wearing a cowboy hat like my father used to wear when he was working cattle, I was touched by converging spirits.

Those who think history is just so many words in a book ought to spend time on the reservation, where the scars from history are still visible and deep. Some say that the Indian refuses to walk across the bridge to the white man's world; I think the bridge was probably never meant to be built.

6

The Black Elks of Wounded Knee Valley

I love driving through the Wounded Knee Creek Valley; the high white bluffs and chiseled landscape is the type of picture Zane Gray used to paint in our mind with his words. It's one of the most scenic places in the country, making these long trips my father and I would take worth the drive.

What also made the drives worthwhile were the people we met and the stories we heard. It was in the heart of this valley, near Manderson, South Dakota, that I met the great-grandson of Black Elk, Mitchell Desersa, and he showed me around the area telling me stories. One story his great-grandfather told was about the spotted eagle who challenged a hummingbird to see who could fly the longest. The eagle, with strong wings, flew towards the morning star. The eagle looked around and didn't see the hummingbird until he felt a movement on his back. It was the hummingbird who had hitched a ride on the eagle's back. The hummingbird waved good-bye to the tired spotted eagle as it flew on toward the evening star.

I told Mitchell that sometimes we called my father Hummingbird. A rancher who lived near the mouth of the Niobrara River had once said, "When Doc Walstrom comes to work cattle, he is a congenial, warm-hearted guy who is fun to visit with. When the work is to be done, he undergoes a transformation and works at a hummingbird's pace. He gets real serious and works fast."

The rancher had gone on to say, "When we ran several hundred head of cattle through the wooden

Mitchell Desera in front of Ben Black Elk's cabin. Mitchell is the great-grandson of Black Elk, cousin of Crazy Horse.

chute for vaccination, the last heifer banged the cottonwood gate down and the heifer ran over Doc. He scrambled up and I went to round up the Hereford heifer so we could make sure she was vaccinated. Doc said, 'That's okay, I shot her as she was going over me.' We never quite believed Doc, but as the years went by, we had him do other work on the ranch and saw how quick he was, and decided that it was possible that he had actually vaccinated that cow."

Mitchell Desersa is a student of archeology and a firefighter on call for the United States Forestry Service in the Black Hills. His great-grandfather, Black Elk, was the great Medicine Man of the Oglala Sioux, and a cousin of Crazy Horse. It was Black Elk who would tell John Neihardt his stories, which comprised the book, *Black Elk Speaks*.

Being related to Crazy Horse, Mitchell Desersa's family lore was filled with the stories of the great chief, as well as the legendary Medicine Man. Mitchell told me that there is a reason Crazy Horse's grave was known only to his parents. Desersa took me on a guided tour of the area, sharing stories with me that illustrated his own understanding of why his ancestors would keep the final resting place of Crazy Horse a secret.

Once, while hiking through the Great White Bluffs, Desersa came across two petrified babies imbedded in the limestone rock. He decided to share his find with two archeologists. They took one of the babies and never returned it. He has since told no one of the location of the other petrified baby because his trust had been violated, and so had the spirits of the babies.

A Native American woman, Julie Lakota, in Kyle, South Dakota, told me that in the 1850s the US Army was known to have taken the bones and crania of Indians and sent them back east to be studied. To the Sioux, graves were sacred. Crazy Horse's parents could reasonably have been afraid that the bones of their son would end up in a museum—a situation that would certainly not be acceptable to Mother Earth and the Great Spirit, and probably not to any loving parents. With so many enemies, it was difficult for Crazy Horse to be certain who was friend and who was foe.

Chips, a medicine man and a close friend of Crazy Horse's, related that the true resting place of Crazy Horse's bones is unknown because the Sioux depended on Crazy Horse as a fighter, but, just before he was killed, many of his people had turned against him. They told lies about him and were jealous of him. Although Crazy Horse sought peace, there was a price on his head—dead or alive.

Desersa explained that Crazy Horse was the greatest of all Sioux chiefs because he had his own medicine, which means a lot coming form the grandson of Black Elk. He explained that the sacred powers were within him, and it is said that Crazy Horse could extend his personal protection in battle to others by simply touching them.

On first hearing some of the stories about Crazy Horse, a person might be inclined to scratch his head and dismiss them as nothing more than superstition and legend, that is, until he learns about some of the bold feats Crazy Horse accomplished during battle. For instance, during a battle with the Arapaho near the Wind River in central Wyoming, Crazy Horse's animal was shot from beneath him. The younger warrior believed his visions that, while on horseback, he was protected in battle by the spirits. He jumped on a loose pony and charged the enemy. Through a hail of gunfire and arrows, he rode untouched to the top of the hill, into the

29

heart of the Arapaho, drove an arrow into a brave, turned in a whirlwind and rode back down the hill. The Sioux warriors were whooping and cheering the brave young Crazy Horse, who took no time to wallow in the congratulations. He immediately charged the hill again to kill a second brave as he fulfilled his vision again.

Desersa explained that Crazy Horse carried with him into battle a stone given to him by his friend, Chips. Before each battle, Crazy Horse would rub the stone all over his body which he believed would give him an invisible shield as tough as the rock itself. He also used a stick to drill a hole through the edge of a larger rock where he threaded a buckskin thong. In battle, he wore the rock around his neck, always holding the rock between his heart and the enemy like a shield.

Crazy Horse was a man who believed in honor, even in battle. The accidental killing of a woman in battle haunted him. The incident occurred in the summer of 1855, along Beaver Creek near Bartlett, Nebraska. Young Crazy Horse, then known as Curly, accompanied his uncle and a band of Brulé on a pony raid in the Loup River region. They crept into an Omaha tribe camp, cut loose horses and drove them north. The Omahas gave chase, and soon a battle erupted. Crazy Horse spotted a figure crawling in the brush, fired his bow and killed the enemy, a young woman.

Nicholas Mignery said a trapper watched the battle with a spy glass from this hill.

The Sioux believed there was dishonor in killing a woman. He was ashamed and slow to admit the truth. His companions had no way of knowing what had happened, but they thought it was strange that Crazy Horse left the scalp behind and teased him about it. When the truth was learned, Crazy Horse was taken to Canada and hidden, in the hopes that the incident would not result in full-scale war between the two nations. To complicate matters, there was a second battle on the same day between the Omaha and the Sioux that heightened tensions even more because it resulted in the death of a great Omaha Nation Chief.

The battles were very close in proximity to each other. One happened near the farm where Michele Mignery Mlinar's (my sister-in-law) grandfather homesteaded. Michele's father, David, told me a story passed down from their grandfather, Nicholas, a blacksmith who built steam engines for the Union Pacific in the 1850s. He became interested in homesteading, and a fur trader told him to look along the Beaver Creek near the forks for a good place to settle because that was where the deer would go to give birth to their little ones.

David Mignery told me that on the same day as Crazy Horse killed the young woman, the celebrated Omaha Nation leader, Chief Logan Fontenelle, was wounded on Mignery land. The story was handed down in the family, Nicholas said, that the fur trapper in 1855 observed with a spyglass from a far away hill an Indian battle between Chief Fontenelle and a band of Sioux Indians who had dug in for battle about a quarter mile northwest of David's present day house.

Fontenelle had been leading a hunting party along the Beaver when a skirmish broke out between the Omaha and Sioux. The chief was wounded, so the Omaha retreated and took the Chief to a location near Albion, Nebraska. The chief died from the wounds just north of what is now the town of Loretto. The news of chief Fontenelle's death led to the decision to take Crazy Horse into hiding, fearing that the chief's death and the killing of a woman would lead to war.

There is a forest near the city of Omaha named for Chief Fontenelle, who is still celebrated as a great leader by the Omaha Nation. I have always been amazed at the twists and turns fate took for Crazy Horse, how his life and times were intertwined with so many other legendary historical figures. This is just another example of that, and one more obstacle Crazy Horse would have to overcome. The killing of that young woman triggered a period of great soul searching by Crazy Horse.

In fact, introspection was the main source of Crazy Horse's medicine. Desersa called Crazy Horse's soul searching process lamenting. He would go off alone many times a year and meditate, open his mind to the spirits and receive visions. Desersa said Crazy Horse would have visions of the rock, the shadow, the badger, the prancing horse, the spotted eagle, each holding a special meaning in his life. Mitchell said that it has been passed down in his family that Crazy Horse was the greatest chief of all. Red Cloud was a great chief, but he was through fighting after the treaty he made with the *wasichus* (white government) in 1868. Red Cloud had gone to live with his band, the Bad Faces at Soldiers' Town. "There were no chiefs in our family before Crazy Horse," Mitchell explained, "only holy men. And Crazy Horse became chief because of the power of a vision he had when he was young."

Desersa explained one of Crazy Horse's visions, a journey to the spirit world, as told to him by his grandmother. "Crazy Horse dreamed and went into the world where there is nothing but the spirits of all things. That is the real world beyond this one. The things seen here are but a shadow from that world," he explained. "Crazy Horse was on his horse in that world and the trees and the grass and the stones were all made of spirit, and nothing was hard, and everything seemed to float. His horse danced around like a horse made only of shadow. This is how he got his name. His horse was not crazy or wild, but in the vision he had, it danced around in a queer way. The great power Crazy Horse had was from his vision."

Mitchell went on to tell me that shortly before his death, Black Elk had been converted to Catholicism by a missionary, but there is reason to believe he had accepted Christ as his Savior before that. When the missionary had asked him which was more powerful the Bible or the Peace Pipe, Black Elk replied, "We will build a fire and you put your book on the coals and I will lay my pipe there, too." So the fire burned the book to ash and the stone bowl of the pipe was only blackened with soot. The pipe Black Elk was using had an L-shaped bowl attached to the stem. Black Elk took the L-shaped bowl of the pipe and laid it in the soft sand and rolled it from side to side. In the sand was left an imprint of a cross.

I knew that, at the time Black Elk died, Christianity was a part of his funeral ceremony. He had been christened a Catholic and given the name of Nicholas. I wasn't sure, but I felt that the imprint of the cross in the sand was symbolic that the cross and the pipe were of one and the same spirit. Mitchell also mentioned that his great-grandfather had envisioned the Oglala Sioux people going forth in numbers as flames to bring about beneficial change in Black Elk's generation.

There are differences between Indian spirituality and Christianity, but there are also many similarities, with the main one being the reliance upon faith in that which you cannot see or touch. As time passes, I can now understand that during my father's illness, this became the real search he was undertaking, the search for understanding, acceptance, and true spirituality.

Over the next several months, I read and researched, and then I thought plenty about why there might be so many alleged burial places of the great warrior Crazy Horse. As a mortician, I am particularly interested in why the body of the most famous of all Sioux war chiefs was so carefully hidden. The many stories of the numerous places he could be buried deepened the mystery surrounding Crazy Horse. I wanted to consider each of those stories carefully. Discovering the exact location of his burial place was not as important to me as understanding how, through the stories from the many people I have met on my journey, the Great Spirit guides us in our care for those who sorrow. Whether my readers are Lakota Sioux or of other races, I hope that they will see that this is a universal story of the courage and love of those who gave their life for what they believed.

7

Close Calls and the Conflict Within

The Lakota Sioux in the Midwest were largely unaffected by the Civil War, and were quite content to be left alone by the white man. Their lodges were filled with buffalo meat and hides, and their lives were normal. During the years of the Civil War, Crazy Horse became a respected leader of war parties. It was during this era also, that he would have his heart broken, a wound from which he would never recover.

Much of the information in this chapter is based on the tireless work of a host of authors, including Mari Sandoz, Jason Hook, H.P. Howard, and Stephen Ambrose, as well as interviews with Eleanor Hinman and others too numerous to mention. When my dad and I first started making our investigative trips into the heart of Indian country, we would pass the time on the journey by reading aloud from these authors' works, educating ourselves, sharing stories from our own investigations, and discovering leads for my dad's book and then for my own. Even though our work has taken different paths, both of us have been inspired and educated by the work of these fine authors.

As we continued to travel the countryside and learn more about the Sioux chiefs, we often stopped to pick a wild sunflower to stick in the grill of dad's Grand Prix to brighten our day as well as the day of whomever we might meet. Once we even put one in the back window. That one was a giant sunflower that my dad had grown on his farm along the banks of the river that ran near his big white barn and flower patch.

In our readings, whenever Dad and I would come to passages about the life and time of Chief Crazy Horse, I was always fascinated by the psychological aspects of how his personality was shaped. This chapter is intended to shine a light on the trials and tribulations that helped mold the great chief. We've discussed much of his younger days and his family life, but it may just be the love he found and then lost that had the biggest impact on his life.

The year was 1862. Crazy Horse was staying in Chief Red Cloud's Bad Face camp. Crazy Horse and Red Cloud's niece, Black Buffalo Woman, fell hopelessly in love. Red Cloud and Crazy Horse had philosophical differences. Red Cloud was older and had become more reflective; he carried the scars of a lifetime of battle etched both in his heart and on his skin. Red

Cloud was deliberate, thoughtful and cautious with age. Crazy Horse was quick to anger, prone to violence and made no secret of his differences with Red Cloud in those matters.

Crazy Horse was proud of his accomplishments in battle, and believed his manhood was measured by his abilities as a warrior. Crazy Horse had been accepted into an elite group known as the Shirt Wearers. Only the bravest of the brave—the best of the best warriors—were accepted into this society. Members were expected to live according to a strict code of ethical behavior. Being a Shirt Wearer was a source of great pride for Crazy Horse. Red Cloud felt that such a society only served to stir up the radical young warriors, which in the long run would cause more trouble for their people, especially with the white man, who just kept coming forth in seemingly endless waves. His reluctance to do battle with the white man had nothing to do with a fear of their ability as warriors, but rather the number of the enemy.

In the middle of it all was the beautiful Black Buffalo Woman.

In 1870 when Red Cloud sent word that Crazy Horse was to lead a war party against the Crow nation, Crazy Horse boldly answered the call. A brave named No Water left the war party early due to a toothache and returned to camp. When Crazy Horse and his men returned to camp two weeks later, he learned that No Water stayed behind to marry Black Buffalo Woman. Red Cloud had used Crazy Horse's eagerness to lead other braves into battle against him.

In anger, Crazy Horse rode away from camp and returned a few days later with two Crow scalps which he threw to the dogs in camp. When Black Buffalo Woman gave birth to a light-haired boy less than a year later, leading some to question the child's paternity, No Water sent two ponies to Crazy Horse's father signaling that the matter of Black Buffalo Woman was closed.

Black Buffalo Woman was as heartbroken as Crazy Horse, because the matter was actually not closed. Black Buffalo Woman ran off with Crazy Horse after years of marriage to No Water. No Water tracked them down and surprised the lovers in Crazy Horse's tent. He shot Crazy Horse at close range with a pistol, the bullet hitting Crazy Horse in the face, nearly killing Crazy Horse. After his long recovery, it was his turn to seek revenge, and he hunted down No Water. He didn't need to inflict a single injury to win the showdown, however. No Water fled with Black Buffalo Woman, whom Crazy Horse never saw again.

To make matters worse, Crazy Horse was stripped of his membership in the Shirt Wearers Society. He had broken the strict code of ethics, by engaging in adulterous behavior. His shirt was never given to another. He Dog, a member of the organization, said that the decision to strip Crazy Horse of his membership was the beginning of the end. "Everything seemed to stop right there. Everything seemed to fall to pieces. After that, it seemed nobody wanted to wear the shirt; it meant nothing."

Crazy Horse was revered. His troubles served only to make him more valiant, or perhaps more carefree when it came to battle. It wasn't that he had a death wish; he just didn't care if he lived or died. This was evident in many instances, perhaps none more telling as his willingness to be a decoy for a trap designed to defeat the cavalry at Fort Phil Kearny.

The Captain at the fort, William J. Fetterman, was a man who held the Indians in contempt. He felt they were inferior in battle, and once boasted, "Give me eighty men and I'll ride through the entire Sioux Nation!" The trouble started when a small group of loggers from the fort rode in wagons to the Big Piney Creek looking for firewood. A small band of warriors swept down the hills toward them. The loggers circled the wagons and signaled the fort for help. Ironically, Captain Fetterman answered the call with eighty men.

The Sioux immediately retreated, disappearing over the hills, except for a small band of Indians who appeared helpless. This group that seemed ripe for the taking included Crazy Horse, Hump, He Dog, and other handpicked braves. Fetterman couldn't resist and gave chase. Since some of Fetterman's men were on foot, they pursued slowly. Playing their parts well, Crazy Horse and his friends moved just as slowly. Just before he reached the big ridge, Crazy Horse jumped off his horse and pretended his horse had gone lame. The other Indians gathered around him, as if to protect him.

Fetterman had been ordered not to chase the Indians beyond the ridge because help was unavailable. This was different, he thought, since there were just a handful of Indians; they were so close. Fetterman shouted for his men to hurry. Shots rang out as they gave chase. Over the ridge the soldiers rode, into the valley…and into the trap.

It is estimated that two thousand braves descended upon Fetterman and his troops when they reached the bottom of the valley. The soldiers were all killed. Thirteen braves lost their lives as well, most killed by friendly fire, the Sioux said. Crazy Horse and Hump searched for their life-long friend, Lone Bear. They found him seriously wounded. Lone Bear died in the arms of Crazy Horse. As Crazy Horse and Hump returned to camp, their hearts were heavy with the loss of their friend.

It is interesting to note that historians recently discovered that the attack on Fetterman and his troops occurred under an unusual moon. In December 1999, during the winter solstice, a lunar perigee occurred. A lunar perigee is when the moon is closest to the earth and literally floods the prairie with light. The last previous lunar perigee was December 21, 1866. It was by the light of this lunar perigee that Crazy Horse's daring warriors led a decoy party to bait the cavalry of Fort Phil Kearny, according to an article published in the *Indian Country Today* on December 2, 1999.

Those who study Crazy Horse's battle plans, such as Donavan Sprague, director of the Cultural Center at the Crazy Horse Memorial near Custer, South Dakota, note that the moon that waxed that night produced probably the brightest moonlight Crazy Horse had ever seen. Hours later, on the hillside just outside Fort Phil Kearny, for Fetterman and his hapless soldiers, that bright light went out.

The aggression of the white men drove Crazy Horse and his warriors to run like the wily prairie coyote. Under a full moon, a coyote becomes as active as a waterbug on the Niobrara River in the warmth of summer when it hunts its prey. A coyote's belly is never empty when the face of the moon smiles its widest. Others who have lived under the stars also understand how nature's gravitational pull can overwhelm the senses. Animals that prey become more aggressive hunters and less inhibited around people. Could the lunar perigee have influenced Fetterman and his men that fateful night just outside Fort Phil Kearny?

Crazy Horse, Hump and Lone Bear had ridden together in many, many battles and had shared triumph and tragedy. Warriors don't like to think about it, but they know that with every battle the chance of death looms like a dark cloud on the horizon. Crazy Horse would know the pain of seeing many close friends die, but none affected him as much as what happened to Hump since Crazy Horse felt responsible.

It was autumn: cold, windy, with rain changing to snow. Crazy Horse and Hump were in a war party searching for Shoshones. The mud and slush were ankle deep. Crazy Horse wanted to turn back, but Hump talked him out of it. "The last time you called off a battle they laughed at us. You and I have our honor to think about. If you do not care about it, you can go back. But I am going to stay here and fight."

Crazy Horse was a loyal friend, "Alright, we will stay and fight if you feel that way about it," he told Hump, "but I think we are going to get a good licking. You have good guns, and I have a gun, but look at our men. None of them have good guns and most of them only have bows and arrows. It is a bad place for a fight and a bad day for it, and the enemy numbered twelve to our one."

It didn't take long for Crazy Horse's words to ring true. The Oglalas found themselves on the run. Crazy Horse, Hump, and a brave named Good Weasel acted as guards on the rear of the retreating Sioux. Hump's horse was shot in the leg and stumbled in the mud. Crazy Horse and Good Weasel tried to hold off the Shoshone, but they could not. Crazy Horse had lost his lifelong friend, and his heart was again heavy.

Within a few moons, Crazy Horse would also lose his brother, Little Hawk. Crazy Horse had always felt that his brother was a better warrior, and they were very close. Little Hawk died while on a buffalo hunt. He and others set off to harass some Shoshones, but were fired upon by white miners. Most of the Oglala fled when they were fired upon, but Little Hawk did not and he was shot and killed.

He Dog was worried about Crazy Horse. His friend was living in his parents' lodge and at times, seemed distant and bitter. He Dog arranged a marriage for Crazy Horse with a

Chief Sitting Bull. Photo courtesy Nebraska State Historical Society.

Cheyenne woman named Black Shawl. Crazy Horse sent a message with his mother to Black Shawl. "You must say that there will be little joy in a life with me." Black Shawl did not listen. They married and brought into the world a daughter Crazy Horse cherished, whom they named They Are Afraid Of Her.

Crazy Horse had formed a close friendship with Chief Sitting Bull. Sitting Bull was resistant to change in the Sioux ways of life, a trait Crazy Horse admired. Sitting Bull and Crazy Horse refused to meet with the white man, but Red Cloud did. There became two camps: those who followed Red Cloud, and those who followed Crazy Horse. The two were diametrically opposed in how they thought the Sioux should deal with the white man. Red Cloud thought treaties and peace would bring freedom; Crazy Horse believed only war could ensure that his people would never be shackled.

Red Cloud and his followers lived on reservations. Warriors like Sitting Bull and Crazy Horse clung to the last vestiges of freedom. But the white man kept coming. There were surveying crews, settlers, and troops, all seeking to "civilize" the untamed frontier. Once again, tragedy struck close to home.

For three days, Crazy Horse mourned his deceased daughter as he lay on a scaffold with her like this one. Photo courtesy Nebraska State Historical Society.

In 1873, Crazy Horse was living in a village near Little Bighorn. Crazy Horse had left camp on a raiding party to fight the Crow. When he returned, they discovered that the village had moved. Signs painted on buffalo skulls and sticks showed the way to the new camp. As he approached the new site, he was met by his father who told him his precious daughter, They Are Afraid Of Her, had died of sickness and lay in a scaffold seventy miles away in land now occupied by the Crows. He was determined to visit his daughter one last time and asked an Indian interpreter, Frank Grouard, to accompany him.

Grouard had been a mail carrier in Montana who was captured and eventually taken in by Sitting Bull. He fought with the Lakota against the government forces on the Yellowstone River. After quarreling with Sitting Bull, Grouard joined Crazy Horse's camp.

In Joseph De Barthe's book, *Life and Adventures of Frank Grouard*, he states that Crazy Horse told Grouard to select a campsite while he visited the scaffold that held his daughter. For three days and nights, Crazy Horse shunned food and water in his deep sorrow. At sunrise on the fourth day, he woke Grouard and said he was ready to go. His people didn't know where he had been, and Crazy Horse did not speak of it.

Tragedy changed Crazy Horse. He withdrew and seldom would speak in public. He did not seek power or leadership roles in the tribe; he only asked that he be left alone and allowed to fight for his people. He became more reckless in battle. His enemies, including the Crows who were the opponents who knew him best, were more afraid of him now than ever. A Crow reported it was well-known among them that Crazy Horse had medicine that would hit whatever he looked at and that he himself was bulletproof.

He would disappear from camp for weeks at a time. No one knew where he went or what he was doing, but over time, several white miners who had invaded the Black Hills were found killed, an arrow stuck in the ground beside their bodies, their scalps intact. Crazy Horse was deeply troubled and he felt powerless to change things. The white man just kept coming…

8

Beckoned to the Battle Site at the Little Bighorn and Dowsing for Gravesites

n the banks of the Little Bighorn River, the battle of that famous name between the Sioux and General George Armstrong Custer was waged. I have always felt drawn to this site in Montana. When I was a child, I had visited it with my parents on a family trip that took us through the Black Hills, around Devils Tower, and then to Custer's Last Stand. At the time, I was not sure why I was attracted to the vast rolling grassland that overlooked a small stream, but I felt that I would return to this area at some point in my life. It was there that my real interest in Crazy Horse may have been born, but it would be many years before a coincidental encounter would again spark my curiosity about the great chief.

Shortly after my mortuary internship in Marysville, Kansas, two young women from California came into our mortuary to pay their respects to their father. I asked them if their father looked all right to them. They replied that they did not think their father looked quite right; he did not look like himself. They found a piece of lint on his suit, then another one; I was sinking deeper into a dark hole. Their mother said softly, "I think he looks good."

I asked the daughters about the last time they had seen their father and they told me it had been a year and half, and "he just doesn't look like himself." I talked to them about the cancer from which he had suffered, the long term illness he had gone through. They knew he had lost weight. I explained how much I wanted to help them through this. I thought I was able to understand why they were upset that their father did not look natural. I had no excuses except that, in this case, I was not able to reproduce nature as it once was. We talked about grief, the denial of death, the negotiation, the hostility, and all the other difficult things one goes through to accept the death of a family member. Throughout the funeral, I could see the daughters gaining an understanding of illness and a comprehension of the spiritual world. They were particular people who wanted things just right. In time, we became friends. Whenever they returned to visit their mother, they would stop at the mortuary to say hello.

On one of their visits they stopped to ask if I knew how to help them find a baby buried in their family plot at the Marysville cemetery. The women told me their plot was very large, with more than twenty burial spaces in it. I told them they should go to the city hall where they would find a record of the death and a map of the cemetery. They had done that, yet still could not locate the small marker they remembered being on the grave.

I went home for lunch and then sat in my easy chair and prayed to help these women. I felt I may have let them down once, and I wanted to do a better job of assisting them than I had in coping with their father's death. A warm feeling came over me; I bolted from the house with two L-shaped wire rods and headed for the cemetery. My father had taught me how to dowse for water, and I had heard George Musil, a guy who occasionally helped at the cemetery, say he could dowse to find vaults and caskets that were buried in cemetery lots; now, I intended to try it.

Dowsing is not only a search for water, but also lost objects. My father taught me how to find the water pipe that went from one building to another on our farm. He showed me that you could also tell the depth of a pipe or well by holding out the L-shaped rod or wire and counting the bounces of the rod. Each time the rod went up and down meant it was one foot in depth; so if you counted twenty bobs, that meant the well was twenty feet deep.

An early experience with my father verified the viability of dowsing for me. A well company was drilling for water on our neighbor's property and we went over to ask the boss of the drilling operation if he ever used dowsing to find water or to check the depth. He said, "I don't believe in it and I can't do it anyway." My dad told him that, according to the bounces he counted with his dowsing rod, they should hit water at 42 feet. Later that day, one of the drillers said he hit water at 42½ feet; the boss did not speak to my dad for a long time.

When I got to our cemetery, I walked across graves to see if my rods would cross, indicating that the grave was occupied. It seemed to work, but I thought I needed a better test. I knew that some people bought their headstones before a death occurred and usually, for a husband and wife, there is one stone with both names on it. If the wife died but the husband had not, I figured that by walking down a row of headstones, I should come across stones that would indicate by the death date that only one person was in the grave. If I walked by a stone that had two names, each with death dates indicated on the engraved stone, and my rods crossed at two different locations, then there was a possibility that two people were there. If I walked over a grave near the headstone that just had a birth date on it and no death date engraved, then I should get no response from the dowsing rods. If they did cross, the possibility still existed that someone could be buried there and the date had yet to be engraved on the stone; if that were the case, it may have been a recent burial and the ground would be freshly turned. I seemed to get positive results with a test where I had another person cover up a recently dug grave with a big black plastic sheet about twenty feet by twenty feet in size, and I was able to determine the two-foot-by-eight-foot gravesite.

I went to the large family plot that the women had asked me about to see if I could find where the baby might be buried. I walked back and forth over the lot which was about eight hundred square feet. At about three feet from the curb of the cemetery road, I found a three-foot-by-two-foot area where my rods crossed, which to me was a positive indicator that something was in the ground below. This was kind of exciting.

I called the daughters to tell them I may have found a way to find the lost grave but that they might find the method unusual and hard to believe. When they arrived shortly, I explained my method of dowsing and they understood how it worked from hearing about dowsers searching for water. I did not tell them that I had located the gravesite of the baby earlier; instead, I showed them how to dowse and they both had immediate responses.

It was a nice, sunny, early fall day and the recently hired sexton, who was out checking on some new road work in the cemetery, came over to say hello to us. We told him we were looking for a baby that had been buried in this large lot many years ago. The family thought at one time there was a small grave marker for the child, but it had since disappeared. The sexton said, "You know, we just did some road work here putting in new curbing. I think there is a cross marker made of concrete and stones that goes there where you are looking. It does not have a name on it." He got down on his hands and knees and felt the surface of the thick grass. He was looking for a receptacle for the cross to fit into. "Here it is," he said with excitement. "I found it. It's underneath the grass." He jumped up and headed to his pick-up, saying, "I will be back in a minute." When he returned, he had a small cross in his hand that fit exactly in the receptacle. He said, "The street crew put the cross over in the cemetery storage shed when new curbing was being put in last spring and this marker was forgotten about. I remember the old sexton saying something about when the curb work is done, the marker is to be placed on a baby's grave in this area."

We were all astonished that the mystery may have been solved. I told the women we could not know for sure if the baby was buried there unless we dug down to find a casket or bones. We could make a pretty educated guess that this was the burial spot we were looking for. They were satisfied that this was indeed the spot they had been looking for and did not feel it was necessary to dig. I knew I had developed an interest in this dowsing process that was not going to go away.

My father belonged to the American Dowsers Association headquartered in Danville, Vermont. I called them to see if they had much information on gravesite dowsing and the secretary there told me that a man had come to their annual convention to give a speech on dowsing and archeology at the Custer Battlefield in Montana. The library at Danville had a tape of the field exercise and the secretary said they would send me one. I soon received the tape recording of Daniel M. Larson describing dowsing the Little Bighorn Battlefield after a prairie fire in 1984 and finding remains and bones that were taken to the Midwest Archeological Center in Lincoln, Nebraska, for further study.

The same week I was reading a book by Thomas Noguchi, *Coroner at Large*, which told about Dr. Thomas B. Marquis' 1920 theory disputing the heroic version of that battle. Marquis was a physician assigned to the Cheyenne Indian Reservation in the early years of the 1900s. Survivors of the battle were still alive, and what they had told him stunned him. There had been no hilltop battle as described by other people. Custer and his troops were surrounded, but the Indians had charged neither on foot nor on horse. Instead, they dismounted and hid in the gullies and draws on the hillside, sniping at the soldiers on the ridge with their few guns, or launching arrows toward the hill from below.

Early in the battle, a few brave detachments of soldiers charged down the hill trying to break out of the encirclement and they were killed. About two hundred soldiers on top of the hill were still in fortified positions, therefore the Indians knew that a frontal attack would be foolish and instead they waited for dark. To their astonishment, there was a flurry of gunfire on the hill above them, then silence. An Indian scout crawled up the hill under cover of the bushes and saw an incredible scene: Custer and his men all lay dead.

That was the way the story went as Dr. Marquis learned it from the Indians, a version of the battle that must be appalling to American patriots. Some of the soldiers had been killed by Indians, but Custer and the bulk of the troops chose to commit mass suicide rather than suffer torture at the hands of the Indians. If it were true, this seemed like an outrageous story. The army said all it really knew was that two hundred American soldiers died there, and perhaps only a dozen Indians.

I went on to read in Noguchi's book that Navy Commander Jerry Spencer of the Armed Forces Institute of Pathology presented the mass suicide theory at a conference of the American Academy of Forensic Sciences. He said that he had requested that the skeletons be exhumed for examination. I knew Jerry Spencer; he'd graduated from Marysville High School and I had helped with arrangements burying members of his family. He told about techniques of modern forensic science that would make it possible to substantiate the suicide theory of Dr. Marquis if the skeletons could be examined. At the time Marquis' book had been written, the skeletons had not been exhumed for examination.

I decided I had to go to Lincoln to the Midwest Archeological Center to find out more about the dowsers and this suicide theory. At the center I met Dr. Doug Scott. Doug knew of Marysville, Kansas. He had a good friend, Merlyn R. Schwarz, who farmed just east of Marysville and was an expert on US cavalry arms. Doug sometimes consulted with him about old guns. Dr. Scott's work on the Little Bighorn Battlefield had been featured in the December 1986 *National Geographic*. I had many questions for Doug. Most of all, I wanted to know if the dowsers who worked the battlefield were accurate. He listened to Larson's tape, and when it reported that they had found a body on the Custer Battlefield, Scott noted that they had, but by a boot sticking up or a bone protruding the surface. "You didn't need a dowser to find remains on the battlefield. The dowsers," Doug said, "were one hundred percent wrong in what they did." I was disappointed, but I wanted his straight opinion of what he thought of dowsing. I told him I was experimenting with it. I thought I'd had some success, but I wanted to test my results. Doug said his father was a dowser who was quite good at finding water and water pipes, but Doug had never had any success at it. "But, Cleve," he said, "you might try this. In your profession as a mortician, do you ever move graves from one cemetery to another?" I replied that we did. Doug went on to say, "That would be a good test. You could take someone with you to verify your dowsing predictions before digging. Then when you do dig down and if you find remains, you will know how close you were to your predictions."

I asked Doug Scott about the Custer suicide theory. He told me that most individuals who commit suicide with a firearm shoot themselves in the head, and the muzzle of the weapon would be close in contact to the head. Besides the bullet, a large quantity of powder residue is driven into the scalp tissue and into the skull, where it would remain indefinitely. Doug acknowledged that the mass-suicide theory has been used to account for the brevity of the battle, since troops, in many other Plains Indian warfare fights, had given a good account of their victorious actions despite overwhelming numerical odds. If suicide were the case, one would expect to find a high frequency of close-range gunshot wounds to the head. Unfortunately, the osteological remains available in this study include no complete skulls, but none of the cranial fragments available for study show any clear-cut signs of gunshot trauma. Because of lack of cranial materials, the absence of evidence of gunshot wounds in the head is not alone sufficient to rule out the suicide theory, but it certainly offers no support for it. Rather, the osteological evidence supports a scenario of events that consisted of a brief firefight followed by the close-range termination of the wounded. It appears probable that the majority of the troopers were still alive but helplessly wounded when resistance stopped, and that many were finished off with massive crushing blows to the head. After death, many were mutilated and dismembered.

Army burial parties arrived the next day and Custer's grave was dug to a depth of eighteen inches. It was also made wide enough to hold the body of his brother, Tom, and the two bodies were laid side by side. The general had been shot twice; one bullet entered the left temple, and the second struck him in the chest. There was a wound in his right forearm that could have been caused either by a third bullet or an exiting fragment of the bullet that caused the chest wound. Tom Custer had been scalped and his skull completely crushed, his body stuck with arrows, and his abdomen cut open. Prior to closing the grave with dirt, the bodies were covered with blankets and canvas tent sheets. An Indian travois found in the abandoned village was laid over the grave and weighted down with rocks. Exhumation teams came later to move General Armstrong Custer's grave to West Point, and Tom Custer to Leavenworth, Kansas, but the probability of their bones commingling with each other's definitely exists.

In the fall of 1998, I was in charge of burial arrangements for a woman by the name of Viola Svea Dean at the National Cemetery at Leavenworth, Kansas. Her family was from Marysville. We found that the grave she was to be buried in was about one hundred meters from Tom Custer's. At least the stone says Tom Custer. Few people who visit this site would realize that some of the bones in the grave are probably George's, too. Tom Custer is the only US Army soldier to receive two Congressional Medals of Honor for heroic efforts during the Civil War. At Manozine Church, Virginia, on May 10, 1862, he captured the enemy flag. The second medal he received when he captured two stands of color, the flags of the enemy, and was wounded at Sailor Creek, Virginia, in April 1865.

Through the years I have kept in contact with Dr. Doug Scott, reporting on various experiments in gravesite dowsing. Most of them have been pleasant surprises with positive results. There is one mystery that remains at the Custer Battleground site and that is that 28 out of approximately 250 of Custer's men have never been retrieved. They are believed to be buried in the area of Deep Ravine on the battlefield. In 1989, when I visited the site on my way to do a disinterment in Montana, a dowsing experiment indicated that a few of the graves of the missing men might possibly be located in the upper end, but, to date, their remains have not been retrieved.

The dowser who worked the Custer Battlefield, Dan Larson, was a person I wanted to visit with to hear his side of the story. The Danville Vermont Dowsing Society said he was from the San Francisco Bay area. I contacted the Bay area's dowsing society and a member told me that unfortunately, Dan had died.

Sitting at our mortuary office one day, I looked through the yellow book, the mortuary directory, for listings in the Bay area. Out of many, I picked one to call. The man who answered remembered that they had handled the arrangements for Dan Larson about two months earlier. They gave me Dan's widow's phone number. When I called her, she related to me that Dan had always been careful to behave in a professional manner as a dowser, and that he'd had no personal gain from it. Dan had paid his own expenses to Montana and never took money for any dowsing, except of water sites. Dan considered it a great honor to be included in the Custer digs, and when he dowsed there, he was satisfied that his gift was real. His widow sent me a letter with a number of articles about Dan's success locating several lost gravesites. He had also worked with anthropologists at East Bay Regional Parks District's Old Somerville town, where graves of old Chinese residents may lie.

How does dowsing work? In 1988, Dr. Doug Scott, an archeologist, claimed that dowsing just did not work. But the wife of Dan Larson believed that Dan's work was credible. I can tell you, ten years later, that they both may be right in their analysis. Here is how that might be the case.

Is it a gift? Most will say they don't know, and that is a perfectly good answer. It seems to be a gift most of us have but few have developed or believe in. When we dowse, we create the idea of the target, whether that target is tangible or intangible. The accuracy of our response, or even whether we get a response at all, depends on the degree of resonance our creation achieves with the desired target. Dowsing may be thought of as an art. The role of the artist is to become an interpreter of the infinite, subtle qualities of the spirit present in all things that may reveal a glimpse of the absolute idea of perfect harmony. In other words, you focus on a target to see if you can find it by receiving a response with your instruments—in my case, wire rods that were nothing more than cut up coat hangers made into an L shape.

I attended dowsing school in Danville, Vermont, in 1988. There were many interesting people there telling their stories of dowsing. Some were laborers and farmers, some were deans of engineering schools. According to Edgar Mitchell, an astronaut, "There is no unnatural or supernatural phenomena, only very large gaps in our knowledge of what is natural. We should strive to fill these gaps of ignorance."

There was an engineer present by the name of Ludger Mersmann who did extensive work on the development of the Geo-Magnetometer. He related his mechanism to the process of dowsing. The device picks up distortions in the earth's magnetic field. A magnetometer works like sonar, sending out electrical impulses that are read by means of a graph that shows the conditions of the earth's electrical field. Dr. Mersmann said dowsing rods probably work much the same way.

The burying of Custer's dead fell to the men in Reno's command. Reno had ridden with Custer, but the command was divided up such that Reno fought the Indians a few miles away and came upon Custer the next day, on June 26, 1876. The burials were hasty, and most of the dead were interred in very shallow graves. Dirt was simply thrown over the bodies, or sage brush was piled over them. In the summer of 1877, Captain Michael Sheridan reinterred exposed bones and removed all the graves he could find. He also drove cedar stakes at each grave he could find. Custer's remains were later removed and reburied at the United States Military Academy at West Point, New York.

I have a brother-in-law, Larry Shaw, whose grandfather was Amberson G. Shaw. Family stories tell of Grandfather Shaw living among the Sioux Indians, and his connections with them were useful when he did scouting work for the United States Army. In the summer of 1877, Amberson Shaw was employed with two four-mule wagons to put up hay at Fort Custer at the forks of the Little Bighorn River. The mule teams arrived in August. Shaw says that he told the officers at the fort there were bones on the Custer Battlefield lying exposed with shameless indifference. He says the bones were put into a vault that year, and the vault was laid in masonry.

Larry told me at a family gathering that his grandfather, Amberson G. Shaw, was in his seventies when Larry's father Ralph was born. Primary memories of A.G. were that he was married many times, and threw knives at one of his wives in a Wild West show. When Ralph was ten years old, A.G. was confined to a wheelchair. A.G. asked his son to wheel him down every Thursday evening to one of the four brothels in Valentine, Nebraska, which catered mostly to the Buffalo Soldiers stationed at Fort Niobrara.

In 1879, the Army sent another detail to the Little Bighorn; this time not only to inspect graves, but to erect a memorial monument. On the knoll just above where Custer had been buried, the detail stacked cordwood eleven feet high to form a memorial. Parts of five bodies were all that could be found at that time and they were placed underneath the memorial. Horse bones were collected and placed inside the cordwood structure, but the many horse bones lead to speculation that Custer's dead were scattered about. The bones found at the site must have been a source of confusion to burial parties and dowsers alike.

Amberson G. Shaw reported seeing five soldiers' graves on the south side of the Little Bighorn River where they had been buried in shallow graves, and also, in a lower place, he saw seven Indians' bodies that had not been buried. Shaw also reported that Tom Custer was killed somewhere close to the river on the north side. Could the five soldiers' graves on the south side of the river be some of the twenty-eight unaccounted for bodies believed to have been buried in Deep Ravine? In *Archaeological Perspectives on the Battle of the Little Bighorn*, Douglas Scott and others state that two years later, in 1881, an officer's report noted that no remains were exposed and that graves were covered with grass. In 1881, these graves were opened and the remains were re-interred in a common grave where they are today.

The ground of the battlefield had been disturbed by the constant digging and re-digging of the army burial details. Such ground disturbances often affect dowsing reception. Dr. Doug

Scott said the ground disturbances also affect the Geo-Magnetometer's ability to give an interpretation of the ground distortion. He said that the Geo-Magnetometer had been used at the Custer Battlefield site; it did not seem to work well because of the many times the field had been excavated.

Both Dan Larson, the dowser from California, and Dr. Scott believed in their work. When Dan Larson would offer an opinion of where a burial site was and the archeologist would dig down and find nothing, the dowsing was dismissed as being invalid. Dan Larson may have been getting dowsing responses from old burial sites where remains had been removed by army details. Both of these people were driven by different spirits, and to each the ghost of the grave speaks differently. In the seasons to come, I wondered what feelings I would sense about the burial grounds of others. What would I find? Where would I be called?

9

Crazy Horse and the Battle of Little Bighorn—Was He Late?

In the late summer of 1998, I stopped to visit with my friend, Darlene Rosane, who lives on the Pine Ridge Reservation. Darlene had been raised by the son of Chief American Horse, a first cousin to Crazy Horse. Each generation selected one person to act as family historian and Darlene had been chosen. Visiting with her is pleasant in many ways, her wealth of knowledge being just one of the things that makes my visits with Darlene so enjoyable.

On this day, I would learn things about Crazy Horse that I had never heard or read before. Much of her information, she said, came from a visit with an old Crow Indian when she was a child. His name was Yellow Tail, a descendant of the Crow Chief of the same name. The Chief was a courier of news, bringing messages to and from various tribes, including Sioux, Cheyenne, Mandan, and Blackfeet. Yellow Tail told Darlene that the older Yellow Tail delivered a message to Crazy Horse, who was camped on Crow Creek at the base of the Rocky Mountains near what is now Littleton, Colorado, that he was to hurry to Little Bighorn and attend a large council of Chiefs.

I stopped her because I had read in history books that the Crow and Sioux were enemies. Why would Chief Yellow Tail help a Sioux? She said the confrontation between the Crow and the Sioux were games to see who was the smartest; they were essentially a contest of wits, not a war, although this warfare seemed serious to me. There were casualties, yes, but they were stealing ponies from each other most of the time and it was a risk they took. In time, the Sioux would steal them back…and so the game went.

Chief American Horse. Photo courtesy Nebraska State Historical Society.

She went on to explain that tribes from many nations were gathering to camp in the meadow at Little Bighorn. There was a young boy who tended to the ponies. When some got free, he gave chase over the hills and was shot by soldiers, who were patrolling the area. Upset over this act, the Indians retaliated and this led to the demise of Custer and his troops. According to Darlene, the mother of the slain boy was allowed to finish Custer off with a knife, though reports from the Army say Custer was shot twice, and no stab wounds were mentioned. Yellow Tail told her that three soldiers were allowed to escape to spread the news of what happened and why, but ultimately only one survived.

Darlene said Crazy Horse was not there, according to American Horse family history, but arrived one day late. He was to have led the charge, but the Indians could not wait to avenge the boy's death.

With all due respect to my friend Darlene, there are those who say that Crazy Horse was indeed at Little Bighorn, and that he led the charge. It has been well documented that Crazy Horse fought in the Battle of Rosebud on June 17, 1876. Here Crazy Horse attacked George Crook. The battle raged for six hours, leaving thirty-nine Indians and ten soldiers dead. Eight days later the Custer massacre took place. Both battles were in southern Montana, not far from each other. It would be difficult to ride from the Rosebud to Colorado and then come back to the Little Bighorn in eight days.

General Custer and Crazy Horse as drawn by Kills Two. Picture courtesy Nebraska State Historical Society.

American Horse and Crazy Horse fought many times side by side, and were friends, but there is evidence that the two had different opinions on the war with the white man, and these differences drove them apart. There are also stories that tell of American Horse's desire to kill Crazy Horse at Fort Robinson, and others that speak of his involvement in the Chief's death. Could a bitter feud and a desire to discredit Crazy Horse result in a revisionist history that excludes him from Little Bighorn?

Eli Ricker, an employee of the Indian Bureau, conducted interviews with various people regarding Crazy Horse, including American Horse, after Ricker retired from Government Service around 1906. His handwritten notes are on file at the Nebraska Historical Society. Ricker verified that American Horse was with Crazy Horse when the Chief died at Fort Robinson, and says that American Horse told him that the stabbing was an accident. American Horse told Ricker that he was about to shoot Crazy Horse as he lay on the ground, but a crowd gathered around the Chief before he had the chance. A scout named William Garnett would describe American Horse as a "...sly diplomat who could play both sides against the other." Not a flattering description of American Horse, and one Darlene was quick to dismiss. She said that

Ricker must have misunderstood what he was told. American Horse supported Crazy Horse; they simply disagreed on whether the white man could be beaten.

American Horse eventually joined Red Cloud's camp, marrying one of Red Cloud's daughters. Like Red Cloud, American Horse wanted peace with the white man. In fact, American Horse's grandson, Joe, told me that American Horse was one of the signers of the 1868 Peace Treaty. [*Joe American Horse is a great Pine Ridge runner who won a gold medal in the 1957 Nebraska state track meet. Gregg McBride of the Omaha World-Herald called it the best mile ever run by a Nebraska high school athlete. It was run in bad weather conditions but, at the time, it was the second fastest mile ever run in state history at 4:28.1. In 1960, he set the University of Nebraska record in the two mile at 9:18.2. Joe American Horse now lives at Pine Ridge and was tribal chairman from 1982-84 and 1986-88. Joe told me that Chief American Horse had five wives until the government handed out land allotments and made him choose one wife. He compromised and narrowed it down to two.*]

Crazy Horse, on the other hand, believed that the white man posed a threat to their way of prairie life, and that the white man must be defeated in battle if the Sioux wanted to live in peace. For this reason, it would seem strange for Crazy Horse to miss a battle like Little Big Horn. But Darlene held firmly to her family history, maintaining that Crazy Horse was a day late for the battle.

I have heard several conflicting stories of Crazy Horse's actions during the Battle of Little Bighorn. One such story comes from Short Buffalo, younger brother of He Dog, as told to Eleanor Hinman:

> In this Custer fight, I was helping fight Reno (whose troops were located just a few miles from Custer's) and never noticed Custer coming. We had Reno's men on the run across the creek when Crazy Horse rode up with his men. "Too late, you've missed the fight," we called out to him.
>
> "Sorry to miss the fight," he laughed. "But there is a good fight coming over the hill." I looked to where Crazy Horse was pointing and saw Custer and his blue coats pouring over the hill. I thought there were a million of them. "That's where the big fight is going to be!" Crazy Horse told us. "We'll not miss that now."
>
> He was not a bit excited, he made a joke of it. He wheeled and rode down the river, and a little while later, I saw him on his pinto pony leading his men across the river. I saw he had the business well in hand. They rode up the draw, and there was too much dirt, I could not see anymore.
>
> The next day we saw Bear Coat (Indian name given to General Nelson A. Miles [actual person was Alfred Terry, not Bear Coat (Buecker)] coming from below along the river. These soldiers are the ones that dug in the ground, and didn't do much fighting. In the morning, they joined forces with Reno on his hill. The Indians quit and went away.

In his book, *Black Elk Speaks*, John G. Neihardt writes about Black Elk's recollection of the great warriors who were at the Battle of the Little Bighorn, including Crazy Horse.

Black Elk described the excitement when Crazy Horse arrived at the Little Bighorn. "A great cry went up out in the dust, 'Crazy Horse is coming!' Off to the west and the north they were yelling, 'Hoka hey!' It was like a big wind roaring and making the tremolo, and you could hear eagle bone whistles screaming. I stayed there a while with my mother and watched the big dust whirling on the hill across the river and horses were coming out of it with empty saddles…" [*The battle saying "Hoka hey!" is used by many white authors who think it means "Today is a good day to die. Today is a good day to fight." But Barbara Adams, who works in the archives at the Piyawiconi Oglala Lakota College in Kyle, South Dakota, told me it simply means "Let's go," like one might encourage teammates at a basketball game today.*]

Darlene said she knew Neihardt. "He stayed with my parents. He drove a little green pick-up truck with a camper on the back," she recalled.

> I was a little girl then and we used to sneak up on him and scare him. He would throw pencils and paper at us; he was just having fun with us. My parents told me that he was in our area to talk to Black Elk. I was young enough I did not know what was going on at the time. But later, I was told he was there to learn the visions of our spirit journey, Crazy Horse and grandmother's land. Black Elk was a medicine man but he was not really the true medicine man for our people. That was Little Warrior. Black Elk was picking potatoes when he met Neihardt. When a question arose that needed to be pondered, Black Elk would quit for the day and seek council with Little Warrior not far from his garden, and a day or so later, the talks would resume.

Everyone needs mentors and guidance. Black Elk took the time to meet the earth, wind, and fire of the Plains and give it the best ride he could. Great learning comes from great stories or parables. Black Elk helped us find some answers from the thunderbeings just beyond the potato patch where he found Little Warrior.

At the Indian Art Market held at the Golden Eagle Casino near Horton, Kansas, in October 1999, my wife was admiring a Lakota eagle pin carved of ivory and Pine Ridge blood agate by artist Pretty Voice Hawk of Lower Brulé, South Dakota. I asked Pretty Voice Hawk if he would consider a trade of some of my father's books about Lakota chiefs. I had brought along some books for the trip to Horton in case anyone was interested in buying one. He looked at the book and nodded his head. My wife made a deal for the beautiful pin. A man standing next to me noticed the books and asked if I was from Marysville, Kansas. I replied, "Yes." He told me that he knew that I had visited with Mario Gonzalez about my research on Crazy Horse. The man's name was Jack Runnels of Horton, Kansas, and he was a member of the Pine Ridge tribe. His grandfather, John Conroy, who also had a Lakota name, White Man, had fought in the Little Bighorn battle. John's father was an Irishman named Thomas who had been at Fort Laramie. I told Runnels I had been making a genealogy chart to keep track of the people I had visited with and how they were related to Crazy Horse. I asked him if he was related to Crazy Horse's father's side of the family through the Standing Bear people. He looked at me in surprise and answered, "Yes, I am."

Crazy Horse and the Battle of Little Bighorn—Was He Late?

"Soldiers charge our village,
to kill our women and children.
So we chased them back across
the Little Big Horn River."
—a Lakota warrior

Ledger Art by Vic Runnels is drawn on authentic Indian Agency ledger paper that was given to the natives to sketch on. Ledger painters carry on an art form that emerged during a difficult transitional period for their people. The art itself combines elements of both worlds—the ledger book of the people who were changing the West and the images of an older indigenous culture.

Jack introduced me to his brother, Victor, an accomplished artist who was showing his drawings at the market. I sat down with the Runnels brothers, swapping stories, and they told me how their grandfather, White Man, was one of twelve sharpshooters who had Reno and Benteen pinned down in the cliffs above the Little Bighorn River. Their grandfather was a member of the Tokala, or Kit Fox, society of warriors who would stake themselves to the ground with a spear and fight until death, or until another member removed the stake.

On the day of the battle, Reno and Benteen were probably about three miles away from where Custer was located. They were attacking from another angle when they were driven back to the cliffs above the river. Here the sharpshooters pinned Reno down. His army men became thirsty would volunteer to be water carriers and run down to the river for water. The sharpshooters would then shoot holes in their canteens. Then the soldiers came with kettles, and the ammunition again penetrated the kettles. They shot one soldier dead who was at the tail end of a group trying to retrieve water. Victor said, "My grandfather and his sharp shootin' friends had a weird sense of humor at Little Bighorn."

From all sides, there are believers and doubters of Crazy Horses' presence at Little Big Horn. I firmly believe that no one is willfully lying; they are simply telling history as they know it to be. These accounts leave us pondering the many mysteries surrounding Little Bighorn. The spirits of the earth, the wind and the fire know the truth, but they are not telling…yet.

Whether or not Crazy Horse was at the Little Bighorn Battle, the Lakota people thought Crazy Horse needed to be some place. If he was not fighting Custer, it is clear that many wanted him at Last Stand Hill. He was the best warrior among the Lakota and the most feared by the white nation. To those who wanted to confront the covered wagons and protect the buffalo, he and his spirit were flowing wide and far like the flooded Platte River in the spring. The massacre of tatanka (buffalo), the Plains' mainstay, would not go without retaliation by the people of Crazy Horse.

Comparing Legends

Crazy Horse and General Custer are both figures of epic proportions in American history and folklore. Both were brave men who stood out from the crowd. Neither consumed alcohol, despite living in societies where it was used abundantly, and they weren't afraid to go against the grain of current wisdom. Some like to portray the two as very much alike, when in reality, there are as many stark contrasts separating the two as joining them in spirit.

Custer wore outlandish uniforms, extremely long hair and loved to have pets and admirers hanging around. Crazy Horse did not wear the traditional feather-laden war bonnet; instead, he wore a single feather. Custer craved attention; Crazy Horse was a solitary soul who sought peace through introspection which is how the Sioux nation distinguishes him from other chiefs.

Custer's men went into battle wearing the same uniform so as not to stand out. Braves riding with Crazy Horse were encouraged to be individuals, decorating their bodies with wild figures and designs. The two men led by example, though each in his own way. Custer, for example, knew that the regiment would follow because of military discipline. Crazy Horse inspired his braves to follow with his courage and proven battlefield skills.

One afternoon, while my son Woody and I were driving through the Black Hills and around the reservations of South Dakota, I was sitting in the passenger side reading of how writer Stephen Ambrose, in his book, *Crazy Horse and Custer*, thought the two might view themselves. Crazy Horse was a humble leader who felt he was part of nature. He believed that when you died, you should be buried in a buffalo skin, exposed to the elements to increase decomposition. The body would then feed the wild grass, which would feed the buffalo, which fed the Indian, forming a circle that ensured life to come. Custer saw things differently. He had a big ego, viewing himself as superior in every way to those around him. In death, Custer believed the body should be buried in metal caskets to keep it free from bacteria, ensuring it would not be fed to the soil (Ambrose, 124).

Custer liked the idea of the writers of the time glorifying his exaggerated exploits. Crazy Horse was quiet and unassuming, even though followers in search of a hero could very well have over-dramatized some of his adventures also. Custer's body was proof that he was at Little Bighorn, and while the debate will rage on about whether Crazy Horse was there or not, it would be fitting for these two warriors to have met on the battlefield.

For me, the spirit of Crazy Horse seems to have touched many people in many ways. If, indeed, Crazy Horse missed the Little Bighorn fight, so be it. No matter where Crazy Horse was at the time of the Little Bighorn Battle, he left his mark; his reputation was so large, he seemed to be everywhere.

Sometimes the price of war is high, even in victory. The changes that would follow the battle of Little Bighorn affected the Sioux in ways no one expected.

10

The Aftermath of Little Bighorn: Another New Treaty and the March to Camp Robinson

The dust had settled at Little Bighorn. The Sioux had seen victory. The smoke from the Indian camps was gone, and they left the area with feelings of uncertainty and concern. What would happen now?

Crazy Horse led his band of about 600 toward the Bear Butte area of the Black Hills. Sitting Bull and his Hunkpapas went back to their hunting ground near the Yellowstone River. And those Indians living on reservations, known as agency Indians, returned home to find that they had been declared prisoners of war because the Treaty of 1868 had been violated at Little Bighorn. The government denied the Sioux all rights to their hunting grounds on the northern plains, and formulated a new treaty that gave the Black Hills, the Big Horn Mountains and the Powder River country to the United States. Furthermore, if the Indians did not sign the treaty, rations to agency Indians would be cut.

The noose of government control tightened around the neck of the Sioux. Chief Red Cloud and Spotted Tail had little choice but to sign the treaty. They then learned they would be moved to a new reservation on the Missouri River. Red Cloud was not happy and was captured trying to escape. Red Cloud was sentenced to time in the Red Cloud Agency, and Spotted Tail was declared head chief by the government (Hyde, 158).

According to Darlene Rosane, oral historian for the American Horse family, Red Cloud's followers reacted bitterly to his attempted escape. They

Red Cloud Agency, 1876. Photo courtesy Nebraska State Historical Society.

Chief Red Cloud. Photo courtesy Nebraska State Historical Society.

declared him unfit to be their chief since he had abandoned them when they needed him most. Red Cloud was forced to drink two cups of buffalo fat as further punishment (ingesting buffalo fat results in severe diarrhea). Red Cloud's position was given to Man Afraid of His Horse. The white people regarded Spotted Tail as an agency chief, but Man Afraid of His Horse was the Indian people's choice. Darlene Rosane said that this was the end of the line for Sioux Indian-elected chiefs.

Those living outside the reservation found that the forces sent to track them down were insurmountable. Chief Sitting Bull agreed to meet with government officials in council. During this meeting, a fight broke out and troops opened fire on the Indians. Sitting Bull's Hunkpapas escaped and headed north. Some made it to Canada with Sitting Bull and Chief Gall, out of reach of the Americans, while others who had been separated grew weary as winter set in and surrendered.

The government then turned its attention to capturing Crazy Horse. General George Crook led 2,200 troops and used 350 Crow and Shoshone scouts to track down the Oglala Chief. Not surprisingly, No Water was among the first to sign up. [*No Water's wife was the woman with whom Crazy Horse eloped.*]

Crook was on a mission, and seemed to be of a mindset that any means of capture was a good means...even ambush. His troops' slaughter of sleeping Cheyenne at dawn on November 25, 1876, became known as the Hole-in-the-Wall battle. Troops attacked the village; a few managed to escape, while the rest were shot and killed. Troops killed the horses and burned the lodges. Those who did manage to escape stumbled upon Crazy Horse three days later, his encampment located along the Tongue River. The Cheyenne people on the run were wounded, freezing and hungry. Crazy Horse was also trying to elude Crook and his men. His own people suffered from a lack of supplies, and he could offer little assistance to the Cheyenne.

Crazy Horse struggled to find ways for his people to survive that winter. The Chief had always been a solitary man, now more than ever. According to Black Elk, Crazy Horse would often wander out in the snow and cold to be alone. "His eyes looked through things and he always seemed to be thinking hard about something," Black Elk recalled. "Maybe he was always partway into the world of his vision. Maybe he had seen that he would soon be dead and was thinking how to help us when he would not be with us anymore."

Writer and researcher Eleanor Hinman interviewed Short Buffalo in 1930 regarding the Cheyenne who escaped the Hole-in-the-Wall battle and turned to Crazy Horse for help. Writers Major Bourke and George Bird Grinnell have portrayed Crazy Horse as being cold-hearted, refusing to help the suffering Cheyenne for no reason other then meanness. Short Buffalo said that such accounts were fiction.

"...we helped the Cheyenne the best we could. We hadn't much ourselves," Short Buffalo told Hinman. Running was futile. His people were suffering gravely. Crazy Horse could see that he had no choice but to meet with the government.

Short Buffalo, who was the younger brother of He Dog, told Hinman that while they were hunting in the Rocky Mountains, a message was delivered to them.

> They asked us to come back to the Red Cloud Agency and quit fighting. When the messengers came to He Dog, we learned that Crazy Horse had already come down to Lodgepole Creek near the Powder River. He was already moving toward the agency. So, at the Powder River, we all met and had a big council and decided to go in together. The Cheyenne chiefs, Two Moon, Ice and Little Wolf, took another course.... When we got to the head of the Powder River, we met Red Cloud with one hundred other chiefs to bring us a welcome message. They said, "All is well, have no fear, come on in."

Short Buffalo told Hinman that they were in good spirits at the point. "On a big flat near Camp Robinson, Red Cloud and White Hat (William Philo Clark) and troops met Crazy Horse. They said they were glad to see him, and everybody had come in peace. Crazy Horse spread out his blanket for Red Cloud to sit on and gave his shirt to Red Cloud. He Dog did the same for White Hat. All of this indicated that there were no ill-feelings toward the whites."

According to reports, Crazy Horse requested that his reservation be located near where Gillette, Wyoming, is today. "There is a creek over there they call Beaver Creek. There is a great big flat west of the headwaters of Beaver Creek. I want my agency right in the middle of that flat." [*There are many Beaver Creeks and this one is different from the one where Crazy Horse killed an Omaha girl near present day Bartlett, Nebraska, and different from the one where Sun Dances were held north of Hay Springs, Nebraska.*] He said the grass was good for horse and game. Although Crazy Horse preferred this place, a second establishment near the town where Sheridan, Wyoming, is today would be acceptable.

Crazy Horse said that after the agency was established, he would go to Washington D.C. to meet with officials but the government wanted Crazy Horse to come to Washington D.C. before the reservation was established. What seemed like a minor misunderstanding would eventually be the source of great friction.

Once inside the Red Cloud Agency, still quite content with things, Crazy Horse offered his left hand to General Clark since he had his war bonnet to surrender. "Friend, I shake with this hand because my heart is on this side; the right hand does all manner of wickedness. I want this peace to last forever." The Sioux were given more food and supplies than they had seen in months.

Clark then issued a stern reminder of who was in charge, and how Crazy Horse could ensure his people always had ample supplies. "No matter how fierce or brave a person thinks he is, if he learns to humble himself once in a while, he will be well-liked and good things will happen to him."

The Oglalas marched to Camp Robinson, led by Clark and Red Cloud's Indian Police. Six hundred people and 1,700 ponies covered the trail, stretching for miles. Beside Crazy Horse were his close friends He Dog, Little Big Man, Old Hawk, and Bad Road. Right behind them were Crazy Horse's braves, faces painted and dressed in their best attire. Two miles behind them, the women and children rode in silence.

As they entered the valley of the White River, where the surrendering warriors saw a vast crowd of Sioux who had been living in dependency at the agency, Crazy Horse's warriors began to sing the peace song of the Lakotas. The agency Sioux joined in, and soon, the women and children in the procession behind Crazy Horse also began to sing the peace song. The valley filled with voices and the government officials on hand sensed the singing was in respect to the great Crazy Horse. One of the officer's commented, "By God, this is a march of triumph, not surrender!"

Crazy Horse and his band were forced to surrender horses and firearms to the soldiers. Luther Standing Bear later wrote that Crazy Horse foresaw the consequences. "It meant submission to a people whom he did not consider his equal. Crazy Horse feared no man, and when he did surrender, it was not from volition on his part, but because his people were tired of warfare."

Crazy Horse kept pressing for his reservation to be located on the northern territory. General Crook spoke of sending Crazy Horse and a delegation to Washington D.C. so they could bring their case before the president, but Crazy Horse had no interest in seeing the president. Crazy Horse began to realize that his wishes might not be granted, and worse, he had little recourse.

Dr. V.T. McGillycuddy, the post surgeon, urged Crazy Horse to go to Washington D.C. and meet with the president. Crazy Horse refused. McGillycuddy said this is what Crazy Horse told him:

> We did not ask you white men to come here. The Great Spirit gave us this country as a home. You had yours. We did not interfere with you. The Great Spirit gave us plenty of land to live on and buffalo, deer, antelope and the other game. But you have come here. You are taking my land from me. You are killing off our game so it is hard for us to live. Now, you tell us to work for a living, but the Great Spirit did not make us to work, but to live by hunting. You white men can work if you want to. We do not interfere with you, and again you ask, why do you not become civilized? We did not want your civilization. We would live as our fathers did, and their fathers before them.

Meanwhile, Crazy Horse was a celebrity among the white officers. Young braves also idolized the fearless chief and tried to get close to him. Crazy Horse was visited often by white officers who were once his adversaries. Other Indians worried that the white man might make Crazy Horse the Chief of all Indians. There were those who did all they could to cause trouble for Crazy Horse, like No Water, who sought revenge against Crazy Horse, and Red Cloud, who considered Crazy Horse a threat to his power.

General George Crook had developed a liking and a trust of Crazy Horse. When he decided that Crazy Horse could lead a buffalo hunt to the north, Red Cloud and Spotted Tail warned that Crazy Horse could not be trusted. They said he would not return and he would use the guns to make war on the white man.

Crazy Horse had grown to trust some of the whites, like Crook and Clark. He decided to go to Washington D.C. to meet with the President of the United States. When this news spread, the jealousy levels rose. Red Cloud's own people warned Crazy Horse that he was in danger; the others were jealous and afraid he'd be named Chief of the Reservation. This would mean that Red Cloud and Spotted Tail would lose their power. Little Big Man warned Crazy Horse that plots were brewing to have him assassinated either at Camp Robinson or in Washington.

Red Cloud, Spotted Tail, and No Water kept telling anyone who would listen that Crazy Horse could not be trusted. In a meeting with agency officials, they again said that he was planning to use the guns and horses to make war on the white man. Not sure what to think, agency officials avoided talking about the hunt, and began watching Crazy Horse for signs he was planning an uprising.

It was a very confusing time…and it would only get worse.

11

The Conspiracy against Crazy Horse as Reported by Indian Scouts Frank Grouard and A.G. Shaw

In August 1877, General Crook asked Crazy Horse to help fight the Nez Perce. Although Crook had confiscated the weapons the Indians had traded for or acquired from previous battles with the whites, he then issued horses and guns to those of Crazy Horse's people who signed up to fight the Nez Percé. Those who signed up paraded around with their new guns and horses. Crazy Horse refused to help Crook. Red Feather later said, "When he [Crazy Horse] came to the agency, the soldiers had made him promise not to go on the warpath anymore. They told him not to fight and then to fight." Crazy Horse was upset about this, saying, "If the Great Father wants us to fight, we will go north and fight until not a Nez Percé is left." Frank Grouard translated this to Crook as "…until not a white man is left."

Crazy Horse was angry. First they had made him swear not to fight, and now they were asking for his help in battle; they had taken the Indians' weapons, and then they issued new ones. Crazy Horse threatened to take his people north again. The white officers were in a panic.

Earlier, Frank Grouard was mentioned as being a good friend of Crazy Horse. On May 20, 1877, Robert Strahorn wrote an article for the *Denver Daily Tribune* titled "Northern Indians" and quoting Frank Grouard:

> He rode three days with Crazy Horse to the death scaffold of Crazy Horse's only child, and he was the keeper of the Crazy Horse family history, later destroyed by fire. Still, some historians maintain that Frank Grouard mistranslated the message on purpose. Frank's mother was of Polynesian descent and the Indians may have teased him about this, causing him to leave the tribe. Grouard may have felt the power of the new government and been aware that the people he could benefit most from were the whites, so he would help them. Could the mistranslation have been done on purpose, as many have suggested? Some Indians claimed that much of Grouard's zeal against them was inspired by his former love for a white girl who was a captive of the Sioux for sixteen years. She was captured when she was four years of

age and was brought up among the Sioux. When the Indians were brought in, she was with them, but she had been married to a buck since Grouard's escape. He, therefore, had lost interest in her. She was said to be very pretty.

In 1873, Frank Grouard fought with the Lakota against government forces on the Yellowstone. Later, after quarreling with Sitting Bull, Grouard joined Crazy Horse's camp. He soon left and went to Fort Robinson where he served Crook as a scout (Bettelyoun, 173). In May 1877, after General Crook had tracked down Crazy Horse, Crazy Horse asked to have supper with Frank Grouard, so it appears that they were still friends at that time.

A.G. Shaw. Photo from Larry Shaw collection.

Grouard said he would often have an Indian bring him all the news they could get from Crazy Horse's camp. Grouard said that he had "heard of their plot to kill Lieutenant Clark and myself and afterwards massacre the people at the post. Thinking that the report was exaggerated, I set about finding when the next Indian council would take place. I thought it would be best to attend myself." Grouard went to the secret meeting (or at least the Indians thought it was secret) which was held around midnight. Grouard reported,

> Dressing myself up as an Indian, I got on my horse bareback and went down amongst them, their camp being situated on the site where Chadron, Nebraska, now stands, thirty miles from Camp Robinson. Tying my horse in front of one of the lodges, I went right through the village looking for the lodge where the meeting was to be held. After traveling through camp for some time, I found the tipi where they were to meet. Standing at the door watching the Indians go into the lodge, I drew my blanket over my head so that I could not be recognized by any of them unless they should pull the blanket off of me, but they very seldom did anything like that.
>
> I took a back seat when the council met and heard everything that was said, how Crazy Horse was to take a few of his best warriors and go up to the office of Lieutenant Clark, and the Indians were to kill all the whites in the room, myself included. They were to give warning to all the other Indians that wanted to join them so they would be ready to massacre all the whites at the post as soon as the shooting began. After listening for some time and finding out all I cared to know, I took the first opportunity that presented itself and departed.

At one time, Crazy Horse and Grouard had been friends, however, now Grouard was employed by the military and plotting against his former friend. Even military scout Amberson G. Shaw had heard a rumor that army officers were to be killed. Shaw asked Chief Spotted Tail whether there was any truth to these rumors. Spotted Tail, at first, denied such a thought. But when Shaw told the chief he knew there was such a conspiracy, Spotted Tail acknowledged that, "Yes, there is a conspiracy, but we will be the winner!" Shaw went on to say that even Little Big Man, an old friend of Crazy Horse's, wanted Crazy Horse out of the way.

It is a fact that General Crook had promised Spotted Tail he would advance him to be a bigger chief than he already was. Shaw noticed that Spotted Tail was an everyday visitor at Crook's house. Spotted Tail also spoke of Crazy Horse being a weak chief, and that he, Spotted Tail, would remain friendly with his own people. [*Many people have stated that Crazy Horse was not a chief at all. Crazy Horse is often referred to as a great war chief, which may have made him a chief only when his people went on the warpath. When Eleanor Hinman asked Red Feather, Crazy Horse's brother-in-law, how long Crazy Horse was a chief, Red Feather replied, "Ever since he was a grown-up."*]

Spotted Tail would not brag about Crazy Horse, but he bragged about his other people, those who followed him. Even though Crazy Horse was a member of Spotted Tail's family, he refused to become an "agency Indian" like Spotted Tail. Crazy Horse wished to remain free, a warrior of the Plains. Shaw, who was married to a squaw at that time, said that Spotted Tail wanted to hold the Crazy Horse people together so he could profit when Crazy Horse was out of the way. Spotted Tail was very jealous of Crazy Horse and did not want him to go to Washington, for Crazy Horse, he admitted, was a great warrior and had become world famous as the most notable Indian leader in the Custer Battle.

Shaw said that the idea was to get rid of Crazy Horse because he had become an object of personal glory and power for some ambitious individuals. Nothing could be more natural than to make it appear to the whites that Crazy Horse was an arch fiend planning to take the life of General Crook and perhaps, the lives of other officers. It would help their secret plan to have the army aroused against Crazy Horse. There was much incentive to inspire the falsehood borne to Crook and Clark by Woman Dress. It was a shrewd plan, skillfully worked and shamefully successful. Whether or not the stories from Woman Dress or those of Grouard were true, General Crook got wind of the plot to assassinate the whites, and he secretly ordered the arrest of Crazy Horse and the disarming of the Indians (De Barthe, 174; Shaw, 1907). [*Woman Dress had grown up with Crazy Horse and had served with him as a warrior, but he was jealous of Crazy Horse because he was named a Shirt Wearer and Woman Dress was ignored. Woman Dress and others were sent to contact Crazy Horse to ask him to move to an agency. Instead, Crazy Horse went to a high hill to seek a vision.*]

In Thomas R. Buecker's *Fort Robinson and the American West*, he states:

There are various accounts that Crook and Clark held a secret meeting at Camp Robinson and met with those chiefs they could trust, which included Red Cloud, Young Man Afraid, American Horse, and No Water. The latter was the one who had shot Crazy Horse over the woman they both wanted. Crook told them Crazy Horse was leading their people in the wrong direction and that they must help the army to arrest him. The Indians wanted to kill him. Crook did not want this, but requested help in capturing him. This would prove the chiefs were not in sympathy with the non-progressive element of their tribe. The chiefs agreed to march with the soldiers the next day.

Woman Dress on right. Photo courtesy Nebraska State Historical Society.

12

The Final Days

An interview Eleanor H. Hinman conducted with He Dog on July 7, 1930, sheds more light on what happened in the final days of Crazy Horse's life at Camp Robinson, which became Fort Robinson in December 1878. He Dog surrendered with Crazy Horse at Camp Robinson on May 7, 1877. At the time of his interview with Hinman, He Dog was 92 years old, but he possessed a remarkable memory. When the Court of Indian Offenses was established at the Pine Ridge Reservation in the 1890s, He Dog was made judge of it and he served for many years in that capacity. People trying to find historical information about Crazy Horse often heard the saying, "He Dog will remember that."

In that interview, He Dog stated:

> I was present at the killing of Crazy Horse. I can tell you just what happened, who was present, and the condition of the weather.
>
> In the year we fought with the white people (1876), the band I led had joined Crazy Horse's band during the fighting. In the winter after fighting, Spotted Tail went north and persuaded Crazy Horse to come down to the agency the following spring. When we started in, I thought we were coming to visit and see whether we would receive an annuity, not to surrender. I thought we would be allowed to go back home afterwards. But when we got near Fort Robinson, I found we were coming to surrender. Spotted Tail had laid a trap for us. Later I found that Spotted Tail was telling the military things about Crazy Horse which were not so.
>
> Spotted Tail and others kept urging Crazy Horse to go to Washington and talk to the president. After a while, Crazy Horse refused to go anywhere or talk to anyone. One day, I was called to see White Hat (William Clark) and asked to bring Crazy Horse in for a talk because I was such a friend of his. I asked Crazy Horse, but he would not come. This made me feel bad, so I moved my people from where Crazy Horse was camping and camped over near the Red Cloud band. There was no quarrel; we just separated.

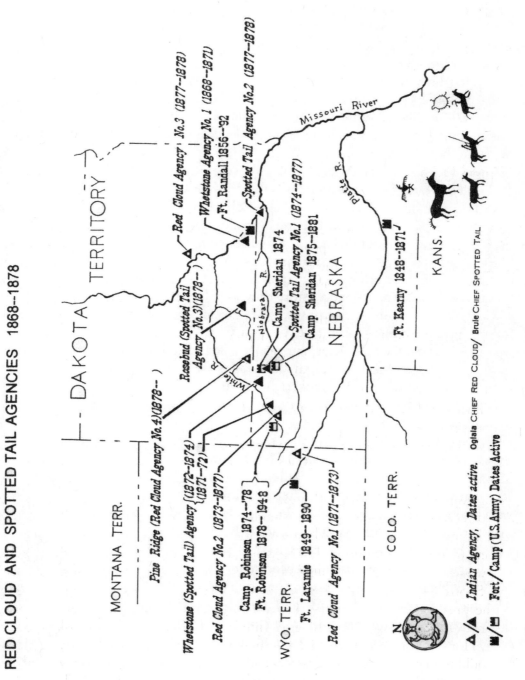

HISTORY OF THE RED CLOUD AND THE SPOTTED TAIL INDIAN AGENCIES' LOCATIONS & DATES. 1868 TO 1878

RED CLOUD AND SPOTTED TAIL AGENCIES 1868--1878

MONTANA TERR.

DAKOTA TERRITORY

Pine Ridge (Red Cloud Agency No.4)(1878--)

Red Cloud Agency No.3 (1877--1878)

Whetstone Agency No.1 (1868--1871)

Ft. Randall 1856--'92

Spotted Tail Agency No.2 (1877--1878)

Rosebud (Spotted Tail Agency No.3)(1878--)

Whetstone (Spotted Tail) Agency {(1872--1874) (1871--72)}

Red Cloud Agency No.2 (1873--1877)

Camp Sheridan 1874

Spotted Tail Agency No.1 (1874--1877)

Camp Sheridan 1875--1881

Niobrara R.

White R.

Camp Robinson 1874--'78
Ft. Robinson 1878--1948

NEBRASKA

Platte R.

Missouri River

Ft. Kearny 1848--1871

KANS.

WYO. TERR.

Ft. Laramie 1849--1890

Red Cloud Agency No.1 (1871--1873)

COLO. TERR.

N

△/▲ Indian Agency, Dates active. Oglala CHIEF RED CLOUD/ Brule CHIEF SPOTTED TAIL

▣/▣ Fort/Camp (U.S.Army) Dates Active

©2000 DAVID HAMMETT

Crazy Horse said to me that if they have the agency moved over to Beaver Creek, then he would go to Washington as they had asked him. The reason he gave for this condition [whether or not to go to Washington] was that Beaver Creek was in the middle of the Sioux Territory, while the location at Camp Robinson was on the edge of it.

After I had moved camp to the Red Cloud Agency, close to Camp Robinson, I was given orders to go and camp a couple of miles east of Camp Robinson at the foot of the White Buttes. Word was brought that Three Stars, General George Crook, was coming that evening and all the Indian leaders were to have a meeting there the next day with Three Stars. But Crazy Horse did not come to that council, and neither did Three Stars. After a while, we were summoned to Camp Robinson and told that it would be necessary to arrest Crazy Horse.

The next day when I went to Camp Robinson, I was told that Crazy Horse had escaped with part of his band. The Indian police were given orders to bring him back. Next day, they brought him back. I was still encamped at the White Buttes, and they brought him past my camp on their way to the fort. I saw them coming and sent orders for them to bring Crazy Horse to my tipi. I meant to give him a good talking-to. But the police didn't stop; they took him straight on to the fort. When I saw this, I could only put on my war bonnet and get on my horse bareback and follow. When I came to the fort, I found Crazy Horse in the lead on his horse, wearing a red blanket. A military ambulance followed; a couple of army officers were in it, but no Indians. I rode up on the left side of Crazy Horse and shook hands with him. I saw that he did not look right. I said, "Look out; watch your step. You are going into a dangerous place."

I was standing just south of the entrance to the adjutant's office at the fort. Red Cloud, with his men, stood to the east of the building which had the adjutant's office in it, American horse with his men to the west. Crazy Horse was taken into the office and, after a little while, led out toward a building just north of it. I knew this building was the jail because I had been sent out by White Hat once or twice to get some Indians who had done something bad, and they had been taken to this building. But Crazy Horse did not know it. Turning Bear walked ahead of Crazy Horse; on either side of him were Little Big Man and Wooden Sword. Behind him was Leaper. Loyal Brulés that were with Crazy Horse were Swift Bear, Black Crow, and Fast Thunder.

He Dog. Photo courtesy Nebraska State Historical Society.

The Final Days

Turning Bear, a Brulé friendly to Crazy Horse, was to have said, "Stop! To avenge Pehin Hunska (the Custer massacre), they have planned to kill you. If you enter those doors, it means your doom. Look around you, for on the outside are countless friends standing ready to defend you" (Bordeaux).

Soon after Crazy Horse had gone into the jail, a noise began in there. Crazy Horse had a revolver with him and tried to draw it, but it was taken away from him. Then he drew his knife. American Horse and Red Cloud shouted to their men, "Shoot to kill!" The white sentry who was on guard outside the jail ran in behind Crazy Horse as he was fighting with the Indian police and lunged— twice—with his bayonet. Crazy Horse cried, "They have stabbed me!" He staggered backward and fell on the ground. I looked around and saw that soldiers and cavalry had formed all around the edge of the parade ground. I stood there, ready to drop.

Then White Hat appeared and said I might go up to Crazy Horse. I did so. There were soldiers standing all around him. The bayonet was lying on the ground beside him and also the knife he had used, and they were red. I tore in two the large red agency blanket which I was wearing and used half of it to cover him. He was gasping hard for breath. "See where I am hurt," he gasped. "I can feel the blood flowing."

I pulled back his shirt and looked at the wound. He was thrust nearly through twice. The first stroke went from between the ribs in the back on the right side, and

Fort Robinson, 1897. Photo courtesy Nebraska State Historical Society.

Guard house where Crazy Horse was killed at Camp Robinson in western Nebraska.

very nearly came through in front under the heart. A lump was rising under the skin where the thrust ended. The second wound was through the small of the back through the kidneys.

There were many observers who have told their accounts of what happened at the scene of the killing. An army interpreter, William Garnett, who was interviewed in 1920 on the Pine Ridge, said a sentinel gave Crazy Horse the death wound with a bayonet. One other account added that the bayoneting was done by William Gentles, a private in the army at Fort Robinson. The sentinel had prodded Crazy Horse in the abdomen in return for the thrust Crazy Horse gave with his knife.

From Addison E. Sheldon and the Brininstool Report given to the Nebraska Historical Society, comes this information in a telegram from General L.P. Bradley, Ninth Infantry, Commander of the District of the Black Hills, which included Fort Robinson.

When he [Crazy Horse] was put in the guardhouse, he suddenly drew a knife, struck the guard, and made for the door. Little Big Man, one of his own chiefs, grappled with him and was cut in the arm by Crazy Horse during the struggle. The two chiefs were surrounded by the guard, and, about this time, Crazy Horse received a severe wound in the lower part of the abdomen, either from a knife or bayonet; the surgeons are in doubt which. Little Big Man, while holding down Crazy Horse's hands, deflected the latter's own poniard dagger, and inflicted the gash which resulted in death.

William Garnett also submitted a statement corroborating this account.

In 1881, at a Sun Dance, Little Big Man told Lieutenant John Bourke that he had unintentionally killed Crazy Horse with Crazy Horse's own weapon, a stiletto which was shaped at the end like a bayonet, and it made the very same kind of wound as a bayonet. He

Little Big Man. He was small in stature, but thought he was the Big Man. Photo courtesy Nebraska State Historical Society.

described how he jumped on Crazy Horse's back and seized his arms at the elbow. He showed how he himself had also received two wounds in the left wrist. In the struggle, Crazy Horse's stiletto was inclined in such a way that, when he struggled, he cut himself in the abdomen instead of harming the one who held him in his grasp. Little Big Man further assured Bourke that, at first, it was thought best to let the idea prevail that a soldier had done the killing, thus reducing the probability of any one of the dead man's relatives avenging his death in the manner of the aborigines. The bayonet thrust made by the soldier went into the door of the guard house where Little Big Man said it could still be seen. Bourke told both stories, although he was strongly inclined to believe what Little Big Man told him (Bourke, John).

Turning Bear was with Crazy Horse when he was killed. Photo from A.G. Shaw collection.

13

Who Wielded the Bayonet?

In Ephriam D. Dickson III's article "Greasy Grass" he states:

Private William Gentles was officially identified as the man who killed Crazy Horse. While most writers have since accepted this claim as historical fact, some questions must still be asked. It was not until 1903 that Gentles was labeled as the man responsible for the fatal bayonet probe. Gentles had died at the age of forty-eight on May 20, 1878, at Fort [Camp] Douglas in Utah. The cause of his death was listed as asthma. It was William F. Kelly of the Fourteenth Infantry who told the story about Gentles to the *Washington Post*. Interestingly, army records do not show a William F. Kelly in any unit stationed anywhere in the United States Army at the time. Muster rolls do indicate that Private Gentles was at Camp Robinson on August 31, six days before Crazy Horse was killed. Some weeks before, Gentles was serving the last of a twenty-day sentence in the guardhouse. He had apparently been released on September 2, and would have been eligible for guard detail.

In January 1999, I set out to go through the Mari Sandoz file at Love Library in Lincoln, Nebraska. Mari's sister Caroline had told me a few years earlier that Mari's notes on Crazy Horse had been donated to the library's special collections and were within the 45,000 hand-written three-by-five-inch note cards in the Sandoz archive collection.

In the process of doing this research, I recalled my father telling me he went to the University of Nebraska during World War II to study chemical warfare. He said he had stayed at Love Library. I asked the archivist on duty if they knew anything about WWII soldiers staying in the Love Library building. She told me that soldiers stayed there on the same third floor where the Sandoz collection is now housed. Since it was my father's interest in the burial sites of Sioux chiefs that got me started on this journey, this was one of the more sublime coincidences that I encountered.

Who Wielded the Bayonet?

I was working my way through the handwritten index cards of Mari Sandoz when I came across the note, "William Gentles bayoneted Crazy Horse, says Kelly, see *Washington Post* story." My hands moved quickly through the many cards until I came upon something that struck me as remarkable. On a card, in Mari's handwriting, was written, "Mac Donald supposedly bayoneted Crazy Horse." Then the word "Shumway." I found another typewritten card that said, "Crazy Horse—bayoneted by Corp. Mac Donald."

I photocopied the cards and sent them to Thomas R. Buecker, the curator at Fort Robinson who was in the process of publishing a book on Fort Robinson and the American West. I thought Buecker could shed some light on this mystery.

That same week I had been invited to a Westerners Club meeting in Lincoln to hear the lecture of Eli Paul on Crazy Horse and Red Cloud. Paul is a noted writer and researcher on Indian wars whom I had met at the Nebraska Historical Museum when I stopped in to do some research.

The evening of the Westerners Club meeting, my wife and I were sitting at the table with Eli Paul and Cynthia Monroe, who tended the Nebraska Historical Society archives. Cynthia

Death of Crazy Horse by Amos Bad Heart Bull, a nephew of He Dog. Photo courtesy Nebraska State Historical Society.

knew my father from when she worked with the State Brand Inspection Agency. We traded old cattle thieving stories and, when we ran out of them, Cynthia directed the subject to another topic, "Tom Buecker called me from Fort Robinson. Someone found some note cards in an old file saying that a MacDonald bayoneted Crazy Horse. Tom wanted me to look up something about a Shumway who may have written a story about the killing of Crazy Horse. His name was on the note cards. I can't imagine how reliable those notes could be," she said, mocking the reliability.

I allowed the conversation to pause for a moment, and then said, "Those note cards came from the Mari Sandoz file in Love Library. I know, because a few days ago I discovered them and asked Tom to find out about Shumway."

Cynthia replied, smiling, "Yes, that probably is a pretty authentic source."

In about a week, Cynthia located an old book printed in 1921 called *The History of Western Nebraska* by Grant Shumway. Shumway's account of the events were as follows:

One of the great mysteries of the famous Custer massacre and Sioux War of 1876 was the death of Crazy Horse, one of the principle chiefs and leaders of the rebellious Sioux—the man above all others who was the evil genius of that stormy period. The telegraph reports sent out from Fort Robinson at the time of his death were contradictory and nebulous. No one seemed to know how he died. While the man who killed him—William Gentles, of the Fourteenth United States Infantry—died with the secret locked in his bosom. There were only two witnesses to the act, and only one of them is now living. His name is Sergeant William F. Kelly, formerly of the Fourteenth Infantry, in recent years a resident of E Street, in Washington. The story he told to the Washington Post reporter of the killing of Crazy Horse had never before been published. Sergeant Kelly had kept the matter a secret for twenty-seven years.

Crazy Horse caught sight of the grated bars and iron doors of the cell he was to occupy. Crazy Horse and Little Big Man struggled for the mastery out through the door and into the alleyway between the prison and office. The guards formed a circle around the two men as they struggled while Captain Kennington was trying every way he could to get someone to part the two men and secure Crazy Horse.

It was an exciting moment when a shot would have started a massacre, and no one knew just what to do. Suddenly, as the two men surged forward in the direction of where I was standing, I saw William Gentles, an old soldier, and veteran of the Mormon Campaign of 1857, give Crazy Horse a thrust with his bayonet. The thrust was delivered with lightning, like rapidity, and the next instant he had his gun at carry, as though nothing had happened. Crazy Horse gave a deep groan and staggered forward and dropped his knife and fell.

Only two men, myself and another, saw and knew how this was done; and the strangest thing of all was that many members of the guard imagined that they were guilty of the killing. Crazy Horse died at midnight. He was conscious all the while and never uttered a word.

While William F. Kelly could not be found to be a member of the United States' armed services at any time, as he said he was, it was possible that he served under another name. William Kelly was able to recall fine details of the Crazy Horse killing as well as other details of Camp Robinson. For instance, he talked about only one cannon at the fort—an old brass affair used for firing the morning and evening gun—and that constituted the artillery. "An old Irishman named Murphy (there were two Murphys at Camp Robinson at the time of Crazy Horse's death, Michael Murphy and Jon Murphy) who argued with the driver because the latter failed to keep the six mules in line with the rest of the command, had charge of the battery, while I was the gunner," said Kelly. There were two other Kellys that served at Camp Robinson at that time: John Kelly and Edward Kelley (with two e's) (Buecker, Tom, 1998).

Grant Shumway told another story about Crazy Horse's death in his *History of Western Nebraska*. Shumway had been sitting around listening to stories by Johnnie Stetter, the first white man married in the county of Dawes after it was officially organized. Shumway wrote,

> You give Johnnie Stetter a good cigar and a half Nelson on your time and he will keep you interested for many hours, telling you how Corporal MacDonald, a regular soldier, skewed Crazy Horse to the wall with a bayonet at the old Red Cloud Agency and held him there until he was dead [five hours later], and how the incident came near causing an outbreak, which only for Antoine Janis, whose wife was Indian, might have resulted in a massacre similar to that when brave Custer with this entire troop was annihilated on the Little Bighorn.

After I read this from Shumway, it dawned on me that my Schwan's frozen food delivery man was named Tom Janis. Tom was from Pine Ridge, and one evening when he called on me, he told me that Antoine Janis was his great-grandpa's brother. Tom's great-grandfather was Nick, who married Chief Red Cloud's niece. The Janis brothers came to that part of the country with the Bordeauxs and a man named Chadron. They were French fur trappers who later acted as interpreters. To think my Schwan's delivery man had a relative that helped simmer things down at the Crazy Horse killing was mind boggling. It was news to Tom Janis, too. By this time, I thought, I should be getting used to these unlikely connections.

Buecker, provided me with a list of men who served at Camp Robinson during 1877, and indeed there was a McDonald who served at that time. There were actually six McDonald's, all of them spelled without an a: George H., Henry, James, John, William, and William H. With that many McDonalds, it certainly increases the odds that a McDonald could have wielded the fatal bayonet thrust.

A few months later, I received an answer from the National Archives to my request for information on soldiers named McDonald at Camp Robinson in late 1877. Archive technician Brewer Thompson provided me with the information that in Boston, Massachusetts, in December 1872 a George H. McDonald had taken an oath of enlistment and allegiance for a pe-

Delegation of Oglala. Back row left to right: He Dog, Little Wound, American Horse, Little Big Man, Young Man Afraid of His Horses, Sword. Front row left to right: Yellow Bear, Antoine Janis, William Garnett, Joe Merriville and Tree Grizzly Bears. 1877. Photo courtesy Smithsonian Institute.

riod of five years. The oath stated that George was five feet six inches tall and had blue eyes with a fair complexion and brown hair. He served with Troop L, Third Cavalry, and was discharged December 5, 1877, by expiration of service at the Red Cloud Agency. His dismissal papers indicated that his character was very good and that he had attained the rank of corporal.

Barbara Adams, the archivist at Kyle's Lakota College and a descendant of the Fast Thunder family, told me that, in her family, the story told is that the army man who wielded the bayonet that killed Crazy Horse had gold stripes and gold braid on his uniform. Tom Buecker, curator at Fort Robinson, doubted that a private, such as Gentles, would have had any gold stripes and braids on his uniform, but a corporal probably would have had yellow stripes.

Mari Sandoz had discovered both stories and recorded them in her notes. In her book on Crazy Horse, she identified William Gentles as the man who took the bayonet to the warrior chief.

In his book, *The Oglala Lakota Crazy Horse: A Preliminary Genealogical Study and Annotated Listing of Primary Sources*, Richard G. Hardorff states:

Who Wielded the Bayonet?

Private William Gentles has always been the prime suspect, and that opinion was supported by the fact that, following Crazy Horse's death, he was whisked away in the dead of night to Camp Sidney on the Union Pacific line at Sidney, Nebraska. It was to this minor, but safe, post that Pvt. Gentles was brought for his protection. He could not have stayed there long for he was to report for guard duty at Camp Robinson on the 16th of September where he stayed until November of 1877, when he was relieved of duty and was ordered to report to Camp Douglas. On May 20th [1878], Gentles had an asthma attack and died. Seven (eight according to Buecker) months after the fatal attack on Crazy Horse, Gentles was buried at the Fort Douglas National Cemetery. His marker erroneously records his death as March 20.

The mystery of who wielded the bayonet that killed Crazy Horse at the Camp Robinson guardhouse grows larger as many moons wax and wane and one more candidate is added to the list of "who done it?"

The Death of Crazy Horse. David Hammett

14

Dr. McGillycuddy's Account of the Death of Crazy Horse

He Dog reported that there were two wounds in Crazy Horse's body. Could Little Big Man and a soldier's bayonet have both been responsible? He Dog also said that the bayonet was lying on the ground beside Crazy Horse, and also the knife that he had used, and that both were red.

Years after Crazy Horse died, William Gentles was blamed for the death. Soon only Gentles' spirit could refute the accusation of his guilt from the grave. Few actually saw Crazy Horse being wounded, but many stories circulated.

American Horse and interpreter Baptiste Pourier Jr. attempted to defuse the situation by explaining that Crazy Horse was merely sick and needed the post surgeon's attention. This strategy allowed sufficient time for the wounded man to be safely removed to the nearby adjutant's office where he was placed on an outstretched blanket on the floor (Dickson, 2-8).

In the days immediately following Crazy Horse's death, official reports from Camp Robinson were ambiguous. Lieutenant Lee was the only witness who filed an official report of the event. From the Spotted Tail Agency, he wrote, "I saw a soldier make a thrust with a fixed bayonet."

On September 14, 1877, the *New York Sun* reported:

> Dr. Valentine McGillycuddy, civilian surgeon at Camp Robinson, attempted to demonstrate that the wound came from Crazy Horse's own knife. Using a sheet of paper to demonstrate, he tried to convince those present that the outline of the knife point most closely resembled Crazy Horse's wound. In his delirium, Crazy Horse spoke indistinctly about bayonets. That created, at least in the minds of the two Indians present at the event, the idea that he had been stabbed with a bayonet. Crazy Horse's knife was a butcher's knife that had been whetted down to a very slender and pointed blade that corresponded exactly with his wound, which was so small as to be barely noticeable.

The story passed down to Darlene Rosane in the American Horse family was that a bayonet had killed Crazy Horse, which would agree with McGillycuddy.

Dr. Valentine McGillycuddy said he had become a close friend of Crazy Horse's after his surrender at Fort Robinson. It was part of his duty, as assistant post surgeon, to look after Indians, friendly or hostile, requiring medical attention. Crazy Horse's wife had tuberculosis and came under his care. In E.A. Brininstool's article in *Nebraska History*, Dr. McGillycuddy described the events which he believed led to the fatal bayonet wound:

E.A. Brininstool wrote in the *Nebraska History* magazine, in 1929:

The day, September 5, 1877, Crazy Horse was brought in as a prisoner from Spotted Tail Agency, 43 miles east, I was ordered to keep within close touch, should there be trouble, hence, was in front of the Adjutant's office on the arrival of the chief, and he recognized me as usual. I saw him enter the guard room next door, a prisoner, out of which he sprang without delay, with a drawn knife, to regain his freedom, and was standing forty feet from him when one of the guards, a private of the Ninth Infantry, lunged his bayonet into the chief's abdomen, and [Crazy Horse] fell to the ground.

Wedging my way through the circle of the guard, I decided that he was mortally wounded, and so advised Captain Kennington, officer of the day.

By that time, the Indians, friendly and hostile, were crowding in upon us by hundreds.

Kennington, the absence of contrary orders, endeavored to put the dying chief in the guardhouse, and all the Indians objected, saying, "He was a great chief, and could not be put in prison." So matters came to a standstill.

I explained the latest development to the general, with the suggestion that the Indians were becoming somewhat irritable, and that while there were one thousand men under arms at the post, and that they could possibly imprison Crazy Horse, there were ten thousand Indians around us, and it would mean death of a good many people, and knowing the Indians, I suggested that we

Dr. Valentine McGillicuddy. Photo courtesy Nebraska State Historical Society.

effect a compromise and put Crazy Horse in the Adjutant's office, where I could care for him until he died.

To this arrangement, the general reluctantly consented, and on my return to the guardhouse, the Indians agreed to the decision, and carried him to the office themselves. That was about 5:00 P.M.

At about 11:30 P.M., Crazy Horse struggled and raised an arm toward the sky and seemed to say something. Only his lips were moving, and then he died. During the evening, and at his death, there were present: Captain Kennington, officer of the day; Lieutenant Lemly, special officer of the guard; John Provost, interpreter; Touch the Clouds, a relative of the mother of Crazy Horse; the old father of the chief, 80 years old; and the doctor.

Chief Touch the Clouds crossed over to the body lying on the floor, drew the blanket over the face, and pointed to it with the remark, "That is the lodge of Crazy Horse." Then standing to his full height of seven feet, pointed upward, saying, "The chief has gone above."

Crazy Horse had the reputation among the whites and Indians generally of being a man of his word, and never breaking a promise. It is my opinion that he had no intention of again going on the warpath and joining Sitting Bull as charged at the time of his arrest.

Dr. McGillycuddy said that the old father made many remarks after Crazy Horse died about his people not being agency Indians, that they preferred the buffalo to white man's beef. The old man also said, "Messengers wanted us to come in to the agency. Well, we came in, and now they have killed my boy. Hard times have come upon us, but we are tired of fighting. Red Cloud was jealous of my boy. He was afraid the white government would make him head chief. Our enemies here at the agency were trying to force us away, so probably, we would have been driven soon back to our hunting grounds in the north."

Bat Pourier was with Crazy Horse when he was stabbed. He did not see the tragedy, but he was present when Crazy Horse was dying, and he told the doctor that he was dead. The doctor said he guessed not, but upon checking him, found it so.

Those present feared to tell Crazy Horse's father because of his deep misery. So Bat suggested giving him a drink of grog, which they did. Bat got his portion, too.

The old man expressed his satisfaction saying it was good, and calling Bat his son which he usually did. He said, "It was good. That will open my heart." Bat said, "Don't take it hard, but your son is dead."

The old man's outburst of grief and remorse was explosive. His expressions were, "Hengh" (a grunt like a bear when it seizes and squeezes), and, "Micinci watoye shi-te-lo" ("My son is dead without revenging himself") (Pourier, 1907).

15

Final Reflections

No matter which of these accounts is accurate, Crazy Horse's death had far-reaching impacts on his people and all he knew. Frank Grouard told of going from their camp about five miles from Camp Robinson to the village of Crazy Horse's people after his death.

The whole camp was talking about the killing of Crazy Horse, but I heard nothing which led me to suppose that there would be any trouble. Everything was quiet around the village. Along about three o'clock in the morning, I thought all the trouble was over, so I went to bed.

I don't know how long I had been asleep when I was awakened by a rapid discharge of firearms. My first thought was that the troops had jumped the village, but as soon as I got out of the door, I heard some of the Indians laughing and talking, and found out there was an eclipse of the moon, and the entire village was shooting at the inconstant old girl trying to bring her back to life.

Grouard went on to say that Crazy Horse was the bravest man he ever met.

Reserved at all times, his counsel was greatly sought after, and even in the most solemn deliberations of the Oglalas, he spoke only through some chosen friend. In leadership, he outranked every man in the tribe. In reality, he was a hereditary chief. His battles with the whites proved his prowess, and he brushed aside the honors. He possessed nothing but his native intelligence and cunning. He gave no thought to acquisition of wealth. He was a warrior at all times and in all places, and he left the counting of his coups to those who were as familiar with them as himself. Quick to act, he was first in battle and shrank from no danger. It was to this man's tepi that I went and found shelter and protection when Sitting Bull sought to destroy me. Crazy Horse was the Napoleon among the Sioux, and the death-knell of savagery was sounded in his murder."

More than a month before his tragic end, Crazy Horse had told Grouard that:

…he [Crazy Horse] was looking for death, and believed it would soon come to him. He had a dream, and in the vision, Crazy Horse saw himself at a lofty height and saw a mighty eagle soaring far above him. He watched it as it floated in the quiet sky, and presently it seemed to fold its wings and fall. The eagle's body anchored at his feet, and when he looked upon it, lo, it was himself. An arrow had pierced its body, and its life was gone.

In the hour when death found him, he lay with his head pillowed upon his father's breast, lost to all thought of fear in his approaching dissolution and happy in the contemplation that the spirits of those he loved were awaiting his coming to the far-off Happy Land. Touch the Clouds, the chief of the San Arcs, bending over the body of Crazy Horse and laying his hand upon the chieftain's breast as his warrior spirit took its flight, said, "It is well. He has looked for death and it has come" (De Barthe, 337-351).

The next day at sunrise, a group of officers placed his body in a coffin and loaded it onto a wagon. Chief Touch the Clouds, with gun in hand, forced the crowd that had gathered away from the wagon as it left to join the camp where Crazy Horse's parents were waiting.

16

In Crazy Horse's Territory and the Story of an Olympic Athlete

It was late June 1996, in the Month of Making Fat (as my father liked to say when he was explaining the native Sioux calendar to my son Wally). I was taking my father and Wally on a trip to see Fort Robinson, the site where Crazy Horse had been killed. As we drove through the rolling Sandhills of Nebraska, we were playing a goofy game, seeing who could spot the most windmills. Doc, with his quick, keen eyes, won a good share of the games. He asked Wally, "Don't you wish you had eyes like mine?"

I told my father about the terrain, the white bluffs and sprawling, grass-covered prairie he would see around Fort Robinson. I knew he would like visiting the fort's stables and veterinary facilities that were once the world's largest remount station. In the late 1940s, the fort reached its peak of 12,000 horses and mules. I told him I had heard that Fort Robinson horses were made available to ranchers for breeding purposes and were also trained there for the equestrian events of the 1936 Olympic games in Berlin.

Mules reminded Doc about the time he was called out to castrate an ornery jack mule for a rancher. We were hoping the castration would settle him down. He told Wally, "The rancher said for me to come out and not do anything until it was time to castrate—that he'd tell me." When I got to the ranch the mule was standing in front of this old red barn with a rope around its neck. The rope was strung up through a pulley near the peak of the roof. This pulley operation is usually used for pulling hay up to be stored above the stalls in the barn. This rancher had the other end of the rope tied to his little Ford tractor and when he saw me drive in the yard he started the tractor, put it in gear and up went the mule—about eight feet in the air until it was even with the hay mow barn door. I yelled at him to let go but he would not. Several minutes went by and the mule wasn't moving so he let it back down. The mule just laid there. I thought I was going to be operating on a dead jack. The rancher yelled, 'Now you can castrate him.' The mule was knocked out from being choked and I didn't need to inject any anesthetic. I operated and pretty soon the mule came to and with a foot nudge, up and away he went. You know, Wally, that guy had two different wives in his lifetime and he told me he did not want to be buried beside either one of them. When he died I guess they cremated him. One day shortly after that I saw a little red airplane circle over his ranch. I later learned that they were spreading his ashes over his land."

As we approached Fort Robinson, I pulled my pickup truck over to the side of the road and called home to check in. My wife informed me that Ed Broxterman, of nearby Baileyville, Kansas, had left a message saying he was in ninth place in the high jump at the U S Olympic Trials. He would be among the twelve to try to qualify for the final three spots on the Olympic team. The finals would be in two days, and he was delighted.

Ed was a Kansas State University student from Baileyville, a small farming community east of Marysville, my home town. His family are grain farming people on the gentle rolling land near there. I first met Ed when I saw his attempt to qualify for state at a regional track meet in Marysville in 1992, Ed's senior year of high school.

It was a cloudy, misty day in May. Coming into the meet, Ed had the second highest high jump in the nation at the high school level with a height of seven feet, three inches. All of the other high jumpers had gone out earlier; the best at six feet two inches. At this meet, Ed opened his jumping height at six foot six. As Ed made his first approach, he accelerated to gain speed and, at the moment he planted for take off, he slipped and went crashing into the pit, knocking the bar off. With two jumps left, he made another approach and planted, only to slip again. Ed had one jump left. If he made it, he would go on to compete in the state championships at Wichita. As he prepared for this jump, I could sense the tension. Ed made his final approach with the bar set at six foot six. He planted and, boom, his feet went out from underneath him and he crashed into the pit with the high jump bar on top of him. The crowd was silent. I thought many of the people did not realize that Ed had been disqualified. Ed walked over to an area of the grass infield where he was by himself and hung his head.

The word spread slowly through the crowd that the state's best high jumper, one of the best in the country, would not be going to state. I went over and placed my hand on his shoulders and told him there would be another day. I asked him if I could look at his shoes. I turned them over to look at the soles and his cleats were worn to tiny nubs. In the geographical area of schools Ed competed in, I knew there were running tracks that had hard asphalt surfaces that would wear a cleat down in short order. I told him that I didn't know if that was the reason he had slipped, but longer cleats may have helped. He was obviously upset, hoping that he could go to state and qualify for the Olympic Trials.

I told him that I assisted at a track meet in Marysville that would take place in about three weeks, and I urged him to come to it. That meet is certified by the US Track and Field Association, and if he met the qualifying standards for the high jump set by the Olympic committee, he'd still have a chance to go to New Orleans for the trials. I asked him if he was registered with the US Track and Field Association. He frowned, squinted his eyes, and said, "No, I don't think so." I explained to him that an athlete must be registered before he can compete at the trials. "Ed, you could have set the world's record in the high jump, but if you are not registered, you can't go to the trials."

I called the Olympic Trials office and they told me we had two days to register Ed, and it could not be done via fax. They sent the form out by FedEx and we carefully tracked the courier who would be delivering the form. The FedEx courier was on time to the minute, and Ed got his form filled out and returned to the Olympic office in New Orleans one hour ahead of the final deadline. Two weeks later, Ed was at Marysville's US Track and Field-sanctioned track meet, trying to qualify as a high school senior for the Olympic Trials.

There were probably more than five hundred people gathered to watch the high jump competition. It was the largest crowd assembled to watch a single track and field event in Marysville. Ed barely missed seven feet, four and a quarter inches. He had almost qualified for the trials.

Ed wrote me a little thank you note, saying he appreciated all the effort I'd made, and someday, if he dreamed hard enough, he would qualify for the Olympics and when he did, he wanted me to join him. Some people, I thought, do not dream big enough—and some do.

When Ed enrolled at Kansas State University, he thought he had a full scholarship in track. A distraught voice called me at home one evening; it was Ed saying that when he went to pick up his books the day he registered for classes he was presented a bill for tuition. Ed was shocked, and he asked me for help. Ed's feelings were similar to those of some of the Lakota people who were promised bountiful land and hunting grounds and saw that dwindle. Then they were promised reservations and those also shrank. Ancestors of those people I have met on reservations around the Great Plains are still angry about those broken promises.

Ed's family wrote me a handwritten note about what they thought Ed had been promised in the way of a scholarship. For insight on college scholarships, I called University Nebraska coach Gary Pepin. Coach Pepin told me at the time Nebraska did not have one man on full scholarship. I asked Coach Pepin if he would be interested in Ed as a jumper but he knew it would be difficult for Ed to transfer and he felt Ed would have a great high jump coach in Assistant Coach Cliff Rovelto at Kansas State. Coach Pepin said if he had a son who wanted to improve as a high jumper he would want Cliff to work with him.

I knew Ed wanted to be at Kansas State; he felt comfortable there except for this misunderstanding of his scholarship. With the help of a local Kansas State booster from the Marysville Pepsi plant, a meeting was arranged with the Kansas State athletic director. At the meeting with the athletic director, I simply said I had heard of over-zealous boosters going beyond what the NCAA allows in the way of compensation to athletes but I never heard of a school breaking promises and acting like an 1860s United States army officer promising big land to the Natives and then granting only a small parcel. I told the athletic director that Ed really wanted to be at Kansas State but that a heavy financial burden was on his shoulders. "I know this guy is going to jump high; make his shoulders light weight and he will fly with the eagles." A week later the head track coach resigned and Cliff Rovelto was named head track coach. In time, Ed received much financial help from the college. A great bond was born between coach and jumper.

I thought of the Lakota people who are now receiving educational aid for colleges that are located on many reservations. I thought of Native Americans who found it difficult to mix into

White society and obtain college degrees. I thought how the government learning institution should be coming around for Ed Broxterman and the Lakota people. I saw Ed soaring with the spirit of Crazy Horse.

Ed went on to jump at Kansas State University where he was a Big Eight Champion and also an Academic All-American. Upon his graduation, Kansas State awarded Ed a huge NCAA Walter Byers post graduate scholarship to study for a masters degree. Ed was awarded a Kansas State University track assistant job by his coach. Coach Rovelto and Ed are great ambassadors for Kansas State and the people of the Great Plains. After his initial disappointment, Ed found that new promises were made, earned, and kept.

Ed was a quiet leader like Crazy Horse. They were alike in many ways; Ed was highly skilled and tenacious in training as a jumper, and Crazy Horse could be described in the same way, only as a hunter and war leader. Each would have a vision and call upon the Great Spirit for guidance.

Ed was a senior at K State in 1996. He skipped a competitive season that year to rest an ankle that he had severely injured. As the summer Olympic Trials approached, his best jump was seven feet even. After qualifying at a sanctioned meet, Ed went to the trials not expecting to do his best; only hoping.

On the night of June 23 that year, I was watching television when the sports network announcer declared that Ed Broxterman from Kansas had jumped seven feet, six and a half inches to place second and qualify for the Olympics! I was stunned, and elated for Ed.

That day my father and I had been at Fort Robinson, meeting with Tom Buecker who worked there and was very knowledgeable about the history of the fort. I enjoyed listening to my father telling the staff about all the horses he treated for sleeping sickness, about how he would vaccinate for the east and west strain and the Venezuela strain of sleeping sickness. He told the staff how mosquito-infected horses with sleeping sickness would swing their heads back and forth often beating themselves against the stable wall. He told about rigging up a gunny sack that was full of ice to keep the aching head of the horse cool to reduce the fever of the disease. He said how he would often inject 50 CCs of calcium gluconate every day for a week to help the horse recover. Some horses suffered from a permanent staggering gait or were slow to commands, but he said he lost only a few.

After we looked at the old Fort Robinson horse barn, we walked the same path that Crazy Horse had walked to the guard house where he was killed. Tom Buecker, the curator of the Fort Robinson museum, enjoyed trading horse stories with Doc. Before we left the fort with the tall old trees surrounding the large parade ground and the well-kept white quarter master buildings, Tom opened his file box and pulled out some information for Doc. It was about Crazy Horse and the many stories Tom had collected about the burial of Crazy Horse.

Tom said, "*You guys have done much research on the burial of Sioux chiefs and I would not touch or write about what I have collected on Crazy Horse. That is for somebody like you to do.*" My father replied, "I suppose someday one of us will; it will probably be Cleve."

Later, my wife relayed another message that Ed had invited me to go with him to the Olympics in Atlanta. He explained that I could go as part of his family and stay with a host family who would get me back and forth between sporting venues.

While I was walking around Fort Robinson, I thought of Crazy Horse and all he stood for, all he fought for, and how he always wore the special stone that had been blessed by a friend to give him protection. There was the hawk feather that he wore in battle, and the colt skin cape that flew behind him as he rode toward the enemy.

I remember telling Ed that Crazy Horse sprinkled himself with gopher dust in order to protect him in battle from bullets. I kidded Ed, saying he could use his Catholic Holy water to sprinkle himself for guidance. He said, "You would not believe it, but to prepare myself before I jump, I listen to a tape that a sports psychologist prepared of Native American drum music. It inspires me to meet the challenges of world competitions." I thought about the Olympics, how it helps our nations sublimate their anxieties about international conflicts into another venue, and how the competition of sporting events, such as the high jump, takes the place of wars that kill or maim.

I also thought that it was amazing that I'd be going to the Olympics at the same time I was finding the stories about someone who, in the 1870s, was really a highly skilled athlete. To become a Lakota Sioux war chief required qualifying in at least one of three ways. The honor required the chief to be a great hunter, a great spiritual leader of people, or a great warrior in battle. Crazy Horse qualified in all areas.

At the Olympics in Atlanta, Ed Broxterman made opening height and then bowed out. At the trials the month before, he'd pulled a hamstring muscle that had not completely healed. After he jumped, I went with him to Olympic Park to see the festivities. A bomb exploded there not long after we left. For someone, those angry anxieties had not been sublimated deeply enough.

Ed was only one of two United States collegiate athletes to qualify in track and field for the 1996 Olympics. The rest were older athletes helped along by corporate sponsors. Ed went on to complete his masters degree at Kansas State. The local paper honored Ed in an article, telling Ed that "as long as there is recorded history you will be known as an Olympian, the best and most honored athlete on planet earth."

The stories of the two young men, a warrior from long ago who fought for freedom on the Plains and an athlete in today's world who worked to gather the accolades that come from training with one's whole heart to be in the Olympics, are similar to each other. On the other hand, they were quite different—Crazy Horse fought until his death.

In the 1870s, white men sought gold and invaded the sacred Lakota Black Hills. Today's athletes, like Ambrose Red Owl of the Santee Sioux, or Ed Broxterman of the Kansas plains, seek gold in the spirit of competition.

17

Mourning a Lost Son

The day Crazy Horse was killed, there were many rumors. People did not know what to believe; everything had taken place so quickly.

In 1998, I visited with Laveda Bark who works at the Holy Rosary Mission north of Pine Ridge. She told me a family relative of hers, Sophie Rock Bear, was at Camp Robinson when Crazy Horse died. Sophie was nine years old at the time and had died in 1954 at the age of eighty-six. Sophie said that other women who viewed the body of Crazy Horse were crying and soon Sophie and her little friends started to cry. But hers, she admitted, was a make believe cry. "Everyone was crying, so we cried, too," she remembered. "All felt sorrow."

Even Red Cloud, rival of Crazy Horse, said, "Crazy Horse was a mystic and was revered by all."

One thing the Oglala people did know was that they could no longer live, roam, or hunt in the way they had before. With Crazy Horse out of the way now, the United States government would be sure to move them all to reservations. The Indians had to make new ways and learn to walk the white man's road. The warriors of the Plains had to be molded like fresh clay out of the creek bed. The Oglala knew they were no longer free to roam for game. They were moving toward what white men called civilization. Crazy Horse, the greatest warrior of all, had no space on the white man's road.

As my father, my son, Wally, and I drove away from our visit at Fort Robinson, I wondered how Crazy Horse's parents might have felt after the death of their son. The death of a child is the most tragic thing I see in my profession. When a parent dies, we lose the past. When a child dies, we lose the future.

About a year after my first child, Woody, was born, I was growing tired of his night disturbances. It seemed he never wanted to sleep; he was always a kid who wanted to be up doing something. He started walking on his exploratory routes at seven and a half months. He liked to travel around at night, and we watched many re-runs of Rat Patrol which ran at 3:30 A.M. Woody's restlessness bothered me until a son of an acquaintance died on a camp out with his parents. The boy may have died as a result of Sudden Infant Death Syndrome, but that experience affected me for the rest of my life. I grew more tolerant of the after-midnight madness and watching Rat Patrol. I recall hugging the parents of the deceased boy, telling them that they had helped me more than I could ever help them understand their loss. Yes, there are still times I may not be understanding of Woody, but when I remember the boy who died at the campsite, I calm down—some—and when I see re-runs of Rat Patrol, it brings a 3:30 A.M. kind of smile to my face.

It is difficult to measure what emotions are evoked when death occurs, but from my observation, the grief a parent experiences over the loss of a child seems more intense than the grief experienced when a person loses a parent. It is difficult to measure but most caregivers who help resolve grief say the same; parents are hit harder.

I knew some people from nearby Hanover, Kansas, who had a son who was an honor student and an active member of the Boy Scouts. There had been a picture of him in the local paper showing that he was in charge of flying the American flag at the town's Memorial Day celebration. A short time later, he was training to develop his aerobic capacity to compete in cross-country by running on the back roads of the community. It was a hot, humid day and he collapsed while jogging in the southeast part of town. The boy had asthma and was found by a telephone employee, lying on the roadside holding an inhaler in his hand. He was pronounced dead at the local hospital. His parents had been married for more than seventeen years before they were able to have that child.

His father made all the funeral arrangements and his mother never spoke a word during the time leading up to the boy's funeral. I knew her grief was such that her speech was almost paralyzed. I tried to comfort her, but I do not know if what I said registered. After the funeral, I told the mother that if she ever needed anyone to talk with, to please call me, any time of day. My words seemed shallow, and I did not think they were very meaningful to her. One month later, she called me at 3:00 A.M., saying she knew it was a terrible time to be calling, but she needed to visit. I listened to her talk about her son for more than an hour, while I hardly said a word; but I have never felt so good talking to someone at three o'clock in the morning as I did that night. One month later, the mother called again during the night just to talk.

I am not sure what one can do to help a parent resolve grief of that magnitude. I would like to think I helped as a sounding board to absorb some of the emotion and to be of comfort, but I really don't think a parent gets over the loss of a child the way a child moves on when a parent is lost. Four short years later, that boy's mother died of cancer, although I felt that her broken heart had also contributed to her death. Not long after her death, the father died as well.

So, it must have been the same with Crazy Horse's parents about whom Colonel Luther P. Bradley observed:

> The father made some remarks as to the life and character of his son. He asked that he might take the body away and give it an Indian burial and consent was given. The offer of an ambulance was declined, and at daylight, September 6, 1877, the gray, bareheaded, wailing wretched old father and mother followed on foot, out of

the post, the travois on which was lashed the body of their only son and protector. Their pitiable condition appealed to the sympathy of everyone, and as they passed Major Burrows' quarters, they were kindly offered something to eat, which they accepted with apparent gratitude, and then resumed their mournful journey.

There is no Indian journalist, author or reporter to present the chief's side of the story of his tragic fate. With the lapse of time, his name and fame may linger for awhile in the traditions of his tribe, and then fade away forever. History will make but little record of him, save to note a point perhaps in the onward march of our Christian civilization....

After Crazy Horse's father had quieted, he made a speech on behalf of his son, saying that Crazy Horse did not want to come to the agency, but he wished to remain north and be let alone, that the troops had hunted him down, and forced him to come in, and that he wished to be put on a scaffold in the customary Indian way, not buried in a coffin. He said that his son had been his only protection, and that now that he was gone, he was poor and friendless. Also, while they were in the north, his son had taken good care of him, and that they had always had plenty of game to eat. But the morning after Crazy Horse died, the old man had been haranguing that his son was obstinate, would not listen to good advice, and that now that he was no more, it was well (Brininstool, 30-31).

In the 1998 interview with Darlene Rosane, she told me that the oral history that had been passed down to her said that when Crazy Horse was accidentally bayoneted, Chief American Horse summoned Crazy Horse's father who was camping nearby. The father rode fast with a quiver on his back. Due to the galloping rocking movement of the horse, the quiver thong wrapped around the father's neck several times. When he arrived at Camp Robinson, he was choking and barely able to breathe. American Horse cut the leather thong from the father's neck. The wounded Crazy Horse told his father at that same time that, upon his death, he wished to be laid in a cool stream for four days so his spirit would come back stronger than before. To this his father had replied, "No son. Let your spirit go on to another place. Look at the skeletons on the hillside. You have done enough."

And so, the father, as well as American Horse and many others, prayed that the power of Crazy Horse would stay in another world.

18

The Crazy Horse Legend: Larger than a Mountain

The stories of Crazy Horse seem to grow larger with time. He is revered for the humble ways in which he spoke. He left the counting of coup to others, for collecting trophies was not his nature. He was not only a great war chief who rode to the front in battle without wearing a war bonnet, but his symbol of guidance was a feather which was stuck in a downward fashion on his headband. This was the way the war eagle's tail feathers point when ready to attack. Crazy Horse was called upon as a medicine man to provide fighting power to others. He defended his people and their way of life in the only manner he knew. He was never known to sign a treaty or touch a pen.

There is a large, looming memorial to the spirit of Crazy Horse being carved out of stone north of Custer, South Dakota, of all places. The figure in the mountain depicts Crazy Horse

Crazy Horse Monument.

with his left hand thrown out, pointing the answer to a derisive question asked by a white man: "Where are your lands now?" Crazy Horse is said to have replied, "My lands are where my dead lie buried." This description of the memorial carving was given by its originator, Korczak Ziolkowski in 1949. Chief Henry Standing Bear invited Korczak to the Black Hills to carve a memorial to Crazy Horse. Standing Bear told his people, "My fellow chiefs and I would like the white man to know the red man has great heroes, too."

How wrongheaded Colonel Luther P. Bradley was, in 1877, when he visualized Crazy Horse going down in history with little honor. Crazy Horse's mark has been made, and his own people, as well as those he has influenced, may never fully understand the spiritual trail that the man who wore a lone hawk feather will fly us to.

19

We Pause to Look Back at the Setting Sun

There are many stories about what happened to the body of Crazy Horse. Black Elk told us that it does not matter where his body lies, for it is grass, but where his spirit is, it will be good. I believe that. I also know that when I was helping my father search for the burial sites of Sioux chiefs, the question that was asked most often and seemed to be of the greatest interest was, where is it that Crazy Horse might be buried?

In September 1996, my father wanted to go for a ride in the country. I walked him down his office steps toward his car. He was growing weak from radiation and disease. An old friend of mine was parked in front of the bank, near my father's veterinary office, in a burgundy colored car that morning. I nodded to the friend; I could not wave because my father needed the support of both of my arms.

We headed west of Verdigre and turned off the asphalt highway onto a gravel road, driving past many of Dad's old clients' ranch places where he had served for so many years caring for sick animals. On the way, we talked and told stories about his veterinary practice. He said it seemed like yesterday that he was just starting out. As we rode through the country, he told me, "You know, you can tell some of these stories we are talking about at my funeral." I had heard his story about his favorite calf incident many times, but I asked him to tell it again. It was difficult for my father to speak because the cancer was affecting his vocal folds. Nevertheless, he seemed delighted to tell, again, about the time he ran a stop sign over by Winnetoon on his way to deliver a calf. A state patrolman saw him shoot his car out onto the highway and gave chase. When he caught him, he asked him where he was headed so fast. Dad replied he had several calls to make and was heading to pull a calf. The patrolman replied that he had never seen a calf being pulled, and asked Doc if he could go along. He followed Doc to the ranch where Doc guided the calf out of the heifer while directing the patrolman to crank the jack.

That September day, driving west of town, we talked about the time I broke Johnny Farnik's (probably one of the best all-around athletes to come out of Verdigre) high school 100-yard dash record. It was a goal I had in mind for many years, and I was really happy when I accomplished this feat. After completing that goal, my dad and I raced from the white barn on our place to the big old cottonwood tree with our tree house up in it, a distance of about forty or fifty yards. I wanted to show my dad how fast I could run and how far I could beat him. My dad beat me; he was forty-seven years old at the time.

Someone told me not long ago that after nearly thirty years, my record of 10.1 seconds still stands. But I was never the fastest in Verdigre, rather the little veterinarian in the white Levi's was the quickest.

As we told stories and drove through the countryside, I stopped the car for a drink of water from an artesian well pipe sticking out of the side of a hill at Raymond Soucek's place. The valley there is thick with cottonwood and oak trees, and a crystal clear stream runs beneath the pipe. This was always a favorite stopping place when I traveled through the country with my dad on calls. I was there this one last time with him.

My father told me about the time he was called to a ranch a few miles west of the Soucek place over towards Dorsey where he was summoned to look at some cattle that had been hit by lightning. The rancher owned several sections of land. It was a hot summer day and several cattle had congregated together in one pasture near some sumac and were standing close together swatting the flies away. Lightning had struck one and the others were touching each other. There were twenty-five cows that lay dead from the lightning strike. Two years later, the same rancher called and said his insurance company wanted a veterinarian to come out and look at his cattle, saying, "Doc, you won't believe this."

When Doc arrived, twenty-four or twenty-five head of cattle had been hit by lightning in the same area of the pasture as two years earlier. They were all lying in a circle. There was one difference: one cow was standing, alive, in the middle of the circle fenced in by the cows that had been struck by lightning.

We continued our trip toward Pichelville, which is little more than a town hall twenty miles from the nearest town. Near there, a bridge spans the Niobrara River and the road heads up a long hill to the north. We talked about a time in the early 1960s when an ice jam was plugging up the river. The ice was putting pressure on the bridge and the *Omaha World-Herald* sent a photographer, Harold Mauck, from Plainview, up to take a picture. Plainview is about fifty miles from Pichelville and Harold did not know where the bridge was, so he asked Doc to take him out there. Doc drove him across the bridge and just as they crossed it, the bridge went out.

The sun was shining that early fall day while I was driving with my father. The trees were starting to turn and their color was everywhere. When we reached the top of the big hill to the north of the Pichelville Bridge, we came across the largest porcupine I had ever seen lying in the middle of the road. Someone had recently run over it. My dad felt bad for it. I reminded him of the many times I had helped him as he pulled quills from the ends of dogs' noses. For years, I kept some of those quills we removed in a baby food jar on my night stand as a reminder of those times I'd helped a dog's nose recover from an encounter with a porcupine.

We continued driving on what the locals call the ridge road, which overlooks the Niobrara River. The valley looked deep and full of autumn light, green and gold. My dad remarked, "Not too many of my old clients are left in these parts. There used to be ten times the farms and ranches in this township than there are now."

We drove past the Mormon monument where my dad reminded me that Mormons are buried throughout the field. Mormons were the first white settlers in this area in 1846. My father told me that many locals thought the Ponca Indians drove the Mormons from the area, but in fact, they were very friendly, and the Mormon deaths that caused them to leave were due to pneumonia, principally affecting the children. My dad did veterinary work for the farmer who lived near the monument. The farmer told him that when he would find their bones when he plowed, he would lay the bones he unearthed near the monument.

About a mile north of the monument, we drove near the Mormon Canal Bridge. This is a bridge that crosses a channel of the Niobrara River. Some folks think it was a canal the Mormons built, but it is just a main channel that ran on the west side of the Niobrara just before it flows into the Missouri River. The channel had been there for many years before the Mormons came.

That day, as my father and I approached the bridge, a woman was standing there who reported that she'd just seen a huge splash. She had seen a car drive up the road, turn around in her yard, and head back down the road towards the river. She could not believe her eyes, as she thought the car had driven into the river. Her son had gone to look and he saw what he thought was a car in the river with just the trunk sticking up. They had called the rescue unit. My father and I stayed and watched the men lining up in the water to reach what did look like a back corner of a car. The current was strong, but the rescuers were able to reach the vehicle and retrieved the body of a lifeless man from the car. No one knew who it was. My father said, "Well, Cleve, between you and me, we know about everybody in this country, so we'd better take a look."

"It is Jamie Kotrous," I said. I could not believe it was the childhood friend who, two hours ago, had been parked in front of the bank in Verdigre near my father's office. I had just nodded to Jamie earlier as my father and I walked to our car to drive out of town. I looked again at the car that was now sinking and there was still a glimpse of the burgundy color of the corner of the trunk. I was stunned. I told someone that I knew that Jamie's sister, Jeanne, and brother, Jan, lived in the nearby town of Niobrara, and that a brother, Jack, was eleven miles down the road at Verdigre.

When we returned to town, I stopped in at the bank and asked the teller if Jamie had been in that morning. She told me he had been and asked me why I wanted to know. I mentioned that I'd seen him out front of the bank somewhere before nine o'clock that morning, and that my dad and I had just identified his dead body. The teller recalled that Jamie had been in a strange mood. He had cashed a check and mentioned that he would not need money now, that it was for his dad.

Jamie's brother, Jerry, told me they had been fishing off that same bridge a few days earlier. "He did not seem much interested in fishing. He just kind of looked at the flow of the river. Things had not been going well for him," Jerry told me.

Growing up, Jamie had been a good friend who was four years older than I was. We enjoyed playing basketball in the barn and shooting pool in the basement of my father's office. Those games will always stay with me.

Years before, in a Sunday School Christmas play, I had some long lines to remember and I was afraid of blowing them. Jamie was at the back of the church making faces at me when I got up to deliver my lines. I relaxed, and things went okay. Since then, when I give a talk to a large group of people, I visualize Jamie standing in the back of the room making faces.

As my father and I ended our drive that September day, we drove toward Verdigre, past my dad's farm, and then past the cemetery. He told me that he had bought some lots there to be buried in. He said, "You know, Jamie is better off where he has gone. I should be there with him."

To myself, I thought of the pain my dad was going through, watching himself slowly lose his health. It would be easy for him to "cash in." I once heard him say that would be a dirty trick to his family. I admired him for sticking in there—coming to terms with his spiritmaker. He believed his spirit would never rest if it did not complete the cycle of going through the process of living out his life the way Mother Nature would guide it. He valued the lessons he was learning of caring, bonding, sacrificing, going for one more ride through the country, and finding delight in telling one more story. These were the things he worked on to prepare his soul for a better journey. He still searched for something valuable to take him to a new spiritual butte that was beckoning to him from the Plains where horses and war paint once rode. No jagged flint spear would intervene, rather he felt his soul had to exhaust itself of disease so it could never be affected by it again. He was a very curious man who felt it was the nature of his soul to grow and to experience the earth. He was realizing it was a natural part of life on Earth to experience mental and physical pain. As his sun was setting, there was a shadow of new riders in the sky coming at him. He was experiencing life's strongest lesson.

He once told me the eagles would take him home. He chose to fight the fight and run the race, and he was finishing the course and keeping the faith. Later he told me that the Bible verse from II Timothy 4: 6-8, (King James version) was the only one he wanted read at his funeral. It is this verse that seemed to hit home with my father. It is here in the chapter of Timothy that the traveling minister Paul, who had started churches throughout the Roman Empire and was awaiting execution in Nero's prison, wrote to Timothy; Paul appointed Timothy to lead the church in Ephesus and carry out the teachings of the Christian faith. As Paul ends his letter to Timothy he expresses confidence in the Lord in the face of death. "When I was first put on trial, no one helped me. But the Lord stood beside me and gave me strength to tell his message, so that all Gentiles would hear it. He will bring me safely into his heavenly kingdom. Praise him forever and ever! Amen" (4:16-18).

To my father, it seemed that life was a vicious cycle with the Christians coming to the Great Plains, bringing their beliefs and establishing boarding schools that took Lakota children away from their families for long periods of time. Lakota warriors like Crazy Horse, defending their spiritual way of life, brought war. The "love thy neighbor as thy self" policy of both cultures was difficult to practice. Treaties were made and then broken. One can only ask: Why does God give us such conflicts to solve?

I could not help but think that Paul, my father, and Crazy Horse each had a confidence in what the hereafter would bring as the sun was going down on their lives that had been filled with turmoil. Each had fought the fight, and was finishing the race and keeping the faith the best they knew how.

How much more work was to be done?

20

In the Area of the Burial Grounds

In my work around funeral homes over the past thirty years, I have seen the importance of going to the cemetery to pay respects to departed loved ones. Many of the concerns of families we serve are about the cemetery. In that short period of time after burial, a grave needs more attention. "Please have more dirt put on Mom's grave." "The grave is sunk, please do something to level it off so it looks nice." "Help. There are tractor tracks that have left deep ruts around my sister's grave." "Please see if you can find out what happened to the flowers we left at Grandma's grave." And, "Oh, dear. The rain washed the dirt away from our son's grave and the vault is exposed, and the cemetery is a mess, and the grass needs to be mowed. Please do something!"

Funerals are a vehicle to help in the resolution of the loss of a loved one no matter what the nationality. The cemetery is a place to go to reflect and remember the life and meaning that the deceased gave. It helps many to be at the foot of a grave remembering the good times. The white man likes graves clearly marked so all can share in the memory of the person. Conversely, the Native American views burial sites as personal places of reflection.

I once worked with a family where the sister was in charge of burying her brother who had been divorced from his wife. He had several children who were living with their mother. The man was found at home lying on the couch. He had died of an apparent heart attack and was not found for a couple of days. The body was not in the best condition, and the family wanted him cremated and the ashes spread. After a day of thinking about this, the sister called me and said, "We have changed our minds and we don't want to sign the papers to cremate. It is important for his body to be buried in the cemetery so the kids have a place to go to reflect on their dad and his life. He meant a lot to them."

Why do we pay our respects to our friends and loved ones by going to the cemetery? Are our feelings more tangible and our thoughts enhanced if we know that we are praying and thinking about the life that has been lived while we are visiting the cemetery? In a cemetery near Marysville, the son of a deceased father missed visiting with his father enough that he erected a bench at the cemetery so he could sit while he visited with him. The stone bench is engraved with the words, "Be Seated."

Cemeteries are sacred, no matter what origin or culture we are. During my search for Crazy Horse's burial place, I asked a Jesuit priest on the Pine Ridge Reservation what he knew about the burial site of Crazy Horse. He replied, "Who should really care? It is the spirit of him that is important. Some of the Sioux people may know and keep it a secret." The question of where Crazy Horse might be buried is sacred to his people and yet many seek to know the location. Not knowing the precise site where he was buried creates a sort of sacred suspense that drives us to seek an answer. In the winter of 1997, Thomas R. Buecker, curator at the Fort Robinson Museum, told me that even the people who make up the questions for the game show *Jeopardy* wanted to know about Crazy Horse.

Well, I must tell you that the trails are many and they are divided. The song of the central plains calls. An occasional eagle can be seen circling over the valley of streams I have hiked, then it glides off over a canyon and the gentle flap of its wings calls me.

© 2000 David Hammett

SIOUX TERRITORIES 1869-1879

LEGEND

~~~~~~~~~ RIVERS R.

= = = = } TERRITORIES AND STATES

——— 1868 TREATY RES.

—·—·— SIOUX LANDS OF 1875 TO 1879.

——— SIOUX RESERVATION BY ACT OF FEB. 28, 1877.

DIAGONAL STRIPES = INDIAN LANDS LOST

■/▓/▨ U.S. ARMY FORT: long term/short term/after 1877

▨ CAMP OR CANTONMENT, DATES ACTIVE

▲/△ INDIAN AGENCY/RELOCATION AFTER 1877 DATES ACTIVE

★ ARMED CONFLICT

★★ CRAZY HORSE'S BATTLES

🐃 BUFFALO SKULL = POOR HUNTING AREA

Scale: 0 50 100 150 200 MILES

N

SIOUX AND CHEYENNE ATTACK NORTHERN PACIFIC R.R. SURVEY CREW AUG. 4 1873

FT. KEOGH Mid-1877–1908 PRECEEDING POST, TO ITS RIGHT Tongue River Cantonment Fall 1876––1877

SIOUX & CHEYENNE WINTER CAMP 1875 TO MAY 1876.

GREAT SUNDANCE OF JUNE 1876. (SITTING BULL'S VICTORY VISION)

BATTLE OF THE LITTLE BIG HORN (CUSTER'S LAST STAND) JUNE 25, 1876

BATTLE OF THE ROSEBUD JUNE 17, 1876 SIOUX & CHEYENNE DEFEAT GEN. CROOK

WOLF MOUNTAINS (BATTLE BUTTE) JAN. 8, 1877 PURSUIT OF CRAZY HORSE BY COL. NELSON MILES

TRAVOIS WITH LOAD

WINTER CAMP

SIOUX LANDS OF 1875 TO 1879

1. LAND ADDED TO RESERVATION BY AGREEMENT OF SEP. 26, 1876.
2. ADDED TO RES. BY EXECUTIVE ORDER, MAR. 16, 1875.
3. ADDED TO RES. BY EXECUTIVE ORDER, MAY 20, 1875.
4. ADDED TO RES. BY AGREEMENT OF SEP. 26, 1876.
5. ADDED TO RES. BY EXECUTIVE ORDER, NOV. 28, 1876.
6. BLACK HILLS CEDED BY AGREE-MENT, SEP. 26, 1876; ACT OF FEB. 28, 1877.
7. RETAINED BY RES. ACT OF FEB. 28, 1877.   1+7
   1. RETURNED TO PUBLIC DOMAIN
   2. BY EXECUTIVE ORDER OF
   3. AUG. 9, 1879.   1+7

NORTHERN PACIFIC R.R. CONSTRUCTION HALTED BY PANIC OF 1873.

ROUTE OF PONCA FORCED REMOVAL TO INDIAN TERRITORY, MAY TO JULY 1877.

TRAIL OF TEARS

FIRST CATTLE CAMPS AND RANCHES APPEAR IN SAND HILLS: 1877.

THE BLACK HILLS AND UNCEDED HUNTING LANDS CESSION WAS IMPOSED ON AGENCY SIOUX BY THE G.W. MANYPENNY COMMISSION NEAR THE RED CLOUD AGENCY IN SEPTEMBER 1876.

THE APPROACH OF THE RAILROAD BROKE THE PEACE OF THE 1868 FORT LARAMIE TREATY WITH SKIRMISHES IN 1872 AND 1873 (ONE SHOWN ON THIS MAP). IN 1874 AN ILLEGAL ARMY EXPEDITION UNDER LT. COL. GEORGE CUSTER DISCOVERED GOLD IN THE BLACK HILLS (SACRED "PAHA SAPA" TO THE SIOUX AND OTHER TRIBES).

FT. STEVENSON 1867–1883

FT. BUFORD

FT. RICE

BISMARCK

FT. ABRAHAM LINCOLN 1872–1891

STANDING ROCK 1873

GRAND RIVER 1868–1873

FT. SULLY

CHEYENNE RIVER 1868–1891

PIERRE

FT. MEADE 1878–1944

DEADWOOD

CROOK CITY

RAPID CITY

CUSTER

BLACK HILLS CESSION 9-26-1876

CRAZY HORSE'S COUNTER ATTACK SEP. 10, 1876

SLIM BUTTES SEP. 9 1876

CROW CREEK 1863

FT. HALE 1878–1884

LOWER BRULE 1868–76 1876–1894

ROSEBUD (or SPOTTED TAIL) 1878–

CAMP SHERIDAN 1874–1877

SPOTTED TAIL 1875–1881

YANKTON DAKOTA 1859

SANTEE DAKOTA 1866

FT. RANDALL

PONCA 1861–1877

SPOTTED TAIL'S CAMP WINTER 1877, SPRING 1878

GENOA

ELGIN

VERDIGRE

FT. OMAHA

OTOE RESERVATION

OKETO

BEATRICE

MARYSVILLE, KS

MANHATTAN

SEWARD

MILFORD

OREGON TRAIL

NORTH PLATTE

CHEYENNE

UNION PACIFIC R.R.

FT. LARAMIE 1875 IRON BRIDGE

FT. FETTERMAN

GOLD RUSH 1875–76

PINE RIDGE (or RED CLOUD) 1878–

RED CLOUD 1873–77

CAMP ROBINSON 1874–78 FT. ROBINSON 1878–1948

RED CLOUD (1873–1877)- SITE OF CRAZY HORSE BAND'S DIGNIFIED SURRENDER TO GENERAL CROOK, MAY 6, 1877.

GREATEST EVER SUNDANCE OF JUNE 1877.

CRAZY HORSE'S CAMP, MAY 1877.

WHERE CRAZY HORSE DIED SEPTEMBER 5, 1877.

SIOUX 1868 HUNTING RIGHTS CESSION. 9-26-1876

SURVEY CREW ROUTE

FT. McKINNEY 1877–1894

CANTONMENT RENO FALL 1876-mid-1877

BIG HORN (WHITE) MTS.

Missouri R.

Little Missouri

Yellowstone

Tongue Cr.

Powder Cr.

Beaver Cr.

Rosebud Cr.

Powder R.

White R.

Badlands

Sand Hills

Part Two
The Burial of Crazy Horse

Over the years, I've collected many stories about the possible burial places of Crazy Horse and the mystery of what happened to him after his death. Along the way, many people helped me in my research. I have discovered that his parents may have carried his body with them on their travels for as long as a year. This part of the book follows their journey as they travel back and forth, crossing Nebraska and South Dakota with their people—and possibly with the body of their slain son.

Through the years of helping my father search for burial sites of Sioux chiefs for his book, I found a number of interesting stories about what happened to Crazy Horse after he died. There are, indeed, many of them, and they reflect the great compassion that his parents had for their son. The following chapters are about the mysteries of those many stories.

As we follow the trail of Crazy Horse's parents as they might have traveled with the body of their slain son, may this journey be a tribute to the sacred ground of a warrior who, like the hawk, was "trying to hold on to its animal yellow."

21

The Feather of a Hawk

My father died in 1997, in the Month of Snow Blindness (March). When he was practicing veterinary medicine, March had always been his busiest month. The day of his funeral was cloudy. The cemetery where he is buried is a mile down the road from where his farm yard was. It was a beautiful old farmstead surrounded by big cottonwood trees, with a huge white barn. We used to have square dances in that barn and play basketball in the hay mow. My dad had worked hard maintaining the place. At the graveside, I glanced up to see the sun had sent a ray that peeked through the clouds and sent a reflection off the tin roof of his barn.

Two friends, Todd Rhodes and Tiff Varney, tore boards of cottonwood from part of the fence around the big barn, made a cross of them, and etched "Doc" on it. It still stands today as his only grave marker. Ambrose Red Owl, of the Santee Sioux, was there wearing a cowboy hat like Dad used to wear. Someone said an eagle flew overhead.

A week before he died, I had promised a friend, Varmit T. Varney, from Mullen, Nebraska, that I'd accompany him on a winter kayaking trip down the Dismal River in the central Sandhills of Nebraska. [*Varmit was an old turtle racing adversary of my father's and mine. We raced against each other for many years. Varmit had owned a turtle named Myrtle who, at one time, held the world's turtle racing record. In front-to-front racing, Myrtle never did beat any of our stock. As an excuse, Varmit would say she was loaded down with pregnancy. Truth was, he just could not find the right high protein bugs to feed his turtle.*]

The Dismal River is in a deep canyon; at least, by Great Plains standards. It is a narrow, fast-flowing river that rarely freezes over in the winter. It is cold and clear, with several hundred-foot deep springs that feed the river. Cedar trees are tight along the river bank and often create obstacles. That name, Dismal, hooked my curiosity. Someone had to have named it that to keep others away, thinking it would repel them in another direction. It is remote; an untouched gem. Crazy Horse and other Sioux had gone there to herd wild horses. It was also a place where they could escape the soldiers because the shifting sands in that area easily covered their tracks.

I knew I probably should not be going. I felt that my place should be near my father, since I knew he might not last much longer. But I could feel a haunting call beckoning me from the edge of the Sandhills. I would soon discover what that was about.

The morning I was to leave to go kayaking, there was an article by wildlife poet Don Welch in the Sunday *Omaha World-Herald* that caught my eye. Don taught at the University of Nebraska at Kearney, a college I had attended after high school. I never had Don as a teacher, but I wish I had. In his writings you can hear the river and the geese, and smell the fish and the valley.

Kearney was halfway between the Dismal and Marysville, Kansas. I decided I needed to visit Don on my way to the Dismal River. I was driving by myself on Interstate 80 which parallels the Platte River in that part of Nebraska and follows the same route white settlers took on their way to Oregon in the 1800s. I thought about all the covered wagons that traveled this road, but the words Don wrote kept haunting me.

At Kearney, in Don's office, I talked with him about a poem (included below) he had written after finding a struggling hawk in a trap. It was his personal favorite. The poem asks the question: Can you turn defeat into victory by refusing to be defeated? Don said, "To me, that is the idea that has influenced my life more than any other."

The Hawk
by Don Welch

Somewhere years from now
I hope I'm saying this
to my sons. Why the hawk
had to hit the trap I couldn't guess.
In the face of it
it was pointless.
But it had hit the trigger
dead center with both feet,
for a moment lifting
the fatal weight
before the blind torque
of the trap had sprung.
After that its wings had clawed
at the sand for hours,
its cries had gradually sunk back
into its throat, although
its beak, thrust defiantly
at the stream, held on
to its animal yellow.
Then it had pulled everything in,
for a moment the hawk
and only the hawk's turn.
In that blind and beautiful light,
trying to hold on,
to what it was.

I told Don it reminded me of what my father was going through, the journey he was taking. A week later, I read that poem at my father's funeral.

100

The Feather of a Hawk

Shortly before Dad died, we had headed west for a drive in his Grand Prix, past the ranches and farms where he had tended to animals in need. We had talked about some of the interesting times he had experienced in his life. After I read the poem at the funeral, I shared some of those stories with the crowd.

One story I told pertained to a trip I took with my father to Colombia, South America, where Danny Liska, an old friend, lived. Danny had been a rancher from Niobrara who had written a book on his motorcycle travels from Alaska to the southern tip of South America. The book was called *Two Wheels to Adventure.* On his South American travels, he had encountered native tribes, some of whom were cannibals.

For a long time, my father had wanted to visit Danny in his new home, and he and I finally decided to make the trip in February 1993. It was a turbulent time in Colombian politics, with a presidential election coming up soon. The day the airplane landed in Bogota, the Rolls Royce collection of Pablo Escobar, a noted drug lord, was bombed by rival cartels. Several other buildings were also bombed.

Near the end of our visit, Danny wished to give my father a special spiritual blessing that he had learned from an Amazon chief he had visited with in the jungle. Danny placed my father in a circle of sulfur powder on the ground, said a prayer of guidance, and then lit the sulfur on fire. Smoke enveloped my father for two or three minutes, and then cleared. My dad suddenly began jumping around and slapping his hands on his pants. His suit was smoking and embers were burning black holes through his pants to his skin. He showed his pants to friends back home, telling them he'd just gotten too close to a bomb intended for Pablo Escobar. Since those pants were blessed, we buried him in them.

Another story I told at his funeral was about his interest in politics. He had been a delegate to several National Democratic Conventions. Every election year, he was always trying to figure out a way to get elected as a local delegate, and he usually succeeded. In 1972, however, he was not elected as a delegate. The party platform had changed, and many of those politicians who had served in the past did not get reelected. The platform called for a representative number of women to be elected, and likewise for people from minority populations. This process eliminated many of the main-line party supporters, but opened up the process for new blood. Since some of Doc's practice was on the Santee Reservation, Gordon Kitto, who was chairman of the Santee Reservation, knew Doc had been to several conventions serving as an alternate delegate, and asked if Doc would represent the Santee Sioux people because Gordon, himself, could not go. Evidently other Santee people were not interested, and so my father accepted. Dad invited me to go to Miami with him.

About the second day we were there, we were walking back from the convention center when we noticed that television cameras were filming the inside of the famous Fontainebleau Hotel. We stopped to get on TV so the folks back home would know we were in town for the convention. We were in the middle of some sort of demonstration. My dad and I were standing close together with our arms over each other's shoulders, each waving our free hand to the folks back home. I turned to someone to ask, "What sort of demonstration is this?" They replied, "Gay Rights." And this was the Santee representative.

101

Gordon Kitto would call my father to treat his sick animals on his ranch that was near the Brazile Creek in central Knox County. He jumped at the chance to tease my father about this "gay" Santee representative in Miami Beach. Sometimes when he called my father, I was not sure that Gordon's animals were really sick, and I do not think my dad charged him much to treat them.

The members of the Kitto family were good friends of my father's, and I had asked them to speak at my father's funeral. They preferred to speak at the graveside in spite of the fact that I'd warned them snowstorms were in the forecast for that day, and perhaps it would be better to speak in the church. Gordon Kitto Jr. said, "The graveside will be fine; we will work with the weather."

The day of the funeral, it snowed twenty miles to the west and several miles to the east of us. At the cemetery, however, the skies were overcast but there was no snow.

Gordon's daughter gave a tribute and a prayer to the Great Spirit, and Gordon Kitto Jr. passed the sacred pipe to our family to smoke. As the casket was being lowered, Gordon's granddaughter, Julie Sage, sang in Lakota to each of the four directions. As she sang, I looked down the road for a mile and saw the buildings of my father's farm.

My father's ancestors had moved over from Europe and located in northern Iowa where they were farmers of the land. They were all proud growers of corn. They showed their grain at the Chicago International Livestock and Grain Show, once winning the best judged ear of corn in the world.

When Dad graduated from veterinary school, he located his practice in northern Nebraska, in the beautiful town of Verdigre. This was a small close knit ranching community where he soon became known as Doc, a moniker that would stick with him the rest of his life.

In his early years in Verdigre, Doc found that few of the local people associated with the Native Americans on the nearby Santee Reservation. I think he had a special affection for the native people he lived near. I believe that is one reason he wrote his book, *My Search for the Burial Sites of Sioux Nation Chiefs*. Of course, he wanted to be remembered, and we all may wish that, but I also think he wanted to apologize for his ancestors' treatment of native people, and for the white government that infiltrated the land and took that land through unfair negotiations. Doc made his living here, but he wanted to acknowledge the people who lost their lands to his ancestors, and to assume his share in the accountability of his people.

Doc was upset when the white missionaries came and, with the support of the government, placed the Indian kids into mission schools to keep them for long periods. This was in direct conflict with his own Christian spiritual beliefs. But not all of the Indians found this to be a bad practice. Anna Fire Thunder, a teacher at Manderson, South Dakota, told me this upset a few of the Indians, but "most of us," she said, "liked to go to the missions to be schooled. It was a new life for us, but they treated us very well. We learned to behave and, just like nowadays, the kids who did not conform to the rules were the ones who said they did not like the mission schools and they made the big noise."

In my father's book about the Sioux chiefs, I could see the two societies coming together, and I think my father would be proud to know he may have played a small part in bringing some of the Native Americans and whites together to pay tribute to lives that had been lived. The pictures he revealed in his book of memorial stone markers that white missionaries had erected over the graves of old Sioux Battle Chiefs told that story.

Cemeteries and burial grounds always fascinated my father, and he would have liked to have known more about the mystery of Crazy Horse and his burial grounds. He found a certain peace in hanging around cemeteries on the reservations. Years after I had become a mortician, he told me that he had wanted to become one himself, but that his father preferred that he work with grains and animals.

A year after my father died, I tried to persuade my mother to come live with me 270 miles away in Marysville, Kansas, near the Big Blue River. But she preferred to be close to Verdigre, Nebraska, where she would be able to put sunflowers on her husband's grave. She did not want him there alone.

Cemeteries tell us much of history by the way we treat and bury our dead. Crazy Horse's parents were unsure of what to do with their son's body. The reward for his head, dead or alive, probably forced his friends and parents to tell many stories about what happened to his body, and to give many directions to his burial site. If that is so, we may have denied the great warrior the honor of people paying tribute to him at his final resting place. Perhaps, only a few of his nearest relatives may have known of and passed down to a select few those secrets.

I suspect, and hope, Crazy Horse is not alone either. May his company, on sacred ground, be more than the Golden Eagle I have seen circling Lakota country then flying into that blind, beautiful light.

22

Bradley's Opinion—Wounded Knee is the Crazy Horse Burial Site

While helping my father research the burial sites of Sioux chiefs, I found an interesting article in the archives at the Nebraska State History Museum. I knew there were several differing opinions as to where the site of Crazy Horse's burial might be, but now it was apparent that there were many more trails to follow than I'd realized.

The first opinion that I encountered about the exact location was that of General Luther P. Bradley, who commanded the District of the Black Hills. Bradley was under higher orders from General George Crook to bring Crazy Horse into Camp Robinson. Bradley was every inch a soldier. An order to him was gospel and law, and was met with prompt, undeviating obedience. Upon returning to General Crook's office, Bradley said, "As I retraced my steps to the office, I had a glimmering hope that on the morrow, Crazy Horse might be heard." He hoped those present would listen to what Crazy Horse told them about his own agency, and he hoped that Crazy Horse would not be harmed.

Following the death of Crazy Horse, Bradley reflected, "With respect to Crazy Horse, I neither eulogize nor condemn. It may be said that he was an intractable Indian chieftain—a bitter hater of pale-faces, insensible to fear in battle, and intensely fanatical in his religious devotions from the Indian's standpoint. I have merely stated the facts as they occurred mainly under my own observations, or as told to me by reliable eye witnesses."

The *Nebraska History* magazine quotes Bradley as saying, "Crazy Horse is forever at peace! He sleeps in an obscure and lonely grave on the cliffs of Wounded Knee Creek where it may be that his hovering spirit, in the closing days of 1890 [referring to the extermination of Chief Big Foot and his people at Wounded Knee], caught once more the sound of the white man's guns that sent to bloody graves in indiscriminate slaughter, men, women and children of a kindred band, imbued with the same fanaticism and contempt of death which had characterized his stormy life and marked his untimely end" (Brininstool, 31-32).

The following chapters describe the other stories I learned over a period of several years regarding what happened to Crazy Horse after he died.

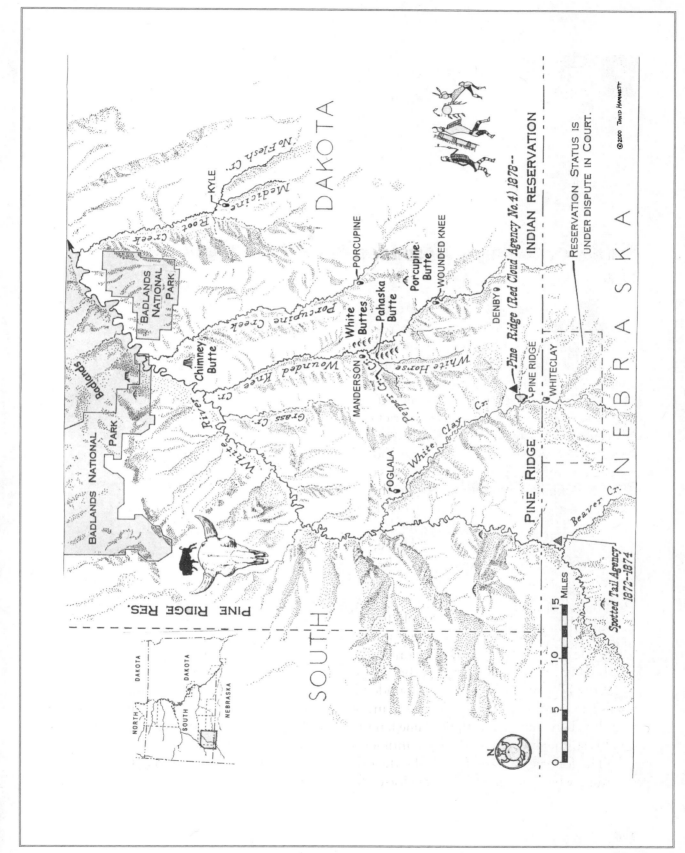

SOUTH DAKOTA

PINE RIDGE RES.

Badlands

BADLANDS NATIONAL PARK

BADLANDS NATIONAL PARK

White River

Chimney Butte

Grass Cr.

OGLALA

White Clay Cr.

MANDERSON

Wounded Knee Cr.

Pepper Cr.

White Horse Cr.

Porcupine Creek

White Buttes

Pahaska Butte

Porcupine Butte

PORCUPINE

WOUNDED KNEE

Medicine Root Creek

No Flesh Cr.

KYLE

DAKOTA

Pine Ridge (Red Cloud Agency No.4) 1878--
INDIAN RESERVATION

PINE RIDGE

DENBY

WHITECLAY

Beaver Cr.

PINE RIDGE

Spotted Tail Agency
1872-1874

NEBRASKA

RESERVATION STATUS IS
UNDER DISPUTE IN COURT.

© 2000 DAVID HAMMETT

NORTH DAKOTA

SOUTH DAKOTA

NEBRASKA

N

0   5   10   15
MILES

23

The Green Highway Sign: Four Possible Burial Sites

A green historical marker erected by the State Highway Department (pictured in Chapter 1) seven miles south of Wounded Knee, South Dakota, declares that there are four possible burial sites for Crazy Horse. My father and I read the sign while driving on the Pine Ridge Reservation in search of burial sites of Sioux chiefs for his book. Cruising along in his Grand Prix, which usually had plastic roses or sunflowers stuck in its grill, I steered the car with my left hand while I used my right hand to tape my father with a video camera. Dad was telling stories about Sioux chiefs and the Wounded Knee Massacre. Viewing the results later, the effect was like quaking earth but, somehow, I managed to keep us from going into the ditch.

One Possibility: The Butte between White Horse Creek and Wounded Knee Creek

The green sign said, "Crazy Horse is buried 14 miles northwest of the sign point." At that location, there is a butte located between the forks of the White Horse Creek and Wounded Knee Creek. According to Batiste Pourier and Jake Russel, Crazy Horse is buried somewhere on that butte.

Pourier was born in St. Charles, Missouri, in 1842. He found employment as a teamster at age fourteen and moved with the Indian traders into the country west of the Mississippi. In this capacity, he gained a thorough knowledge of the country and of the Sioux Indians. He married an Oglala mixed-blood French woman, Josephine Richard. Military authorities employed him as a scout, guide, and interpreter for many years. He was among the party that brought Crazy Horse's body back to Beaver Valley for a wake following his death at Camp Robinson.

Today, Batiste Pourier's great-grandson, Loren "Bat" Pourier, runs a convenience store in the town of Pine Ridge, South Dakota which is not far from Wounded Knee. His place is a hub of activity in Pine Ridge. Bat is a new breed of warrior among the Oglala Sioux—an economic warrior. He employs many Native Americans at his store. He believes that welfare programs have reduced the importance of the male in Indian culture. Once hunters and warriors, these men have become less important economically than women who can bring in more welfare money by having children. Pine Ridge is one of the most impoverished areas in the United States. This reservation has a seventy-three percent unemployment rate, and there are serious alcohol problems here. Most social welfare programs have failed in the past, and there are few new ideas. Many efforts have been made by the government to work with both tribal leaders and the private sector.

Broken treaties and the decimation of the buffalo hunting grounds in the last century have demoralized the spirit and culture of the Lakota people. Poor attempts by the federal government to assimilate the Lakota have made things worse. In recent years, demonstrations by Indians against a beer distribution center in White Clay, Nebraska, just a few miles south of Pine Ridge, South Dakota, exposed a tragic paradox. There is no beer allowed on the reservation, but just south of the border in Nebraska, White Clay bars sell ten million cans of beer every year. As some Lakota protest this reality, others stand in the beer line.

Crazy Horse disapproved of alcohol. Today, descendants of the Crazy Horse family have filed a lawsuit against one brewery that labeled its product Crazy Horse Beer.

According to Bat, the relations between Indian tribes and the federal government may be improving. At one time, the Great White Father would summon the tribal chiefs to Washington, D.C. to receive directives. In July 1999, President Clinton visited the Pine Ridge Reservation on a tour of economically devastated areas. This was a notably more respectful overture to Lakota people than was often the case in earlier government dealings with the tribe. That visit resulted in proposed new programs and allocations for improvements, along with hope that the president's efforts would create positive effects.

Possibility 1: On green sign: Butte between White Horse Creek and Wounded Knee Creek. Looking southeast of Manderson, SD. In the foreground is Whitehorse Creek and in the background is Wounded Knee Creek.

While President Clinton promised to help, what the Lakota people need now is inspiration. There are many problem drinkers on the reservations. The spirit to turn lives around must come from within.

Bat has been one such example of the spirit of transformation. He sees business as a way for men to reclaim the role of providers. The propane company that Bat owns with two brothers and a nephew is called Pourier Tiyospe, a word which means "family" in the Lakota Sioux language. "In the tiyospe concept, both the man and woman are very important," Bat explains. "Before, the warrior was the provider. We're trying to create a modern-day warrior who can create income."

One hot summer day in 1998, I stopped at Bat's store to pick up a couple bottles of Sunny Delight fruit juice. Then I headed down the road at a fast pace and was about thirty miles east of Valentine, Nebraska, when I drove past a golf course and recognized a guy putting on a green close to the road. I slammed on my brakes, parked, and went over to say hello to him. He was the funeral director from Ainsworth, and I would often hang out with him at state conventions. We chatted for a few minutes, and I was on my way. As I was departing, he alerted me that the highway was carefully patrolled by police troopers, and that I should watch my speed.

I was back on the road for about five minutes when the two bottles of Sunny Delight suddenly caught up with me. There were cars on the road coming toward me and cars behind me. There was too much traffic to just stop along this road. I couldn't see any side roads coming up either. I knew that I was just a few miles from the next town, so I chose the option to step on the gas and find a convenience store. At eighty-five miles per hour, I spotted a patrol car, and when I glanced in my rear view mirror, there were red lights flashing. I pulled over and the patrolman asked for my driver's license.

At that time, I was driving my mother's car. She was with my wife in our car about thirty miles ahead of me. Mom had accompanied us from Valentine west to the Pine Ridge. On our return, we'd decided to drive Mom and her car back east the 150 miles to Verdigre and stay a day or two with her.

When the patrolman asked for my license, I realized that I was driving a Nebraska licensed car while carrying a Kansas license. My knees were squeezed together tightly. The officer asked for the vehicle registration, which I could not find. Now the patrolman would think the car was stolen! I explained to him that it was my mother's car, and about our travel arrangements.

The officer went back to his car to radio in for information on the vehicle I was driving. While he did that, I desperately tried to find the registration card in the glove compartment. I finally found it and I walked, knees together, back to his car to show him. He nodded to me. I could not stand it any longer. Since I saw no cars coming at that moment, I explained to him about the effects of the Sunny Delight and asked if I could visit the ditch in back of his car. Again, he nodded at me.

When I returned from the ditch, the officer handed me a paper ticket and said, "I gave you a warning and I really don't know why." I replied, "I think I know why," and I extended my hand to thank him.

Back in my mom's car, I grinned in relief and thought about how I could have been the first guy ever ticketed because he drank too much Sunny Delight fruit juice. At the same time, I wondered about those out west in White Clay—the demonstrators and the slumped over Lakota standing in line for beer. If they only knew how good Sunny D was for them.

A Second Possibility: The Bluffs East of Wounded Knee

Ben Black Elk claims that Crazy Horse is buried on the bluffs east of Wounded Knee Creek. Driving between Wounded Knee and Manderson, South Dakota, and looking east across Wounded Knee Creek, there are bluffs all along the way.

At Manderson, I met Mitchell and Aaron Desersa Jr. Their mother, Esther, is Ben Black Elk's daughter. Ben's cabin, built by the Black Elk family, still stands. Ben's father was the Oglala Holy Man, Black Elk, whom John Neihardt wrote about in *Black Elk Speaks*. Mitchell told me that Black Elk was a cousin of Crazy Horse. He said that Black Elk had seven wives, and the government had made him choose one. He picked the youngest.

I was told by a Desersa family member that the location of the actual burial site of Crazy Horse has been passed on to family members from one generation to the next. This is sacred family oral history that is to be respected and held with tight lips. Each generation, two family members, or possibly just one, will receive this information to carry on. It is passed down to those who are best able to keep the knowledge within their speaking breath. The Desersa's grandmother saw where Crazy Horse was buried.

Mitchell showed us a painting that has been handed down in his family for some generations. My mother, Jean Walstrom, was traveling with me that summer to visit the Lakota lands. She had taught art for many years in Verdigre, Nebraska. Her art classes were top of the line

Possibility 2: On green sign: Bluffs east of Wounded Knee Creek. Looking east of Manderson, SD. Wounded Knee Creek is in the valley. This is the area where Ben Black Elk says his mother fed the grave of Crazy Horse. (S5 T37 R43w).

Wounded Knee Valley and White Buttes looking east.

and her students won many awards. I introduced her to Mitchell Desersa, telling him she was an art teacher. He brought the painting outside to show to my mother.

The painting showed a man up on a butte in a landscape similar to the one where we stood. Mitchell explained that the man was having a vision of the unity of the races: black and white, red and yellow. The man was seeing a flaming rainbow and the six grandfathers, and each one gave him a gift. They gave him the golden arrow, the tree of life and the four directions, and they gave him a bowl of water. He was supposed to plant this tree and, from the tree, the four races of flowers would grow, and they would save all the people in the world. They would never have to work for the devil. When bad spirits were present, a warrior would bring forth a turtle to protect the people. When lightning struck the turtle's shell, the shell protected the turtle and the meat inside. The shell would absorb the lightning, and the meat would disperse the bad energy force into seven areas; this is why there are seven types of turtle meat.

I told Mitchell that I used to race turtles for fun and money with my father. We had raced all over the Midwest—sometimes for purses that were way up into two figures! We'd done silly things to make our turtles faster, such as train them by putting light bulbs in front of them to attract bugs so the turtles would leap at the bugs. That way, the turtle would get faster starts when the box was raised in the center of the racing circle. My dad's favorite racing method was to take the water the turtle had been living in and put it outside the circle edge that the turtle raced toward. He believed it sensed the water it had inhabited and would run for it, fast. Homing water, I guess.

Mitchell explained that the eagle in the painting symbolized the carrying of prayers up to the Great Spirit. The eagle is not the Great Spirit, but symbolizes access to it. Mitchell said that this painting showed the vision of Black Elk, his great-grandfather. Neihardt wrote about that vision as Black Elk described it:

I know that it is a good thing I'm going to do. And because no good things can be done by man alone, I will first make an offering and send a voice to the Spirit of the World that it may help me to be true. See, I fill this sacred pipe with the bark of Red Willow. There are four ribbons hanging here on the stem. They are the four corners of the universe. The black one is for the West, where the thunder begins to live and send us rain. The white one for the North from which comes the great white cleansing wind. The red one is for the East whence springs light and where the morning star lives to give men wisdom. The yellow for the South whence comes the summer and the power to grow. But these four Spirits are only one spirit after all, and this eagle feather here is for that one which is like a feather and also it is for the thoughts of men that should rise high as eagles do. Are not the sky a father and the earth a mother, and are not all living things with feet, wings, or roots, their children? Here, at the four corners of the world a relative I am, give me the strength to walk this soft earth. A relative to all that is. Give me the eyes to see and the strength to understand that I may be like you with your power. Only can I face the winds.

My mom thanked Mitchell for sharing the painting and its meaning with us. She told him that she recalled it from the information in Neihardt's book which I had given to her. She said, "I have used passages from that book as a benediction at funerals when I have been asked to speak. You ought to give that painting to a museum for others to see." Mitchell told her, "No, this is for family. But we are trying to get interest going for a museum around Manderson. We're working on that now." He then showed us around Manderson. Somewhere, in the White Buttes that surround the valley, may be Crazy Horse's grave.

A year later, I visited with Mitchell's mother, Esther, who told me that Crazy Horse was buried somewhere up in the White Buttes just east of her house in Manderson. When the evening sun sets, the White Buttes catch a beautiful reflection that reminds one that the walls of the valley provide a fortress that is comforting to those it shelters.

A Third Possibility: The Bluff on White Horse Creek

On the green highway sign, it says that in 1905, eighty-year-old Sleeping Bear guided Ben Irving to Crazy Horse's burial spot in a bluff on White Horse Creek, four miles south of Manderson.

Mitchell Desersa took me to White Horse Creek, a dry creek that runs only when the snow melts or when long periods of rain soak the valley. The creek lies south and west of Manderson. Large white limestone bluffs loom in the background.

Driving towards White Horse Creek, Mitchell told me that he'd studied archeology in Rapid City and he'd passed the course with ease. He's a man who loves to tell stories, and it's easy to imagine that he inherited the Black Elk storytelling trait. Mitchell told us that when he was working as an archeologist, he went up to the Home Stake Gold Mines near Lead, South Dakota, where the front of one of the shafts had caved in and was covered with rocks. It was

Possibility 3: On green sign: Bluffs on White Horse Creek. Looking south of Manderson, SD with White Horse Creek in the valley.

believed that an old Indian chief had been buried under those rocks and the archeological team that Mitchell was with went there to uncover him. The chief was found, still with his war bonnet on, the feathers of the bonnet still standing upright, perfectly preserved. There was a spear lying next to the bones of the chief. Mitchell liked to tell stories like this while riding around thinking about the possible burial sites of Crazy Horse.

A Fourth Possibility: The Badlands

The last suggested burial site included on the green historical marker south of Wounded Knee is based on an army report dated 1877, which indicates that the body of Chief Crazy Horse was taken from hostiles at Red Cloud Camp near the mouth of Wounded Knee Creek and given to his parents who disappeared with the body on a travois into the Badlands. [*Hostiles were Native Americans who revolted against what they called the white infiltration.*]

Those who saw the parents return to camp the following afternoon believed that the length of time they had been gone established the burial site as somewhere in the Badlands. The mouth of Wounded Knee Creek is approximately twenty miles north of Manderson, South Dakota and the Badlands lie to the north of the green highway sign.

One bright, sunny afternoon in September 1998, I went into the archives room of the library on the campus of Lakota College, west of Kyle, South Dakota. I had many things on my mind at the time. I was thinking about what I might be looking for, such as old maps and information about Crazy Horse. There were many old photographs of Sioux culture on the walls that caught my interest. I glanced from wall to wall, taking mental notes of photos of Indian characters and scenes from long ago, when an archivist walked up to me with a sheet of paper in her hand. She asked me what I was looking for. Her voice was rigid and strong; her eyes pen-

Possibility 4: On green sign: Badlands. Badlands north of Manderson.

Possibility 4: On green sign: Badlands. Chimney Butte in the Badlands.

etrated into me. I told her I was looking for maps of the Pine Ridge area from long ago. She told me to write down my request on a form, which she forcefully handed to me. She was on her way to lunch and would return to help me in thirty minutes. I told her I would stay and browse around the library until she returned.

In the archive room, there was a silver-haired fellow with whom I struck up a conversation regarding writing and publishing books. The man's name was Rollin Curd, a retired surveyor working on a book about old land surveys in western Nebraska and South Dakota.

Possibility 4: On green sign: Badlands. Looking north to Badlands from Chimney Butte.

The two of us visited for about forty-five minutes, sharing stories about producing books, each in our areas of interest. We talked about maps and places to find such materials. During our conversation, I had been leaning on an oak glass case that looked as if it contained special documents regarding Sioux culture. I was listening to Rollin when I glanced down into the case and noticed a map. It was a map of the Pine Ridge and the Sioux camps on the reservation in 1890. "This is just what I was looking for!" I exclaimed loudly. I had been leaning on it all the time.

The archivist, who had really looked me over when I first walked in, had just returned from lunch. She overheard my exclamation and came up to me, saying, "You know, I thought by the way you first walked in here and slowly looked around, and by the way you dressed and took notice of things, that you were an FBI agent." She smiled, and I smiled back, saying, "You must have gotten to know the Feds down at the Wounded Knee shootout in 1975 pretty well if you think I fit that description." She explained that FBI agents had stayed at her house for about two weeks before the shoot out. She'd fed and housed them while they were trying to settle things down with the American Indian Movement (AIM) and the Guardians of the Oglala Nation (GOONS).

During the 1970s, racial strife was at a high point on the Pine Ridge Reservation. The FBI and Bureau of Indian Affairs were in force on the reservation. Under the Nixon administration, FBI agents covertly infiltrated AIM and started harassing its leaders. The traditional tribal members believed that the land must be protected and preserved for future generations. This contradicted tribal chairman Dick Wilson's self-serving interests that promoted the multi-national corporations who wanted to exploit the land. He started the organization known as the GOONS to enforce his policies. Many who disagreed with him were beaten, harassed, and even assassinated. An ad paid for by the Free Leonard Peltier group in *Indian Coun-*

Map courtesy Oglala Lakota College, Kyle, SD. Donated by Elder Johnson Holy Rock.

try Today on June 22, 1999, stated that the "GOONS were trained and armed by the FBI who was mainly responsible for the reign of terror."

The American Indian Movement was started by tribal elders to help with security on the Pine Ridge Reservation. A spiritual camp was set up on the Jumping Bull ranch. The camp promoted self-sufficiency. For example, they would appoint somebody to their patrol who had a bad drinking problem; of course the twist was that to be on the patrol one must be sober. The camp also offered encouragement and support to the local people who were living in poverty and fear.

On one tragic day, three lives, a Native American and two FBI agents, were lost at the spiritual camp. A Bureau of Indian Affairs policeman killed a young Indian named Joe Stunz who had been staying at the AIM camp on the Jumping Bull land. The following morning there was a shoot-out at the Jumping Bull camp, and two FBI agents went down. What took place following the shoot-out was the largest FBI manhunt known in American history.

I told the archivist that I was from Kansas and that I had helped my father with a book on Sioux Nation Chiefs. When the two of us had been researching around the Wounded Knee area of Pine Ridge, people told us that Leonard Peltier was not the one who had killed the agents. They said that Peltier was wrongly put in prison for the shooting murders of the two FBI agents. I asked her what she believed about Peltier.

She then introduced herself as Barbara Adams, and said, "Peltier did not kill the FBI agents. It was Jimmy Eagle. Jimmy was sixteen at the time of the shooting and he lived just down the way from me. After the shootings, he was scared and came to my house and stayed for a week. It was not until he left at the end of the week that I learned he had shot the government agents." She told me that she'd written a story about Jimmy Eagle, and that it is in the archives at Washington State University where it can be read, but not copied.

I told Barbara that I had driven by where Peltier was incarcerated at the federal penitentiary in Leavenworth, Kansas. I'd transported the deceased wife of an old army veteran to the National Cemetery at Fort Leavenworth to be buried. After the graveside service, I'd driven past a building to the west of the cemetery and honked the horn of the hearse, waving to Leonard as I drove by. Barbara chuckled at my imagination.

In April 1999, I was sitting in the Rosebud Casino eating dinner when a tall man with an official casino badge approached me. He was the casino gaming official who had overheard me speaking earlier to a blackjack dealer about my research on stories of Sioux chiefs. The man, Ben Jensen, told me he had many stories to tell as he had worked on several reservations as a policeman. He had worked on a New Mexico reservation, he'd worked on Pine Ridge, and now he was on Rosebud. He had seen the siege at Wounded Knee in the 1970s. I asked him if it was true that Leonard Peltier had not killed the FBI agents. He said, "Leonard did not do it, but he was the ringleader. Jimmy Eagle may have done the actual shooting. He [Jimmy] and a couple of others were charged with the death of the agents, but a month or so later, the charges were dropped against them for lack of evidence."

Ben had been present when the bodies of the two agents were discovered on the Jumping Bull ranch. Ben told me that the FBI agents had been held at gunpoint and shot with hollow point bullets through the palms of their hands as they tried to protect their own heads by covering their faces. The bullets penetrated their skulls.

Back in Marysville, Kansas, I related this story to Father George Bertels. Before he came to Marysville to serve St. Gregory's Catholic parish, he was a chaplain at Leavenworth Federal Penitentiary. There he had met with Leonard Peltier to offer guidance. Father Bertels told me that Leonard had always maintained he was innocent of killing the FBI agents.

A few months later, Barbara Adams, the librarian at the Lakota Indian College, told me that Woodrow Respects Nothing had a story that had been handed down in his family about where Crazy Horse's parents had taken his body. Barbara is related to the Fast Thunder family and the Black Elk family, which makes her distantly related to Crazy Horse's father. Barbara's grandmother, Jenny Wounded Horse, was married to Fast Thunder. Crazy Horse gave his medicine bundle to Fast Thunder when he went in to Camp Robinson to meet with the United States government. Crazy Horse had put the bundle under the seat of a buggy wagon and asked the members of Barbara's family who were driving it to be the keepers of his medicine.

Lakota people make medicine bundles after a vision. The fur or feathers of an animal that appears in the vision are used in the bundle, thus, the spirit of the animal is captured and carried with them. The vision-seeker regards the animal or bird as an advisor.

For example, recently the seniors on the Marysville football team asked me to guide them on a kayak adventure to the Dismal River. It was a trip designed to bring the guys together and to help them to be leaders for the underclassmen for the coming season. Sitting around the campfire, I asked the spirits for help in bringing a meaningful experience to the team. I was moved to play a simple game by walking off with my camp stool in one direction for twelve minutes. Then the participants could try to find the stool. The team was divided up into pairs and the object of the game was to see who could find the stool the fastest. As the sun was setting on a cool July evening I walked up the canyon hills to a grassy spot overlooking the valley. Instead of hiding the chair in a cedar tree, I just sat on the stool. I reflected on the kayak trip we had taken on the river that day. I had promised the guys they would see a porcupine sometime on the trip. The animal is not seen in our part of Kansas and they were eager to see one. Sitting on the stool, I noticed something like a tumble weed that was moving. I stared at it for several seconds. It was a porcupine, not a round bristly old tumble weed. I just sat on the stool hoping for two guys to find me. It was not long. They were amazed to see the porcupine munching away on blue stem grass. They were excited and went to fetch the rest of the senior team and coaches. The porcupine was startled and started to roam off (at porcupine's slow pace). We all stood still and I talked soothingly to the porcupine and he responded by coming back to my pant leg without ejecting his quills.

To the Native American this might be a symbolic vision. The presence of a porcupine is symbolic of how to resist the barbs of others. Porcupines can teach you how to enjoy life and how to maintain a sense of wonder about it. When negative conditions exist, they can teach you how to achieve and be protected from the barbs that life brings. A porcupine can show you strength when you might be vulnerable. Thus the encounter with the porcupine (the animal advisor) was like a spiritual vision that had meaning and purpose for the team, and it came to be a real life experience in the land where Crazy Horse went for protective cover when the United States Army was searching for him.

To the Lakota, the animal that appears in the vision is like a person's twin, and it may come to them when they are sick or dying. This twin spirit is known as Chekpa. If one were to kill the bird or animal whose Chekpa is carried by a person, illness may come to that person because of the death of their Chekpa. Crazy Horse's medicine power was that of an owl. Barbara thought that owl feathers must have been part of his medicine bundle. She also told me that the owl is a symbol of death. The wandering and vigilant part of the soul can take the form of the owl to warn of injury or death. The owl gave Crazy Horse his power to kill.

Barbara recalled that the medicine bundle had been kept in the Fast Thunder family until the 1940s. Family members guarded the bundle at all times. After Jenny Wounded Horse died, another relative, Nellie Ghost Dog, became keeper of the medicine bundle. It eventually passed to Barbara's father, Theodore Means, who was called to the armed services during World War II. He did not know if he would come back from fighting, and he wanted to prevent the medicine bundle from falling into the wrong hands. That fall, the family had been picking corn and potatoes along the North Platte River, near Minatare, Nebraska, not far from Chimney Rock. For safe keeping, the family decided to bury the Crazy Horse medicine bundle. A six foot deep hole was dug to place it in. Just before putting the medicine bundle in the hole, they decided to unwrap the bundle to see what Crazy Horse had put in it. They unwrapped several pieces of cloth until they got as far as a buckskin pouch. Many flying owls suddenly surrounded their tent, their wings making a loud clapping sound like thunder. Barbara said her family wrapped up the medicine bundle and buried it quickly.

The area of Chimney Rock was one I knew well. I stayed there one summer before my senior year in high school. I was living on an island in the North Platte River with the Roland Warner ranch family. They became my friends for life, and I frequently go on white water adventures with their sons Steve and Jack.

While I was visiting with Barbara at the library, she suggested that I check in on Woodrow Respects Nothing who had stories about Crazy Horse. She assured me that he could usually be found at his home in Manderson.

On a steep hillside in Manderson, I found Woodrow Respects Nothing living with his family. Woodrow was in his middle seventies. His father, George Respects Nothing, had been born during the massacre at Wounded Knee in 1890. The family was able to escape the battle and flee to safety. George's parents, Sophie White Cow Tribe and Jacob Respects Nothing, had been with Crazy Horse's family when his body was brought to the Manderson area. The family camped near White Horse Creek, south of present day Manderson. The next day, the family packed up their camp and headed north following the Wounded Knee Creek Valley. That night, they camped near a large rock formation called Chimney Butte, named so because it looks like a short, stubby chimney. Camp was set up for the night, and, when the sun set, the parents of Crazy Horse and the wives of the great chief took the body into the nearby Badlands that begin just to the north of Chimney Butte. They returned to camp before the sun came up the next morning. [*This unusual rock formation called Chimney Butte is thicker and wider on top than the Chimney Rock formation on the Platte River east of Scottsbluff, Nebraska.*]

Woodrow Respects Nothing told me, "It was never told where his body was buried."

24

The Beaver Creek Theory

In February 1995, my father and I visited with David Kadlecek at his home in Hay Springs, Nebraska. His parents, Edward and Mabell Kadlecek, wrote *To Kill an Eagle: Indian Views on the Last Days of Crazy Horse*, which provided some of the information for this chapter. They had started writing their book in 1962, and it took them about twenty years to complete it. The Kadleceks gathered quotes from Indians who had lived around Beaver Creek and heard the stories when they were young.

After Crazy Horse's death, American Horse took charge of the body, wrapping it in a blanket. Four soldiers brought a spring wagon hitched to a team of mules. Thunder Hawk, with the help of some others, placed the body on the wagon, but it was impossible to find anyone to drive it until, at last, two Indian scouts volunteered. There was general fear that the anger in the camp would erupt and warriors would kill those who carried the body. The wagon was driven a short distance over the hill east of Camp Robinson, and there they waited for Crazy Horse's father to come for the body.

A reward had been offered for the capture of Crazy Horse. Ironically, Crazy Horse was killed at Camp Robinson and no one was able to claim the reward because he had not actually been captured; he had come in on his own. When Crazy Horse's parents came to Camp Robinson, they were told about the "price on his head." Not understanding the English idiom, they thought that someone wanted their son's head and was willing to pay money for it.

The body was moved from the wagon to the travois, and the group headed for Beaver Valley, over land that today belongs to the Kadlecek family. The area is about forty miles northeast of what is now Fort Robinson. Throughout their journey, Crazy Horse's parents feared that someone might still try to cut off his head for the money. There probably were some white men who thought they could collect the reward money. In the Kadlecek book, *To Kill an Eagle: Indian Views on the Last Days of Crazy Horse*, Julia Hollow Horn Bear of the Rosebud Reservation remembers that her grandfather told her that the old people were followed back to camp at Beaver Creek by men with just that in mind.

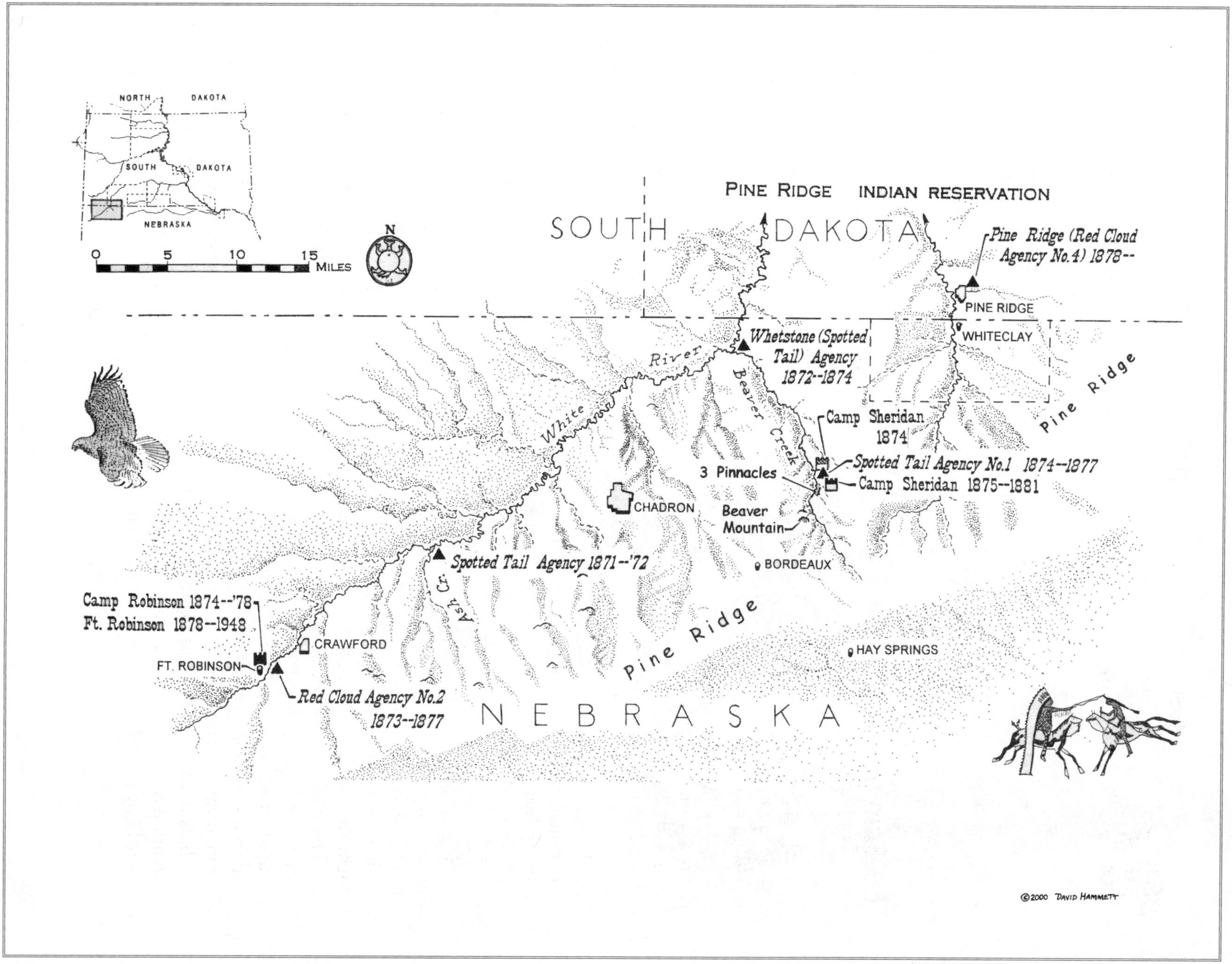

PINE RIDGE INDIAN RESERVATION

SOUTH DAKOTA

NEBRASKA

Pine Ridge

Pine Ridge (Red Cloud Agency No.4) 1878--

PINE RIDGE

WHITECLAY

Whetstone (Spotted Tail) Agency 1872-1874

Camp Sheridan 1874

Spotted Tail Agency No.1 1874--1877

Camp Sheridan 1875--1881

Beaver Creek

3 Pinnacles

Beaver Mountain

BORDEAUX

HAY SPRINGS

White River

CHADRON

Spotted Tail Agency 1871--'72

Ash Cr.

CRAWFORD

Red Cloud Agency No.2 1873--1877

Camp Robinson 1874--'78
Ft. Robinson 1878--1948

FT. ROBINSON

N

0   5   10   15   MILES

NORTH DAKOTA
SOUTH DAKOTA
NEBRASKA

© 2000 DAVID HAMMETT

Old Bear drumming. Drumming ceremonies took place during mourning such as when Crazy Horse was taken to Beaver Creek when he died. To the Lakota, the beat of the heart is the beat of a drum—the beat is the life force. Players of the drum become a channel between earth and heaven. A Lakota drum maker who advised drum making and design said that once you have formed your drum, you then make one intentional mistake in your work. We strive to be perfect but we must be reminded that we are not. Photo courtesy Nebraska State Historical Society.

White Woman One Butte, an aunt of Julia Hollow Horn Bear, washed the dried blood and dust from Crazy Horse's body. He was then wrapped in new deer skins, and a large buffalo robe secured with rawhide strings served as an outside cover.

Louis Bordeaux also told of the death scene at the camp on Beaver Creek. Louis' father was James Bordeaux, and his mother was a Brulé woman. Louis was a government interpreter who accompanied the first Sioux delegation to Washington, D.C. in 1869. He was known among the Lakota as Mato, or Bear, because he was boisterous in his manner. He was with the parents when the body of Crazy Horse was brought to the Sioux camp on Beaver Creek. He remembered that the body was elevated upon the branches of the sepulcher tree on a temporary scaffold for a night and a day.

There have been many ideas over the years about where Crazy Horse's body was buried. A number of people think it was in Beaver Valley; among them, Pete Catches, an interpreter and others such as Ben Black Elk, Thomas White Face, and John Galligo believe it was near Beaver Mountain. Beaver Creek flows through Beaver Valley and the base of Beaver Mountain is within a hundred yards west of Beaver Creek. A man named Austin Good Voice Flute said, "From what I hear, this place is about where Mr. Edward F. Kadlecek lives" (Kadlecek, Edward and Mabel, 6). The Kadlecek ranch house is on a plateau that overlooks Beaver Valley to the west.

According to Ben Black Elk, who tells more than one story about Crazy Horse's burial site, things are more complicated. Ben is quoted on the green highway sign saying that Crazy Horse is buried in the buttes east of Rosebud Creek near Manderson. Perhaps he is suggesting that Crazy Horse was first buried on Beaver Creek and then moved to the Rosebud Creek area but his exact meaning is unknown to the author.

Crazy Horse's father hated the jealous chiefs and scouts who he believed had betrayed his son, and he didn't want any of them to touch the body and offer a blessing because he knew the act would not be from the heart.

The Beaver Creek Theory

Sioux death scaffold at Standing Rock. This is like the scaffold tree that Crazy Horse's body would have been put in at Beaver Valley. Photo courtesy Nebraska State Historical Society.

Crazy Horse's father was a medicine man and he knew how to care for the dead man's spirit. He began making preparations for a spirit bundle. Before the body was wrapped in new skins he braided a lock of hair at the back of his son's head and tied it at both ends, and then he carefully severed it close to the scalp; this braid now contained Crazy Horse's spirit. The lock was purified in the smoke of burning sweet grass, and was then wrapped in a buckskin bundle.

According to Lakota belief, making a spirit bundle, or "spirit keeping," requires great personal effort. It is regarded as a sacred ceremony. The spirit keeper must live in a sacred manner, for the spirit of the departed will inhabit the tepee that houses his body until the Great Spirit releases his soul. The spirit keeper must remember that the habits he establishes will stay with the soul for its eternal life. Harmony must always be within the tepee, because whatever happens will affect the soul of the departed.

Some of the men in the party of Crazy Horse's family selected a burial tree. The body would be placed in the branches of the tree overnight and through the next day. During this time, warriors would sit around the sepulcher tree and hold a wake.

Slightly up the creek from the lodge of the parents of Crazy Horse was a tree that was often used for this purpose. Thomas American Horse remembered that, as a boy, he had seen as many as a dozen bodies lying in the branches. David Kadlecek showed my father and me a large burial tree, and there was evidence of about five substantial limbs branching out perpendicular

David Kadlecek looking over Beaver Valley. He is near the area where Stinking Bear said Crazy Horse was buried.

On the Kadlecek ranch overlooking Beaver Valley Sundance area.

from the trunk; some had broken off. The tree he showed us was not Crazy Horse's burial tree. The tree that was chosen by the friends and relatives of Crazy Horse stands on the west bank of Beaver Creek. The branches in that tree were spread apart like fingers holding a ball of clay. A platform was constructed from poles and crosspieces tied with rawhide strings, and placed between the branches. Wrapped in the buffalo robe, Crazy Horse's body was lifted up to its temporary resting place. Thomas White

Face was told by his parents, who had been with the Crazy Horse family at that time, that the body rested there for a day. From around the area, Indians came to join in the ceremony. Stories were told around the tree about Crazy Horse and his great deeds and songs of mourning were sung.

A feast was held at night and again when the sun was high. When darkness came, the parents and relatives loaded the body onto a travois and the two old people moved off into the night. Their desire to be left alone was honored (except for two little night eyes, that belonged to a young child. In later years a man named Stinking Bear would tell friends what those eyes saw).

At sunrise the next morning, the parents returned with their hair ragged and cut short. Their arm and legs were bleeding where they had cut themselves as a sign of their grief. None of the others asked where Crazy Horse had been buried and the father told them not to look, a request that they respected. Today, many still believe that no one knows where the grave is.

Chief Stinking Bear. Photo courtesy Nebraska State Historical Society.

The Beaver Creek Theory

Stinking Bear said Crazy Horse was buried in the rocks of the three pinnacles that overlooked Beaver Valley.

David Kadlecek told my father and me that, in 1929 or 1930, Chief Stinking Bear told this story to his young Osage friend, Lawson R. Gregg, who related it to the Kadleceks. Gregg said, "Unknown to the father and mother of Crazy Horse, Stinking Bear had followed them out of the camp on Beaver Creek to where they took their son's body off the travois. He watched them when they buried Crazy Horse. The body was wrapped in the buffalo hide and was placed standing up in a crevice in a bluff. The parents pried and dug with sticks and started a big slide of rocks that covered him."

David invited my father and me to hop into his four-wheel drive pick-up truck. He took us over an old travois trail that went up the hill from where the camp of the Crazy Horse family and friends would have been on Beaver Creek. David told us that in 1979, Lawson Gregg spent some time in the area following the trail of Stinking Bear's story. According to Lawson Gregg, three rock pinnacles mark the spot where Crazy Horse is buried. The ridge with three pinnacles lies on the east side of Beaver Creek. Today, pines and cedars cast shadows over the pinnacles on this ridge, and they are not easy to recognize. Just past the third pinnacle headed north is a small cliff. Near the foot of this cliff is a small pocket-like enclosure strewn with boulders that have fallen from the cliff that could be the top part of a filled-in crevice. Mr. Gregg reasoned that it would have been necessary for the parents to carry the body with the help of a travois, following the travois trail from their camp up the hill to the crevice.

Mr. Gregg also told David that the cedars that cover this area near the crevice may be important. When he was a young child, other Indians told him that they always carried seeds from this type of brush-like cedar and planted it around burial grounds.

According to Stinking Bear, when the parents returned to the camp, the father went into his tepee. The mother walked over to a hillside and sat down on a rock. Stinking Bear sat outside of his parents' tepee where he could watch as the old woman sang a death chant. He sat watching her for the rest of the night. She sat where she could see the three pinnacles that appeared black in the moonlight against the sky. Stinking Bear supposed that she was looking out at the place where her son's body lay. She sang the death chant all night, her songs only interrupted when she paused to smoke a pipe. When the morning dawn broke, she laid the pipe on a rock.

Years later, with my wife and my mother, I revisited the three rock pinnacles where Crazy Horse may have been taken to be buried. Someone had left an offering and blessing to commemorate the spot with antelope antlers. As the sun was setting in the west, golden rays of light reflected off the antler.

The Vision on Beaver Mountain

Two miles southwest of the three pinnacles, another memorial to Crazy Horse has been erected. This is in Beaver Valley at the foot of Beaver Mountain. David Kadlecek told us that the flat area at the base of Beaver Mountain is the Sun Dance grounds where Crazy Horse people had their gatherings. They would find a sturdy tree and tie rawhides onto it, then the dancers performing the Sun Dance would pierce the skin on their chests, tie the rawhide strips onto their skin, and dance facing the sun, pulling on the rawhide thongs until they broke the skin. The last Sun Dance was held here in 1877, after the Battle of the Little Bighorn in Montana. David showed us five rocks placed in a "V" with the opening to the east. They were placed there in honor of Crazy Horse—either in reference to the five bands of the Sioux, or the five dancers that danced in his honor. David showed us the fire pit where gophers still dig up pieces of charcoal from fires long past.

It was here where Crazy Horse prepared himself for his own Vision Quest ceremony. Friends built a fire enclosed by the five rocks. The fire heated the living rocks so that Crazy Horse could purify himself in the sweat bath. He would have scented and purified his clothes and his horse with the thick smoke from fragrant sage. He then rode his horse to the top of Beaver Mountain to spend four days and four nights fasting and praying.

At the base of Beaver Mountain, still another monument to honor Crazy Horse was erected by some Indian people

Monument erected by the Lakotas at the Sun Dance area near Beaver Mountain close to Beaver Creek and the three pinnacles.

in 1995. A medicine man was there to offer a blessing. The people brought the monument as far as the gate just off of a gravel road on a pick-up truck and then loaded it onto a travois to be pulled by horse across the stream. The inscription on the monument reads:

> Crazy Horse was key to the Lakota resistance to the white man. He thought first of his people, the Lakota, but never refused assistance to any friendly Indians and always took them into his camp. Crazy Horse was, in his way, a visionary—a thinker and a planner.
> All he wanted was freedom for himself and his people.

The Beaver Creek Theory

Overlooking Beaver Creek Valley where an offering was made. The antelope horns are near the site of where Crazy Horse was buried as told by Stinking Bear.

"We had some Indian high school students from Pine Ridge come to the site of the monument," David said. "They sat up on that little knob drumming and singing, blowing on a whistle made from the wing bone of an eagle. An eagle makes a very shrill, high-pitched whistle." David asked one of the boys what they were singing and he said, "It is the eagle song." David recalled looking up as five bald eagles came over from out of the north, "in formation like the Blue Angels' jets and made a pass over us, going up over to the south along the side of Beaver Mountain. That is the first time I have even seen five. There are sometimes two or three eagles together, but it is very rare to see five all at once." Had they been summoned by the song?

"After my folks wrote *To Kill an Eagle*," David said, "the Indians blessed the manuscript before they had it printed, and they placed these five rocks here to make an altar. The four rocks around the outside represent Mother Earth, and the one on top the Great Spirit." David continued, "Warfield Moose Sr. had been in that place for the ceremony, and he told me that the Lakota people may tell the seventh generation where Crazy Horse is buried. Well, I figured that would make the current generation around twelve years old." David questioned Warfield, asking him if it was wise to entrust that knowledge with someone so young, and Warfield admitted that he was not too sure. "I think it may be best left as a myth where his body may be." David told Warfield, "It's like this: whether he is buried around here or up near Manderson, or up in the Badlands or at Bear Butte, it is probably best left a mystery. I think those Lakota people who know may want the rest of us to wonder."

25

At Camp Sheridan on Beaver Creek

The story of Crazy Horse's burial site gets even more confusing from this point on. For example, in Chapter 24, there is evidence that Crazy Horse's body was first placed in a sepulcher tree and was then taken to the area of the three pinnacles on the east side of Beaver Creek where he may have been buried. Other stories say Crazy Horse's body was taken further downstream and put on a bluff overlooking Camp Sheridan. This chapter examines those stories.

Lieutenant John G. Bourke, who was present at Camp Robinson when Crazy Horse surrendered and was killed, wrote in his diary, "The Indians said that Crazy Horse has always told them a bullet could not kill him and they looked upon the manner of his taking off as supporting in great measure the pretensions he had always made as a prophet and great medicine man. The photograph of the crude grave in which this renowned chieftain now reposes is given."

Bourke provides us with a picture of the crude grave. This picture was taken by the Great Western Photograph Publishing Company, Omaha, Nebraska, and is on file at the West Point Military Academy.

Crazy Horse death scaffold overlooking Camp Sheridan in September of 1877. Photo courtesy of West Point Military Archives.

There is a fence around the scaffold to help protect the scaffold supports from being knocked down by army beef cattle grazing on the grass. This grave is on the bluffs that overlook Camp Sheridan, the Spotted Tail Agency is nearby. According to a news story in the *Sidney Telegraph* on September 15, 1877, there was a large attendance and some excitement that the

Camp Sheridan. Crazy Horse's death scaffold was located high on the bluffs overlooking this camp in 1877.
Photo courtesy of West Point Military Archives.

dead brave was laid in the air on the traditional platform and, stated the newspaper account, "now he is a good Indian."

The Spotted Tail Agency, in 1877, was about two miles north of the three pinnacles of rock on Kadlecek land that Stinking Bear says mark the spot of the Crazy Horse burial. A mile and a half to the north of the agency, downstream on Beaver Creek, is Camp Sheridan. It is situated so that the white soldiers overlooked the Indians at the Spotted Tail Agency. The government helped the Indians with rations and supplies; Chief Spotted Tail was often a guest at the army camp and provided great stories for entertainment at the officers' dinners.

In 1910, a Lakota holy man by the name of Chips said that Crazy Horse was first put on a scaffold in a coffin at the Spotted Tail Agency. A house was then constructed over the scaffold. Susan Bordeaux Bettelyoun, who wrote *With My Own Eyes*, states in her book that the body on the scaffold was given back to the old parents at Camp Robinson where they sat on the hill opposite the garrison at the agency for two or three days.

Even *The New York Times* reported on September 28, 1877, that "Crazy Horse could have been the Chief of all the Indians…he only wanted to roam around the country with this band and fight the Snakes and Crows and steal horses. The day after he died, he was taken to Spotted Tail Agency where he is buried."

The Red Cloud Agency, located along the White River about a mile southwest of the present town of Crawford, Nebraska, was established in August 1873 as a distribution center for annuity goods. In a telegram from the Red Cloud Agency, a *Chicago Times* reporter wrote on September 6, 1877:

> Crazy Horse died last night from the effects of the wound received while attempting to make his escape. The body was taken to his village where the mourning friends paid their humble tribute to his memory, after which the village moved toward Spotted Tail Agency to lay the remains away. They say Red Cloud Agency is not on hallowed ground, so he was taken to the Spotted Tail Agency area.

Minneconjou camp at Spotted Tail agency south of Camp Sheridan. Army Fort would have been just to the left. The small clumps in the foreground are piles of manure from the army horse stables. Photo courtesy Denver Art Museum.

The *Chicago Times* article continued to say that the feeling among the Indians was generally good; they said that Crazy Horse was "the man without ears, who would not listen to counsel." His father remarked that the whites had killed his son, but he had been a fool and would not listen. It was a good thing, the voice of a Brulé cried. "The Indians do not blame the whites for killing Crazy Horse and he brought it all on himself."

A special edition of the *Chicago Tribune* dated September 11, 1877, reported that

> …the father of Crazy Horse said his son did not want to come to the agency, but that he wished to remain north and be let alone; that the troops hunted him down, and he had to come in; that he wished to be put on a scaffold in the customary Indian way, and not be buried in a coffin. The father said his son had been his only protection, and that, as he was now gone, he was poor and friendless; that, while they were north, his son had taken good care of him, and they always had plenty of game to eat.

The *Cheyenne Daily Leader* sent a reporter to the Spotted Tail Camp on September 11, 1877, to describe the scene. The account was published in the *Leader* on September 18. Crazy Horse had been escorted from Camp Sheridan to Camp Robinson where he was killed. His body was later taken back to Camp Sheridan, close to the Spotted Tail Agency. The article read:

> The excitement among the Indians here, which had to a great extent disappeared with his [Crazy Horse's] departure, was revived and augmented by that event. Several attempts upon the lives of white men were made by his friends and

relatives. The brother-in-law of Crazy Horse, fully armed, entered the house of Maj. D.W. Burke and coolly avowed his purpose to take the Major's life. The Major displayed great coolness and fortunately so serious an event was averted.

At his own request, Crazy Horse was buried here, there was no particular excitement attending the ceremony. The body now lies on an elevation in plain view of the Post.

Too much praise cannot be awarded the Agency Indians for their noble conduct during the crisis. The northern chiefs behaved well as soon as they properly comprehended the situation, and realized that no harm would come to them or their people if they conducted themselves properly.

A *Chicago Times* reporter romanticized the traditional Indian burial:

The burial of this big chief will be made the occasion of a ceremonial blow-out. His favorite ponies will be slain and their carcasses piled up around his grave, convenient for mounting when he gets ready to doff the habiliments of his tomb and go galloping over the Plains of paradise. For the next six weeks, his wives and children will howl their anguish at his grave at daylight every morning, and boiled beaver, fried buffalo tongue, and other delicacies known to the Indian cuisine, will be heaped on his tomb in prodigality, that he may not want for grub while on his route to the 'happy hunting grounds.'

To complicate matters even more, a diary entry made by Lieutenant Jesse M. Lee on September 13, 1877, claims that "Crazy Horse's wife died, and her body was placed on the platform beside his body." Lieutenant Lee had escorted Crazy Horse to Camp Robinson.

It is not known to which of Crazy Horse's wives Lieutenant Lee was referring. Crazy Horse had eloped with Black Buffalo Woman in the summer of 1870 and was followed and shot by her husband, No Water. He later married Black Shawl, with whom he lived for at least ten years. Black Shawl died in 1927, at the age of eighty-four. Crazy Horse's last wife, whose last name was Laravie, had a father who was a French trader and a mother who was Southern Cheyenne. Richard Hardoff, who has published much research on Crazy Horse, thinks that the deceased woman could not have been Black Shawl, since she died in 1927, but, he ventures to say, that it was one of the two Brulé women married to Crazy Horse's father. These two women were Spotted Tail's sisters (Brininstool, 38-40).

General Lee wrote in his journal:

Thursday, Sept. 6, 1877: No one can imagine my feelings this morning. I often ask myself, "Was it treachery or not?" To the Indian mind how will it appear? My part in this transaction is to me a source of torture. Started with Touch-the-Clouds and Swift Bear to Spotted Tail Agency in the ambulance, and told them to look out for the driver. Explained matter to Touch-the-Clouds and he seemed fully satisfied that

I was not to blame. He thought his people would censure him for coming down with Crazy Horse.

I had a long talk with General Bradley. He did most of the talking. I felt so miserable that I could scarcely say anything; but told the general how our course was to get Crazy Horse, and that I felt that my power had departed; my influence over the Northern Indians had gone; that I was shorn of my strength; that this whole trouble as was the result of mismanagement on the part of Philo Clark, and mis-interpretation on the part of Grouard.

Saturday, Sept. 8, 1877: Everything is quiet and I think will remain so. Crazy Horse's body was brought to his agency and put on a little platform, Indian fashion, on the hill overlooking the post not half a mile away. Whenever I go out of my quarters, I see the red blanket in which his body is wrapped, and thus is recalled to my mind and heart Crazy Horse's pathetic and tragic end.

Wednesday, Sept. 12, 1877: I think it was yesterday that I received word from Crazy Horse's father and mother, who were mourning in Indian fashion beside the body of their son, from daylight to dark, that the cattle at night would not disturb his body. They asked me to have a skeleton fence put around his body. So Jack Atkinson and I loaded a spring wagon with a few posts and some rough planks and went up there, and in an hour made a fence to protect Crazy Horse's body. The old gray-headed father and mother were bending over their son's body and crying loudly. With tears flowing down their cheeks they grasped the hands of Jack and me, and old Crazy Horse said, in sobbing tones, 'Ottah [Father] you and the other white man are my friends in the great sorrow. Our Indian friends seem to have deserted us, but you are my real friends.' Then old Crazy Horse and his wailing wife gently stroked my face in devoted affection—an Indian way to demonstrate their love to a friend. I gave some good food to the wretched father and mother. I found they were attached to me, and in a few months they went with me to the Missouri River through the winter storms and blizzards, 280 miles east, through all kinds of hardships.

E.A. Brininstool, in his article in the *Nebraska History* magazine, quotes the widow of General Jesse Lee:

When I think, and remember, all the deceit, lies and mistreatment of the Indians at the hands of the whites, it fairly makes my blood boil—as it did the General. The treatment they received makes a black page in the U.S. history.

I was at Fort Robinson at the time of the murder of Chief Crazy Horse, and saw and heard much of the trouble. The father and mother of Crazy Horse took his body to Spotted Tail Agency and buried it on the bank of White River, just opposite our quarters at Fort Sheridan. [*Mrs. Jesse Lee is confused about the river's name. She probably meant Beaver Creek, which flows north and then west into the White River and was about twelve miles farther downstream from Beaver Creek and the Spotted Tail Agency at the time of Crazy Horse's death.*]

On the third day of the burial, my general came home and said, "That old father and mother have been all alone. I am going over there to see what I can do."

Many—even Indians—protested his going, but go he would, and go he did. He was soon back and said, "Those poor souls have had nothing to eat all these days; can you fix up something for them?"

While he went for his carpenter and some lumber to fence in the body, so it would not be disturbed by wolves, I filled a basket with good food and a bottle of hot coffee, and again the general went, and he stayed until the fence was made secure, and then he took the aged parents of Crazy Horse to the agency and made a place for them. They were most touchingly grateful and spoke of the white man, the first to come to their relief.

When the Indians moved to the Missouri River, the parents went along, and my general took watchful care of them as long as he remained at the agency. It may be they moved Crazy Horse's body along with them, but I doubt it because of the many little things I can remember…

When I am asked about my most thrilling experience in the army, my thoughts at once revert to the Crazy Horse episode. I can never forget my general's grief over the results of it all; and I am glad that, despite the protests of our friends, he went to the Adjutant's office and saw the dying man who had asked for him.

When the request came, he looked at me and said, "Shall I?" and I nodded, "Yes." Our host, Major Burroughs, reproved me, saying, "He may never come back," to which I replied, "He is surrounded by friends."

It was a harrowing day, and the next day was equally so, and fraught with much danger. The general felt that he must hasten to his own agency, knowing that his Indians would hear all about this tragedy, become alarmed and some of the bands might stampede.

So we left Camp Robinson early next morning. General Crook had left word that I was not to go, but my general insisted I go, saying he would feel very worried in leaving me there in all that seething excitement. He told General Bradley that if we ran into danger we would die together.

We left with the protection of 20 Indian soldiers, and he said to them, "I am leaving our lives in your care to get us safely to Camp Sheridan." They had one of their number go ahead to spy out the land, knowing the country was full of fleeing Indians of Crazy Horse's band.

I saw this advance guard suddenly halt, take a look around and then hurriedly join us. Instantly our soldiers loaded their guns and closed in around our ambulance.

Before starting, we had decided that should we be attacked, and not able to defend ourselves, I was to shoot myself, and my general to shoot daughter and himself. He examined my pistol and his own, and with them in our hands for instant use, we waited for what was ahead of us.

We reached the top of a hill we were climbing, and in the distance we saw a group of Indians. My general said, "Keep steady, and shoot to kill!" As we drew nearer, I exclaimed, "Oh, they are our Indians. I see Johnny Bordeaux's gay saddle blanket." At the same moment our guard recognized it. I won't lengthen this tale, but I want you to know that the women of that time were equal to all emergencies.

Frank Leslie's Illustrated Newspaper *October 13, 1877 shows the funeral procession as it passed Camp Sheridan on the way to a grave somewhere.* Photo courtesy Nebraska State Historical Society.

Frank Leslie's Illustrated Newspaper *showed this drawing of the late Sioux Chief Crazy Horse in an elevated grave near Camp Sheridan. Horses were slain in the chief's honor.* Photo courtesy Nebraska State Historical Society.

[*General Lee's party had come upon a group of Indians friendly to the United States Army, and Bordeaux would have served as a scout and interpreter.*]

On October 13, 1877, Frank Leslie's *Illustrated Newspaper* published an account of events that tells of the Camp Sheridan commanding officer's efforts to furnish the best coffin the quartermaster's department could turn out. This was elevated about three feet above the ground by means of a rude scaffold, an unusually low grave for an Indian, many of whom sleep their last sleep in the tops of trees. The reporter describes Crazy Horse's burial and wake:

Here upon an exposed mound of bluff, not far from the Agency, repose the remains of the famous Minneconjou, who is said to have taken the scalps of thirty whites with his own hands. His favorite war pony was led to his grave and there slaughtered. In his coffin were placed costly robes and blankets to protect him from the cold, a pipe and some tobacco, a bow and quiver of arrows, a carbine and pistol, with an ample supply of ammunition, sugar, coffee and hard bread, and an assortment of beads and trinkets with which to captivate the nut-brown maids of paradise.

Bob Buchan of Gordon, Nebraska, did research on the location of Crazy Horse's death scaffold on the bluff that overlooked Camp Sheridan.

Then dancing began in all the villages, this being an exhibition of grief as well as of gladness, and was kept up throughout the night and following day. Eight of the chief mourners, stripped to the skin and most fantastically besmeared with paint, were left without food or drink to guard the corpse and do the howling for the friends. All Sioux, whatever the sex or age, in passing the elevated grave, for several days after the funeral, prostrated themselves and joined in the lamentation.

The late Bob Buchan, curator of the Sheridan County Historical Society Museum in Gordon, Nebraska, thought that he and some friends researching the Camp Sheridan area may have located where the scaffold bearing Crazy Horse's body was. The site is on the bluff overlooking Camp Sheridan.

Bob had obtained a grant from the United States Office of Education to finance a project researched and reported on in 1969. Chadron State College and the Sheridan County Historical Society assisted with this study. Their primary sources of information were the military records from Camp Sheridan. The surgeon's daily report from September 1877, states: "the notorious Chief Crazy Horse was captured near here on the fourth, killed at Red Cloud and was buried here." [*The Red Cloud Agency was near Camp Robinson where the death actually occurred.*]

The discovery of a photograph of the fenced-in scaffold of Crazy Horse in the diary of Captain Bourke, aide to General Crook, led to a decision to excavate in an attempt to locate the scaffold post holes or other evidence of the burial. The photograph of the scaffold was matched to the terrain and a five-foot square grid was laid out in native pasture land. A hearth was uncovered. It was the only evidence of human use of the site.

The hearth site could be authentic. Mari Sandoz's notes for her book, *Crazy Horse*, contained a reference to a vigil fire at the scaffold. According to an army report, the body remained on the scaffold from September 8 to October 29, 1877.

From the periodical *Journal of America's Military Past*, in an article by Thomas R. Buecker titled, "History of Camp Sheridan, Nebraska," comes this report of the events following the death of Crazy Horse:

In the fall of 1877, after the death of Crazy Horse, the Oglala and Brulé agencies were moved to the Dakota reservation. One of the two military companies at Camp Sheridan escorted the Brulés to their new home. When the Oglala column moved past Spotted Tail Agency, family members took Crazy Horse's remains with them. All the buildings and supplies at the agency were eventually moved to the new site. When the Indians departed, many of their dogs remained at the old site. Most were destroyed by the soldiers because they "became wild as wolves."

Spotted Tail and his band with Crazy Horse's parents headed for the Ponca Agency east to set up camp on the Missouri River. The area is in Knox County, Nebraska just west of where the Niobrara River flows into the Missouri River.

The Red Cloud Agency was moved north to central South Dakota on the west bank of the Missouri River at the mouth of Yellow Medicine Creek. In 1878 it was proposed to abandon Camp Robinson and keep a garrison at Camp Sheridan. It was ultimately decided to keep a permanent post at Camp Robinson as it was a better location on the road to the Black Hills and better accommodations for troops. Late in 1878, the designation "Camp" was changed to "Fort," signifying the permanent status of the post.

Beaver Valley, the Spotted Tail Agency, and Camp Sheridan, all within a radius of three or four miles, have documented history of the Crazy Horse funeral scene. We have two good stories of what happened in the area of Beaver Valley on the Kadlecek land, and then the military history and various newspaper accounts about the Camp Sheridan area that have been referenced above. The Oglalas added a story of their own. In Eleanor Hinman's interviews as reported in Oglala Sources, it was told that a spotted eagle—a war eagle—descended from the heavens every night to walk about on Crazy Horse's scaffold while his remains were sepulchered near Camp Sheridan.

I asked David Kadlecek what he thought about the reports that Crazy Horse's death scaffold had been a couple of miles downstream overlooking Camp Sheridan. He replied, "Well, yes, there was some research done on that, and there may well have been a scaffold there. I would not doubt that. Whether or not Crazy Horse was placed on it or not, I have a real hard time accepting the fact that Crazy Horse was put in front of a white man's camp on a scaffold. You know, since they were enemies, that did not make sense. Since they gave his body back to his people, why would they display it up on a bluff overlooking the army camp? It doesn't make sense to me."

Indeed, one has to ask, why would Crazy Horse's body be placed in front of a white man's camp? It had been back upstream where he'd gone for his vision quest on Beaver Mountain, and he had told his father that he wanted his body to be placed on a tree scaffold if he should die.

If Crazy Horse was placed in a coffin, as so many white newspaper accounts report, and as is corroborated by army reports as well, what message was the army trying to send? Would this make the agency Indians and the hostiles who had recently surrendered from their vast hunting grounds of the north conform to the white man's ways? Was it to show the power of the big white cannon? Was this a way to intimidate the Sioux?

Maybe the real question is, was Crazy Horse's body really put in the white man's coffin? Perhaps the Crazy Horse people buried the body in an area near the Three Pinnacles Bluff on Kadlecek land and then pretended to go along with the coffin being placed on a scaffold overlooking the white army's Camp Sheridan.

Within a month's time of the death of Crazy Horse, a delegation of well-known Sioux, including Red Cloud, Spotted Tail, and American Horse, and the man who held and assisted in the capture of Crazy Horse, Little Big Man, were meeting with President Hayes in Washington.

The Sioux left the Spotted Tail Agency on October 27, 1877, and headed for new agencies. Crazy Horse had been dead since September 5, but some stories passed down through the generations say that Crazy Horse's parents took his body with them on their travels. What kind of condition was his body in if the parents, indeed, took his remains with them on the exodus to the Missouri River? Wouldn't it be more likely that he was secretly buried in the area of Beaver Creek rather than his body hauled around by his parents?

26

In the Pine Ridge Area

Through the years I have accumulated many more stories about where the body of Crazy Horse was taken after his death. At least nine of these possible locations are within the Pine Ridge Reservation area. These burial locations were either identified by Lakota people, or information about them was found in archival files. Three were previously discussed in Chapter 23: (1) Butte between White Horse and Wounded Knee Creeks; (2) Bluffs east of Wounded Knee Creek; (3) Bluff near White Horse Creek. In this chapter, I will discuss those sites in more depth, as well as other places identified as burial locations on the Pine Ridge Reservation.

Crazy Horse Butte

In the April 15, 1954 issue of the *Sheridan County Star*, Jake Herman wrote an article recounting Bat Pourier's story of trailing Crazy Horse's father and mother to Wounded Knee Creek and White Horse Creek.

Jake Herman grew up on the Pine Ridge Reservation listening to the old warriors who had known, fought, and hunted with Crazy Horse. These were half-breed Indians, scouts and interpreters, whose words Jake thought were above reproach. Jake, who himself was a Sioux, was born in 1893 and died in 1970. He was a writer, trick-rider, and fancy roper, but most of all, he liked being a rodeo clown. He had a mule he called Creeping Jenny and a skunk he called Stinky. Jake is convinced from the years he spent researching Crazy Horse that the remains of the Great War Chief lie on lonely Crazy Horse Butte.

Jake heard that Crazy Horse was first buried on the banks of the White River. Recall that Jesse Lee's wife referred to Beaver Creek as White River, and we know that the White River is about twelve miles downstream from Camp Sheridan. It may have been a common error to refer to Beaver Creek as the White River. Jake had been told that the grief-stricken parents moved the body and placed it in a sepulcher tree on a butte—referred to as Crazy Horse Butte by Jake and others—on the Pine Ridge Reservation. Later, Jake heard, the body was removed from the forks of the tree and reburied in a cave on the same butte; only the parents knew the exact place where they had buried their son's body.

Crazy Horse's father died a few years after his son's death and Crazy Horse's mother, referred to as Mrs. Crazy Horse, is believed to have died around 1884. Jake was told that her body was buried on this same butte as her son. She personally told Black Elk, the great Medicine Man, that it was her last wish that she be buried near her son.

Jake Herman started researching the Crazy Horse stories in 1940 when he lived near Manderson, South Dakota, near Crazy Horse butte. The famous Indian scout, Bat Pourier, repeatedly told Jake that he had been detailed out by the army to trail the aged and grief-stricken parents. Bat said he trailed the travois to that same butte where Crazy Horse is reputedly buried.

According to Jake Herman, Alex Adams, an old friend of Jake Herman's family, described a touching moment. "Crazy Horse's mother had stayed and, one day, they were driving by this butte and she said to Alex, 'This is the very trail that my husband and I brought the body of your cousin, Crazy Horse, along.' Then a tragic look appeared on her face and she sat silently as they drove along until the butte disappeared from view."

Looking south of Manderson, SD, across the White Horse Creek Valley. Jake Herman called this Crazy Horse Butte.

Jake also reported that the only known relic of Chief Crazy Horse was his war club, which is now owned by Mrs. Red Cloud. Jake says that back in 1940, Antonie Randall came to Jake's home and showed him the war club of Crazy Horse. Randall said the club was given to him by Horn Chips the Medicine Man. Years ago Horn Chips told Randall, "Tomorrow I am going to that butte to pay my obligation to the departed spirit of my warrior friend."

People around Manderson today do not know of a place called Crazy Horse Butte. The only butte with a name is Porcupine Butte, about ten miles southeast of Manderson. Even the descendants of Black Elk, the medicine man, do not know of Crazy Horse Butte, but there is some talk of the possibility that Crazy Horse was buried up in the White Buttes that surround Manderson. The green highway marker states that the second possible location of the burial site, according to earlier statements by Batiste Pourier and Jake Russel, was fourteen miles northwest of the sign, where there is a butte between the forks of White Horse Creek and Wounded Knee Creek. Perhaps this is what is sometimes referred to as Crazy Horse Butte.

In the summer of 1998, I was headed north after spending the day with the Black Elk family where they lived south of Manderson. In the valley of the White Buttes, I came to a bend in the road and off to the west I noticed a large hide stretched out on a square frame of logs. Two men were scraping away on the hide in the hot sun. I stopped and told them I was interested in the process of preparation of the hide. Charles Comes Killing and his helper told me they were brain tanning a woodland buffalo hide. This method of tanning is the old way, the way the Plains Indians used to tan their hides. Nowadays, chemicals are used along with tannic acid to preserve the hides. It is rare to see people practice brain tanning anymore.

Brain tanning is done by the actual brains of the animal being worked into the skin. After several applications, the hide is smoked over cedar or cottonwood

Charles Comes Killing working on buffalo hide.

chips. Smoking adds oil (creosote) to the skin, waterproofing the individual fibers of the fur. If the hide were to later become wet, the smoking will prevent it from drying stiff. This is a tedious process, and anyone doing this successfully has my utmost respect.

Charles told me that he donates every fourteenth hide he tans to a local alcohol abuse prevention program for youth around Manderson. He had also donated a buffalo robe for his uncle's funeral. The robe was placed on the casket during the funeral ceremony. His uncle's family kept the robe for the good memories. It is Sioux tradition to give meaningful things away to the family of the deceased, and Sioux families give gifts to those who have been of the most help to a bereaved family. A brain tanned buffalo robe is regarded as much more valuable than a chemically tanned hide.

It was a warm July day and, in preparing the buffalo hide, Charles was using an elk bone scraper to separate the meat, membranes, and fat from the future leather, or dermis. His bare skin was glistening in the light. I could see scars on his chest and back, and I knew that he had participated in a traditional Sun Dance.

I visualized him at the sacred tree brought in for the ceremony. Usually it is the tallest cottonwood tree available that is placed in a hole with buffalo fat and sacred food. Rawhide thongs are attached to skewers implanted in the skin of a man's chest and he is then suspended from the cottonwood tree. Participants dance looking into the sun until their minds fill with the bright light from another world, and then they pray until the skewers are ripped from the skin. The gods can hear their thoughts when they have made a sacrifice with their bodies.

Charles invited me to Crow Dog's Paradise, on the Rosebud Reservation, to participate in a Sun Dance ritual and a vision quest. Charles had lived in the Manderson and Porcupine area most of his life. He says, "People sometimes refer to the big butte southwest of my house as Crazy Horse Butte, but it is not officially called that. We call the butte Pahaska, which means White Butte. The only real Crazy Horse Butte is the one they are carving in the mountain over by Custer, South Dakota."

Charles said his neighbor, who lives a mile southwest of him, had recently died. His family's house was near the base of that large butte. "You could stop and see them," Charles suggested. When I drove into the front yard, I noticed that the burial had taken place out in the pasture, about two hundred yards northeast of the house. White Horse Creek runs just to the southeast of the grave. I told the family I liked the burial spot they had chosen and I wondered if Crazy Horse might be buried nearby.

As darkness came that evening, I drove north away from Manderson, following Wounded Knee Creek into the Badlands. I was thinking about Charles Comes Killing's work to restore the heritage of his people. I admired the hard work that went into brain tanning a hide. His Lakota hide venture is a rare undertaking and a noble cause worthy of many tributes.

One time Charlie mailed me a hide in a box, sent by the United States Postal Service. It cost him seventy dollars to send. When I got the box, I noticed he had licked each stamp on one at a time! The big box was covered with stamps!

A Tributary of Wounded Knee Creek

The following information comes from the book by Mari Sandoz, *Hostiles and Friendlies*. In her story about the burial of Crazy Horse, Sandoz writes about a place in South Dakota where the passing seasons chill and warm a little nest of bones that was once the most beloved and most feared man of the Teton Sioux—the man called Crazy Horse, meaning *Holy*, *Mystical*, or *Inspired Horse*. Apparently, every few years, there had been letters from the public in newspapers offering the bones of Crazy Horse for sale. Like pieces of the True Cross, it was reasonable to suspect the authenticity of the bones. An authentic upper jaw bone would be marked with the path of an embedded bullet that Crazy Horse acquired a few years before his death. People were suspicious of all the folks trying to sell the bones of Crazy Horse. It was a hard time for bone sellers. Over in Iowa, one man offered to fake a jaw bone with the precise wounding to fit the requirements.

Blue Eagle tells that a man who helped with the burial showed him the grave on the tributary of Wounded Knee Creek. The battlefield of the Wounded Knee massacre is seven miles south of Manderson, South Dakota.

A man who calls himself Lone Eagle, and who was interviewed in the January 16, 1955, *Colorado Springs Gazette*, knew of this Blue Eagle. Lone Eagle is not, himself, an Indian, but was the son of missionaries on the Sioux reservation. He was adopted by the tribe and given his In-

Headwaters of Wounded Knee Creek.

dian name, which he used until his death in January 1955. His birth name was Floyd Maine and he later married White Faun, a daughter of Chief Luther Standing Bear. Blue Eagle was a member of the Sioux tribe, and was supposedly the only person still living who has seen the actual burial site. The article stated that Lone Eagle was to get together with Blue Eagle that summer to see if they could rediscover the site. It was their hope to find enough clothing of Crazy Horse's, or perhaps some of the equipment buried with him, so that identification of the bones would be possible. Apparently Lone Eagle and Dick Spencer, editor of *Western Horseman*, had been looking for the grave of Crazy Horse for some time but nothing much ever came of their search.

Lone Eagle told Mari Sandoz that Chief Crazy Horse's body was first taken from Fort Robinson to a rocky cave site on the forks of Scabby Creek and the Little Beaver Creek, about ten miles southwest of the present Pine Ridge, South Dakota. There it was buried and his old father stayed by the grave for days.

In October 1877, Chief Spotted Tail and his band of Brulés made camp at the mouth of Wounded Knee Creek on the White River. They had brought with them the remains of Crazy Horse. There they met a small band of Oglalas, among them were relatives of Crazy Horse. The question arose as to who should have the remains. It was decided they should go to those present who would be the nearest of kin. The remains were never seen again until 1883 or 1884 when a white trapper by the name of White brought a skull into the trading post at the mouth of Wounded Knee Creek. White reported, "We found it with some bones and a set of travois poles, up in the Bad Lands [*sic*] between Wounded Knee Creek and Porcupine Creek. The skull had two marks on it. One on the upper jaw and just below the corner of the nose, also one mark higher up between the cheek bone and the eye."

Sandoz's file of notes tells that an old Indian woman, Mrs. Respects Nothing, who had known Crazy Horse well, said that it was definitely the skull of Crazy Horse. Sandoz had gotten this story from Lone Eagle. Louise Pourier, another relative of Crazy Horse's, took the skull in a piece of blue woolen blanket and, after crushing the skull with an axe, buried the remains in her backyard near present Rockyford, South Dakota. Rockyford is near Chimney Butte where Woodrow Respects Nothing told me a story that had been passed down in his family. He said that Crazy Horse's parents had camped in this area with the body of their son and then had disappeared into the Badlands, returning the next morning without the body.

After I read this story in Mari Sandoz's file at Love Library in Lincoln, Nebraska, I called Woodrow Respects Nothing and related Mari's story to him. He told me the Respects Nothing woman in the story was probably his grandmother Sophia. No one in the family had passed along to him the story of the crushed skull but he felt that it may very well have been true, as he knew that there were stories about Crazy Horse that had been kept secret from him.

On January 15, 1954, the *Anadarko Daily News* reported that Dick Spencer and Lone Eagle were consulting with Leo M. Shea, known to the Indians as Chief White Bear, who told them they had little chance of finding the grave. Chief White Bear did say that the secret to identifying Crazy Horse had been told to him by Old Red Bear, a brave who served with Crazy Horse during the Indian wars.

"We will know after examining the skull whether the remains are those of Crazy Horse," White Bear explained. "We will not allow anyone to commercialize on Indian history unless the remains presented are authentic. Only I and Arnail, a 92-year-old Indian living on the Rosebud Reservation in South Dakota, could identify the remains." If successful, the plan was to move the remains to Granite Mountain in the Black Hills where a huge statue of Crazy Horse is being carved in the face of the mountain.

In Mari Sandoz's own search for the body of Crazy Horse, she explained that it might be interesting to find just where the man's bones are buried—or, perhaps, those of the half dozen other Sioux called Crazy Horse as the name had been passed down for many years. There were three other Crazy Horses who were old enough and important enough to be signers of the Proposed Division of the Great Sioux Reservation in 1889. Additionally, the body of one Private First Class C.P. Crazy Horse was returned to Pine Ridge from the Pacific as recently as December 1948.

At Pepper Creek

In John Neihardt's work, *Black Elk Speaks*, there is a chapter titled "The Killing of Crazy Horse." Black Elk told Neihardt that he knew the parents brought Crazy Horse's bones down Pepper Creek and later, the travois moved along nearby White Horse Creek—empty.

Black Elk, cousin to Crazy Horse, was a Sioux holy man, tormented throughout his life by visions of power to restore the traditional ways of the Sioux. In the 1930s, when Black Elk shared his visions with Nebraska poet and author John Neihardt, he passed along to future generations information about the lives of the Oglala Sioux. The old camp circle, the sacred hoop of the Lakota, and other old ways have been shattered by the machines of a modern era. If the old traditional ways are to be no more, perhaps Black Elk's vision gives new hope for the emergence of a new sacred hoop, or a new circle of hope. The people of Pine Ridge live in one of the most impoverished areas of the United States, where such hope is greatly needed.

Black Elk told this story:

When Crazy Horse was killed, my father and I went back to our camp at Red Cloud Agency.

Crazy Horse was dead. He was brave and good and wise. He never wanted anything but to save his people, and he fought the Wasichus (whites) only when

Pepper Creek Valley.

they came to kill us in our own country. He was only thirty years old. They could not kill him in battle. They had to lie to him and kill him that way.

I cried all night. So did my father.

When it was day, Crazy Horse's father and mother brought him over to our camp in a wagon. They put him in a box, and I heard that they had cut him in two because the box was not long enough. They fastened the box on a pony drag and went away alone toward the east and north. I saw the two old people going away alone with their son's body. Nobody followed them. They went all alone, and I can see them going yet. The horse that pulled the pony drag was a buckskin. Crazy Horse's father had a white-faced bay with white hind legs. His mother had a brown mare with a bay colt.

The old people never would tell where they took the body of their son. I know one thing, and this is it. The old people came with the body right down Pepper Creek which is just a little way south across the hill from where we are. [Neihardt notes that Black Elk's log cabin is situated about two miles southwest of Manderson Post Office on the Pine Ridge Reservation.] There were two hunters who were hunting along the creek there, and they saw two old people coming with a pony drag, and when they told my father about this, they said a buckskin was pulling the drag that had a box on it; that the old man rode a white-faced bay with white hind legs and the old woman rode a brown mare with a bay colt. These hunters saw the old people coming down Pepper Creek, and later on they saw the old people again on White Horse Creek which is just a little way down Pepper Creek from where they were before. And the hunters said the box was not on the drag any more. So I think that maybe they hid the body somewhere on Pepper Creek over there because the hunters had seen them, and maybe they went back again at night and took the box away into the Badlands. But Crazy Horse might be lying over there just a little way from us right now on Pepper Creek across that hill yonder. I do not know.

It does not matter where his body lies, for it is grass; but where his spirit is, it will be good to be.

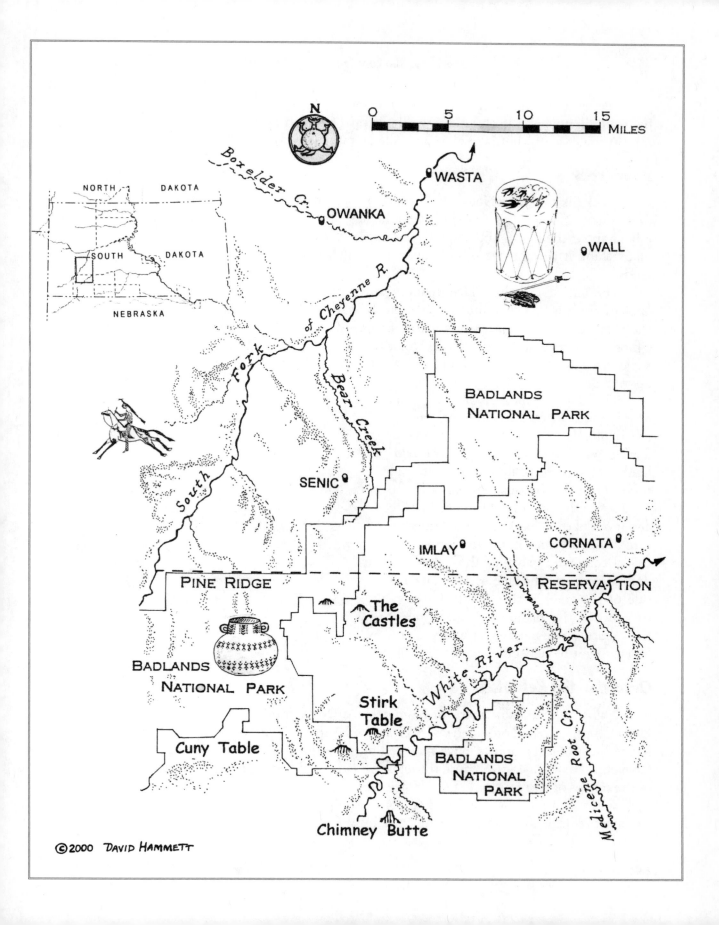

N

0   5   10   15
MILES

NORTH   DAKOTA

SOUTH   DAKOTA

NEBRASKA

Boxelder Cr.

OWANKA

WASTA

WALL

South   Fork   of Cheyenne R.

Bear Creek

SENIC

BADLANDS
NATIONAL PARK

IMLAY

CORNATA

PINE RIDGE

RESERVATION

The
Castles

BADLANDS
NATIONAL PARK

White River

Stirk
Table

Cuny Table

BADLANDS
NATIONAL PARK

Medicene Root Cr.

Chimney Butte

©2000   DAVID HAMMETT

Pepper Creek lies southwest of Manderson about three miles. It is a dry creek that only has water in it when the clouds bring rain. Pepper Creek runs into White Horse Creek, which runs at the base of what Jake Herman called Crazy Horse Butte.

Bear Creek

Black Elk told John Neihardt, "The old people would never tell where they took the body of their son. Nobody knows today where he lies, for the old people are dead, too. Many have talked about the place, and some have said they knew where it was and would not tell, and many think it is somewhere on Bear Creek which flows from the Pine Ridge into the Badlands."

The Lakota call that place Maka Sica, the place where earth itself was misshapen. The ancient animals had been hurled to the earth by the gods and the earth became strange there; the place resembles a battered skeleton. People say this is the place where the medicine man, Chips, found a small stone for Crazy Horse that he wore behind his ear for medicine that would serve as a bond with Chips and the Great Spirit. It would act as a guide when he needed to call upon it.

The day my mother and my wife, Mony, and I visited the Bear Creek area in the Badlands, rain had fallen for several days. It was early August 1998. The Badlands are usually scorching hot at that time of year, but on this unusual visit, the creeks in this desert-like region were about out of their banks and the temperature was cool and comfortable; I liked that. Bear Creek swivelled through a vast desolate region. The land was flat on each side of the creek with many buttes popping up in the distance. Could one of these buttes be a marker for where Crazy Horse might have been buried?

Bear Creek.

Chips and the Reburials

Chips, the medicine man, was a member of No Water's Oglala band. It was Chips (or Horn Chips) who had provided Crazy Horse with protective power. Chips was known to have located lost objects, and to have received answers through prayers. He was revered on the Cheyenne River Agency because through the spirits, he had been able to receive the location of the bodies of two sons of Palmer Horse Shoe who had been lost in a blizzard.

When Crazy Horse was killed at Camp Robinson, Chips was there. He was involved in the short struggle during the stabbing, and his shoulder was dislocated. Chips gave two infor-

Chips and his wife. Photo courtesy of Nebraska State Historical Society.

mative interviews that tell similar stories; the first in 1907, and another three years later. It is somewhat confusing to follow the number of times Crazy Horse's body was moved, according to Chips (Ricker Collection, 1907).

According to Ricker, Chips said that Crazy Horse was buried on the Beaver Creek by the cliffs. When the Indians went down the Missouri River, his body was removed to White Clay Creek and buried. After they returned, Chips and his brother went and took up the body to see if it had been disturbed; finding that it had not been, they reinterred it. The first burial was near the cliff in a frame house that was lined with scarlet cloth. His body was also once buried on White Horse Creek, above Manderson, but it was moved from there to Wounded Knee where it is now.

Chips said that he'd put Crazy Horse's bones into a black blanket and laid them in a butte rock cave. "There is no petrifaction—no flesh—nothing now but bones. The place where No Water shot him in the head showed in the skull."

Three years later, in the summer of 1910, Chips was interviewed by Walter Camp. Camp did considerable research on Crazy Horse. He found that, in 1878, or later, the father was assisted by a medicine man in the first burial. The two agreed to keep the burial spot secret. There were rumors that if the remains were to fall into the hands of white people, they would be placed in a museum. From that time on, it was generally understood among Oglalas that no one but Crazy Horse's father and the medicine man knew the location of the grave. Camp was told this by several reliable old men.

Camp had known a first cousin of Crazy Horse, a man he described as intelligent, gentlemanly, and a good friend of Chips. The cousin and Camp planned to persuade the old medicine man, Chips, to reveal the gravesite. The cousin had been working on Chips cautiously, and thought he could represent the situation to him in such a way that he would consent. But the old medicine man died, and when Camp went to Pine Ridge in 1919, he could not locate the cousin of Crazy Horse. In a letter to Eunice Anderson, the State Historian in Wyoming, Camp told her that he was somewhat reluctant to reveal the name of the cousin, since it might not set well if some stranger were to get the cousin's name and go to him with pointed questions.

Chips served as Crazy Horse's medicine man and he had made Crazy Horse's war bag, which was actually a medicine bundle stored in a bag made from tanned animal skin, which contained the claws and dried heart of the spotted eagle. These objects, blessed with protective powers, were given to Crazy Horse after No Water shot him in 1870. Chips and Crazy Horse had been raised together. Chips told Walter Camp much the same story he had told Ricker three years earlier. [*Camp's notes, while quite informative, are clearly unpolished.*]

When Crazy Horse's old tribe moved to the Missouri River, the parents took his body and unjointed the legs so as to get into a small space and Chips and Old Man Crazy Horse carried it above the head of Wounded Knee (not on the creek) and buried it in the ground in a box.

Later on, Chips and his wife and another woman buried the body in another place. Later still, Chips took up the body and buried it again, and now he was the only one who knew where. This time he buried it in a rawhide sack. This was in 1883. The reason why they don't tell where bones are is because the Sioux depended much on Crazy Horse as a fighter, but just before he was killed many of the Oglalas, including Little Big Man, the principal enemy of Crazy Horse, turned against him.

At the time of the second interview, there were rumors circulating that Chips wanted to sell Crazy Horse's bones. Chips says that in that interview this story is false and that he had never offered them for sale.

Crazy Horse's brother-in-law, Red Feather, was implicated in similar rumors. A map drawn by Red Cloud in 1895 includes a comment in Lakota that Red Feather would not reveal the burial location of Crazy Horse's bones unless Red Feather was given money.

In an April 24, 1992, interview with the *Rapid City Journal*, Charles Chipps, whose grandfather was the medicine man Crazy Horse called on, said, "Crazy Horse was buried in the Manderson-Wounded Knee area. Only the Chips family knows exactly where. That knowledge is handed down from generation to generation." The name Chips eventually evolved into Chipps.

In the late spring of 1999, my son Woody and I were in Wanblee, South Dakota, on our way to kayak the Dismal River, when we pulled up to a house to ask directions to the home of Richard Moves Camp. Mario Gonzalez, an enrolled member of the Pine Ridge Reservation, told me to stop and see Richard because he is the great-grandson of Chips, the medicine man. Gonzalez, who lived not far from me in Marysville, was the tribal attorney for the Kickapoo Reservation in Kansas. When we asked for directions to Richard Moves Camp's, the occupants said they knew where he lived, that Richard's mother lived next door, and they offered to call him for us.

While we were at the house asking directions, some Native American children jumped in the kayaks we had loaded in the back of our pickup; they pretended to be guiding them in water. Woody wanted to take them down to the lake and to give them rides. The kids were cute and full of energy. One of their parents called the Moves Camp family for us.

When I spoke with Richard on the phone, I said that I was from Kansas and that Mario Gonzalez had told me to call him. The family directed me to the Moves Camp place on the west side of the base of Eagles Nest Butte. They told me, "Hey, Richard is a very revered medicine man. Hollywood actor Steven Segal was here to see him, and Willie Nelson pulled up here last week in a big bus and was looking for him."

I thought to myself, *Yeah, I can understand Willie needing a medicine man.*

Richard Moves Camp had us come out early the next morning around 7:00 A.M. I called before we headed to his place but I did not realize we had crossed the time zone, so when I called, the current time was well before 6:00 A.M. A sleepy-voiced little boy answered the phone and told us to come on out. Later I found out it was his birthday, so I gave him some money to spend on his trip to Rapid City later that day.

Woody and I knew Medicine Man Richard Moves Camp lived near Wanblee, SD. We pulled up in front of a house to ask directions and unknown to us we had stopped right in front of his mother's house. The neighbor kids went into the house to get their parents to explain the directions to Richard's house which was about five miles out in the country. Woody wanted to take the kids down to a nearby lake for a kayak ride, so we visited with Richard Moves Camp the next morning.

Woody and I drove down a long winding two-mile driveway that was full of ruts. Usually I wake myself up mornings by jumping on a mini trampoline, but bouncing down the road did the job that morning. Woody liked the road. "I think I'd like to have a long driveway like this one," he said.

Richard was in a good mood. He told me that he was a fifth generation grandson of Chips; the Lakota word for Chips is Woptura. Iron Whistle had been Chips' father. Chips had two sons: Charles Chipps and James Moves Camp. James received his name because he moved his camp away from the rest of the family.

"At the time of Chips," Richard explained, "the United States government arrested many medicine men, but not Chips. After Crazy Horse died, the soldier people took Chips back to Washington where he performed a ceremony for them. He was given honors for his medicine. He did many great deeds for people. I am but a small twig compared to what my grandfather Chips was."

Richard told us that the Great Spirit gave Chips the power to be an invincible warrior, but that Chips asked the Great One if he could pass those powers on to Crazy Horse. Chips wanted to be a medicine man and to help his people with healing. Calling upon his own powers, Chips asked the spirits to guide Crazy Horse.

I asked Richard Moves Camp about the sacred stone that Chips gave Crazy Horse to wear in battle. Richard says it was just a simple stone, but it was a reminder of the great spiritual power that Chips gave Crazy Horse. It was Crazy Horse's medicine. Richard went on to say that it was rarely talked about out loud, rather, one normally talked about this only with the spirits.

I visited with Jack and Victor Runnels in October 1999 at the Golden Eagle Casino in Horton, Kansas. They were members of the Crazy Horse family, and they told me that the stone would have had power only to Crazy Horse. They said that everything has a soul and the power to change. In the stone given to Crazy Horse, the power is not transferable; it was special to the owner. That power was to be respected.

Richard Moves Camp told me that Chips and Crazy Horse were not related, as far as he knew, but there had been a bond between the two of them like that of true brothers. As the keeper of his family's oral tradition, Richard maintained that Chips had been in Canada when Crazy Horse was killed. He believes that Eli Ricker misunderstood in his interview with Chips that he was at Camp Robinson when Crazy Horse died.

"You, Cleve," Richard told me, "are on a journey with your son. You are traveling. You are taking time to kayak together. You are helping your son learn about Native Americans and your bond is growing and you are on a wonderful voyage. That togetherness is what Chips and Crazy Horse had."

"Worm and Chips knew the burial spot of Crazy Horse," Richard told us. "The grandson of Chips, Samuel Moves Camp, also knew, but as far as I know, Samuel died with that knowledge in 1973. Chips died in 1913. Samuel is buried in an Episcopal cemetery near Wanblee, South Dakota, on the west side of the road. Contrary to what others say, the information about where Crazy Horse is buried is now unknown to our family.

"What was important to Crazy Horse was to be humble, simple, and help people. Crazy Horse belonged to the earth."

Two days later, Woody and I met two other fathers and their sons in the Sandhills, and went kayaking on a spring-fed river. It was a good time to be with the boys who were soon to be men. Near the end of the seven-hour trip, I found a long stick that a beaver had been gnawing on. The bark had been removed, and there were a few short jagged twigs left. There was evidence of fresh teeth marks, otherwise the six-foot stick was smooth. At camp we talked about beavers and how they work with their parents to build their homes, and how they work together as a community to accomplish tasks—the younger consulting the old, and the old patiently guiding the young. When their homes flood or are broken down, they quickly work together to rebuild. This was what Crazy Horse was trying to do for his people when white men were destroying their hunting grounds. The Native Americans were constantly moving and rebuilding.

A slight breeze calmed to perfect stillness as we moved about the camp. We cut the beaver stick into six equal parts —a piece for each of us—and asked that it be our medicine.

The Cliffs of White Horse Creek and the Medicine Root

Information about another possible burial site comes from the Ricker interviews archived at the Nebraska Historical Society. Mrs. Richard Stirk, a member of the Oglala tribe whose husband was in charge of distributing beef to agency Indians, recalled stories told to her husband by reliable informants: "Crazy Horse's body was afterward removed by the Indians to a place in the side of a cliff on White Horse Creek between Pine Ridge Agency and Manderson, four miles below Manderson." Richard had heard the Indians discuss this event while they were sitting and smoking together and he is sure it is correct. Richard said, "The hole in the cliff is in full view of the road on the east side of the road; he [her husband] has seen it many a time, and it is about fifty feet above the bottom of the cliff. He has understood that the body was placed there with the aid of ladders."

This story adds validity to the story that Chips may have indeed put the bones of Crazy Horse in a cliff cave.

In 1999, I visited with Jake Little Thunder, a tribal elder at Wanblee. Jake was in his mid-eighties at the time and he is a direct descendant of Chief Little Thunder. It was Little Thunder's warriors who were almost completely wiped out in 1855 by General William Harney at what was known as the Battle at Blue Water after Little Thunder had asked for a peaceful understanding with the authorities and white people in the Platte River region. The Blue Water Creek drains into the Platte River.

Jake is known for his keen memory and carries much family history. Outside of his house, his grandson worked on a car that badly needed repairs. Jake was in a wheel chair at the time my son Woody and I stopped to visit him.

Jake told us that after Crazy Horse died, one of his wives, Nellie Laravie, married a man named White Squirrel who took the name Crazy Horse so he could use the ration ticket for supplies that Chief Crazy Horse had been given by the United States government. Nellie Laravie was a spy put into the Crazy Horse camp to report to the army. Jake said Crazy Horse's other wife, Black Shawl, had tuberculosis which she contracted from an infected blanket of Crow origin. White Squirrel, who was a half brother of Chips, went by the name Crazy Horse for the rest of his life. He is buried in a

Valley of Medicine Root Creek.

cemetery near Hisle, South Dakota, with the name Chief Crazy Horse engraved on his stone.

Jake believed that the real warrior Crazy Horse had, indeed, been buried by Chips in a cave near Kyle. Jake said that Chips had lived on No Flesh Creek, near where it runs into the Medicine Root Creek. It is this area Jake believed to be the final resting place of the great warrior Chief Crazy Horse. As a crow would fly from White Horse Creek to Medicine Root Creek, they are about twenty miles apart.

The number of stories about Crazy Horse's burial site created considerable confusion. At times it seemed like a mixed up mess to keep track of all these locations. My son Woody suggested that I needed to make maps with all of the possible sites.

In March 1999, my sister, Julie Walstrom, of Lincoln, Nebraska, sent me an article about a woman, Lillian Fire Thunder, who told stories of being a nurse at Wounded Knee, South Dakota, during the American Indian Movement's occupation in 1973.

I drove to Lincoln to meet with Lillian and her family. Her great great-grandfather was Fast Thunder, a right hand man to Crazy Horse. Fast Thunder had been involved with the burial. Lillian's son, Norman, told me the old people told stories that the bones of Crazy Horse were buried many different times at a number of different places. Rituals were performed at each burial site by the keeper of the bones. The keeper or Wanajagluha was a medicine man. One such burial place, Chief Fast Thunder told his family, was the white cliffs east of Manderson and just east of White Horse Creek.

Lillian's husband, Mark, said his great-grandpa told him that Crazy Horse always ate from a bowl that had four holes in it. Mark said, "This would drain the liquids and the remaining food would serve as his special medicine. Crazy Horse would make three or four passes as a decoy in front of the cavalry. He was different than a chief or a holy man. His spirit was of a different aura."

We burnt sage together before we parted. *Pela My Ya* (thank you).

Pahaska

In an interview by Eli Ricker with US Indian Scout Standing Soldier, who had been sent from Fort Robinson to the Spotted Tail Agency to get Crazy Horse, Standing Soldier recalled that when they arrived at Spotted Tail, they were told that Crazy Horse had said if anyone came after him, he would kill him—or them. So, it was arranged that some of the Brulé Indians should go out and get him, which they did. They took him under guard to Fort Robinson. The object in taking Crazy Horse was to transport him to Washington to see the president, and the agent at Red Cloud wanted the Rosebud Indians in charge to stop with Standing Soldier and Crazy Horse at the agency so he could tell Crazy Horse the purpose for which he was being brought in. The plan was to leave him at the Red Cloud Agency, but the Brulé did not stop there. They took him on to the fort where he was killed that same day.

Standing Soldier said, "Crazy Horse's body was removed by the Indians to Rosebud; from there they removed his bones to the cliff on the east side of White Horse Creek, four miles above Manderson, and thence it is not known where they have been moved." Ricker, who conducted the interview with Standing Soldier, said that this account of Crazy Horse's remains is apocryphal. It is disputed by some Indians whether any Indian's remains have ever been put up in that cliff.

Pahaska Butte.

Ricker did not want to include this story in his interview. Since that time, we have similar stories from other reliable sources, such as Chips and Mrs. Richard Stirk. Earlier in this chapter, there is reference to Jake Herman's research that mentions such a cliff in the same area. This butte to which they all referred is probably the same butte that, today, Charles Comes Killing says people around Manderson call Pahaska, or White Butte.

On June 2, 2000, I revisited Lillian Fire Thunder in Lincoln. She revealed a more exact location that time, telling me Crazy Horse was buried at the base of White Butte. That information had been passed down to her from her grandparents. We had a long conversation about her family, and she explained to me who was related to whom. Lillian was fun to visit with as she helped me straighten out her family's genealogy. I could see in her that she could have inherited the ability to ride the winds of the prairie with Fast Thunder and Crazy Horse. At that time, she was in her seventies and full of spirit.

As it neared noon, I needed to leave to meet a plane at the Lincoln airport. We were transferring a deceased woman who had lived for many years in Illinois back to where she had been born, in Marysville, Kansas.

As I left Lillian's place, she gave me the gift of a small ceremonial drum painted with the shadow of a lone warrior with one feather on his head. The horse he was mounted on was bending down to eat. There was a deep aqua blue background and a still reverence that portrayed a rider who seemed to be seeking direction from the wind; the hair of both horse and rider were blowing towards the open prairie. Lillian also sent along a dream catcher with a gold eagle feather medallion for me to give to my wife whom she had met on an earlier visit. I thanked her, and told her that our paths would connect again.

On the Pine Ridge

From the Fort Robinson files, George Kills in Sight tells another story that Crazy Horse is buried around Manderson. Kills in Sight was chairman of the tribal Land Enterprise at Rosebud. The information he gave in a 1967 interview with Professor Joseph H. Cash, of Eastern Montana College, was passed down to him from his grandfather, Big Crow. Kills in Sight says that Crazy Horse is sort of related to George's grandmother on his father's side, making Crazy Horse a cousin.

With others, Big Crow was on a hunt in the northern part of the state on what is now known as the Cheyenne River Reservation. Pine Ridge Indians went up to tell Crazy Horse he was wanted down at Fort Robinson. Crazy Horse was hesitant to go, but they finally talked him into going. The hunting party followed Crazy Horse and caught up with him about the time they came to Camp Robinson. Kills in Sight says his grandfather had a six-shooter with a holster, and he told Crazy Horse to put it on. Kills in Sight thought something was going to happen and that Crazy Horse might need it, so Crazy Horse belted it on around his waist. The hunting party did not go with him to the camp. They only went to a point that army guards stopped them from proceeding.

The Pine Ridge members who had gone to find Crazy Horse escorted him into Camp Robinson, but instead of delivering him to the army officers, they took him straight to the jail. Those from Pine Ridge who accompanied him told him, in Lakota, that the place they were leading him to was a jail. There were two guards on either side of him. Suddenly, Crazy Horse turned around and one of the guards ran a bayonet through his guts. The guard did not shoot Crazy Horse, but just let him lie where he fell. The Pine Ridge group claimed that Crazy Horse was their relation, but, if the truth were told, he might not have gone there. It is reasonable to presume that they must not have told Crazy Horse what their real intentions were or he would not have gone into the camp with them. He may have believed that the camp officials simply wanted to talk to him, but then this guard killed him.

My grandfather, Big Crow, and his bunch claimed the body and they made a travois and brought the body home to the camp where the Northern Cheyenne were. Crazy Horse's father and mother bound him up in a buffalo robe that was tied with rawhide, and wherever they go they take him along. They didn't bury him. The way they told it, they had him almost a month. His body was preserved so that it didn't spoil in that time.

They camped at the Pine Ridge Reservation in the area now known as Manderson. They were in an area around the pines and breaks. They asked the father of Crazy Horse if they could bury his son, and he agreed to it. He was willing to bury his son, but only under one condition. He filled his pipe and those who would not ever tell where he was going to be buried would smoke the pipe with him, pledging not to tell the place. Any who were planning to tell should leave because he was determined not to bury him until they had. Only a few stayed and smoked the pipe as their pledge. They then dug a hole in a sort of washout in a ravine. They put the body in there and then put rocks and dirt tightly in around the body so that no one would recognize the place as a grave. Those present at the time promised that they would never reveal the location.

George Kills in Sight had an uncle whose name was Coffee. Every spring or summer, Coffee went down to the site and visited the grave. He had in his possession whetstones and knives that Crazy Horse once had, but he did not want to show them to anyone so he had hidden them in the Badlands northeast of Parmelee. George continued:

> One day, I was working for the government, and Coffee sent word for me to take him over there to the burial site and he'll show me the place where he was buried. But he was sick with pneumonia and he died soon after. Wherever he is buried, a big cedar tree grows and it is right on the corner of a white man's land now. The southeast corner, I believe he said. Nobody is alive that knows where he is buried and knows the whole story. My grandfather Big Crow told me this story.

In 1998, in Kyle, South Dakota, Darlene Rosane told me that her father's grandfather had passed down information that a man named Coffee, or Wakalyapi, was appointed caretaker of the Crazy Horse grave. As a friend of the family, Coffee had been present when the body was buried. Coffee did not want anyone to know where the grave was, but he went himself to tend the grave each summer until some time in the 1930s.

Darlene, who had been raised by Chief American Horse's son, also told me that Crazy Horse's real name was His Horse is Crazy.

One August day in 2000, I visited with Johnson Holy Rock who had given the Oglala Lakota College at Kyle some maps he came across that showed Sioux tepee camps during the time of 1878 to 1890. I was seeking permission to use those maps. Holy Rock was in his eighties and had a deep smooth voice sprinkled with hearty laughs. He told me his grandfather was a member of the Badger Band of a Northern Sioux tribe. When Johnson Holy Rock was a little guy, he remembered Coffee coming to visit his father, Jonas. Sioux tradition did not allow young children to sit and visit with the older people, therefore, Johnson was not even allowed to listen. However, he would sneak around and peek through a window to watch his father and Coffee communicate. This was in the early 1930s and Coffee was very old and also deaf at the time. The two communicated in sign language. Johnson said he did not think his father knew Sioux sign language but he used some sort of signing to communicate with Coffee. Johnson laughed with gusto when he said, "I was ornery and it was a big game to dart around to watch Coffee and my father visit."

Jonas Holy Rock told his family that Coffee was with the body of Crazy Horse when it was removed from Camp Robinson the day Crazy Horse died. Coffee knew where Crazy Horse was buried but he swore never to reveal this location or he would be eliminated. When Mari Sandoz was researching her book on Crazy Horse she was attempting to determine the hero's physical characteristics so she turned to a friend, Eleanor Hinman, who had traveled the Pine Ridge and Rosebud Reservations doing much research on Crazy Horse. Eleanor had talked with persons who had seen him and she shared this information with Mari from her notes: "I have the honor to present to you Coffee and Black Elk, both cousins of Crazy Horse and said by the Indians to resemble him in person and in features." Coffee, the Indians thought, looked more like Crazy Horse than any other man living. Eleanor observed that he was slender, lightly built, of middle height, with a very light complexion. His narrow pointed face, straight nose, and long expressive eyes were well proportioned, but she felt he lacked the fire of his cousin's personality. She described Black Elk, whom she had met on the reservation in 1930, as darker and taller than Coffee, with the most expressive face she ever saw on any man. Hinman said, "For just that fraction of a second I saw Tashunkhe Witco reflected in his cousin's face as in a mirror."

Most of the stories about Crazy Horse's burial site center around the Manderson, South Dakota area within seven miles of the town of Wounded Knee and the 1890 mass gravesite. Years before, when I was helping my father with his book on burial sites of Sioux Nation chiefs, we had always wondered where Crazy Horse's parents might be buried. Father Thomas Simonds, at the Holy Rosary Mission north of Pine Ridge, suggested I check with the tribal census at Pine Ridge. At the office, a pleasant clerk by the name of Mary Bett told me that someone else had been working on a project similar to ours. She said, "I just read an article last week that some guy wrote telling about his experiences trying to find Crazy Horse. It is around here somewhere," and, within a few minutes, she had a copy for me to take along to read while we drove around the Pine Ridge Reservation.

On this trip, my wife and mother were accompanying me. My wife was driving as I sorted stories of Crazy Horse in the back seat of our Suburban. I was reading the article Mary Bett had given me, "Searching for Crazy Horse," by Fredrick Turner, published in *Men's Journal* magazine. Turner began by referencing the same green historical highway marker near Wounded Knee that had gotten my attention. Turner wrote that he'd heard stories of the parents of Crazy Horse bringing his remains along on the trek north from Nebraska in 1878, less than a year after his death, when the Oglalas were being resettled at Pine Ridge. Twelve years later, the place Turner suspected they had chosen for the burial would be etched in blood from the Wounded Knee Massacre.

When Turner had questioned a Manderson store owner about the burial of Crazy Horse, he reported that a change had come over her face. She'd recognized Turner who'd been in the area seven years earlier working on the centennial ceremony at Wounded Knee. His question seemed to hang in the air as they were having lunch together. Her black eyes ranged the shelves, and then she stopped and looked directly at Turner.

"Well," she said at last, "he's supposed to be buried up here. But he's wherever he needs to be." Turner knew he was not supposed to know where Crazy Horse was buried, nor even where anyone thought Crazy Horse was buried.

Turner arranged a meeting with two members of Crazy Horse's extended family (tiyospaye). Within minutes, it was clear that neither had any intention of telling Turner anything. One of them said, "I know the thing my mother told me, and that my grandmother told her, but I'm not going to tell it to you."

The store owner also said, "He's always been a mystery, and I have a deep, ingrained respect for him. It's because of who he was and what he stood for. He was a warrior for his people, and I think he saw a lot farther than anyone else of his time in terms of how things were going to go, how we were going to be treated and are still being treated. Other than this, I have no further comment."

She did tell Turner about the Native American, Yellow Hair, who had helped with a 1990 PBS documentary called *The Spirit of Crazy Horse*. Neither in that film, nor face-to-face in his office, did he speak directly about the strange man, Crazy Horse. Crazy Horse was still so charged with wakan (sacred power) that he was much too dangerous to talk about with the outside world. What Yellow Hair did talk about was that his people see Crazy Horse as a messiah who will come back and lead them to the resolution of all of their problems, which is unfortunate because essentially, that spirit of resolution must live in each of us, in our personal values, in how we conduct ourselves.

Yellow Hair concluded with these words:

To the white outsider, you sense the unspoken presence of an oral history of Crazy Horse running beneath the documented facts like an underground river. The spirit is strong, dark, and deep. It may not be meant to be reached. There were always things his vanquished people wished to keep to themselves. Crazy Horse had a tenacity to cling to his land and it is tradition that makes him one of the most mysterious and intriguing figures in the history of America.

Fredrick Turner tried to tap into that subterranean river. A tribal man lined up other family members for him to talk with, but the family said that, because of the monument and the beer, they don't talk about Crazy Horse. The monument issue, Turner supposed, centered around the fact that admission is being charged to visit the site where the monument was being carved in rock, but the chief's family and tribe will receive none of the proceeds. Turner also learned that there was a Crazy Horse beer on the market. The tribe was suing the brewing company because Crazy Horse would have detested having a beer named after him. He had always been vehemently against white people's alcohol.

That story brought back memories of my father who had once told me that the state patrolman in his area would never give him a ticket for speeding his white Grand Prix down the road on his way to tend a sick animal. "Doc, it is because we know you stopped drinking alcohol long ago," the man with the silver badge had told him.

Turner's article talked about a burly man storming into the tribal office where a meeting had been arranged and confronting him at point-blank range. "You're going to have to leave," the man told him. "I'm gonna give you twenty minutes to get off the reservation. If you don't, I'll put you in jail." The man looked at Turner's notebook and said, "I ought to take that from you," as he jabbed a forefinger at the pages. The man was the tribal sergeant at arms, and he told Turner, "If you speak his name again, I'll put you in jail."

Turner left, heading north down the road through the beautiful, treeless grasslands that led to Custer State Park where buffalo grazed on the knee-high grasses, just as they had in Crazy Horse's time when buffalo were his people's staff of life.

White Clay Creek runs into White River in this valley.

The sun was setting when I traveled down the road that evening, still sitting in the back seat while my wife drove and my mother sat in front with her. We were headed for the Nebraska border where our plans were to stay at Fort Robinson that night.

It was evident from his article that this Turner fellow was wondering what had happened back in the office. Had Crazy Horse somehow made it known that he wanted tribal authorities to throw him off the reservation? Was he visiting with the wrong people? Had he, perhaps, run into some of Red Cloud's old people? It had been Red Cloud who had actively conspired to bring about the imprisonment and death of Crazy Horse, and I suspected that the spirits were haunting Turner.

During the time on the Pine Ridge and Rosebud Reservations when I did research on Crazy Horse, I met many wonderful Native American people willing to share their stories. Gary Coats, a clinical psychologist who'd grown up in Mission, South Dakota, did alcohol abuse counseling on the Pine Ridge. He'd told me, "Cleve, you will not have a problem like Turner's if you are sincere, and it sounds like your work is a continuation of a wonderful adventure you started with your father. It is hard telling what Turner did to provoke the people, or else he just created some controversy for what he thought would make a story. Tell the people about yourself and they will understand what is guiding you."

I thought of Crazy Horse and the hawk's feather he wore for protection as part of his medicine. From the back seat, I stared at the backs of my wife's and mother's heads and then said, "You are my hawk's feather." They smiled and laughed. I silently hoped that my heart would push me in the direction where the eagles circle together, for there I might find Crazy Horse.

In the coming months, as I visited with many Lakota people, I knew I had flown in the gentle winds that lifted me to where the eagles circled.

At White Clay Creek

In his book, *Spotted Tail Folk*, George Hyde describes the events following the death of Crazy Horse. The United States government constructed and renovated agencies (now called reservations) along the Missouri River for the Sioux to live on. The Sioux did not want to relocate because it was three hundred miles away from their homeland and they did not like the Missouri River as it was a conduit for white steamboats and travelers they wished to avoid. They would just as soon stay in northwestern Nebraska. The government thought it would be easier to ship supplies to them if they relocated on the Missouri. The situation reached a critical point when Crazy Horse was killed at Fort Robinson.

In an attempt to solve the problems, the government ordered the Sioux chiefs to Washington for a conference. President Rutherford B. Hayes told the chiefs that if they would move as close as they could to the Missouri during that winter, the agencies would be able to return west the following summer to choose their own agency sites, as long as the site was within the reservation. The Sioux felt they could live with that promise through the winter.

The Oglala and Brulé tribes left their northwest Nebraska agencies during the last week in October 1877. The columns made up of each tribe's members extended for miles. Some rode on horseback, many walked, the old and disabled rode in government wagons. Cowboys drove accompanying herds of cattle which were the Indians main food supply.

Spotted Tail marched from his agency on the West Beaver Creek, ten miles south of the White River, and then went east. Red Cloud's group went down the valley of the White River.

Most of the Indians with Spotted Tail were terribly upset about being forced to move to the Missouri and, near the head of Wounded Knee Creek, they broke away from the column and fled northward. With them went Crazy Horse's old father and mother, carrying the bones of their great son. Somewhere in the Wounded Knee area, on the present Pine Ridge Reservation, the parents are believed to have hidden the bones. They then returned to Spotted Tail's column on its way three hundred miles east to the Missouri River.

In *The Killing of Crazy Horse*, Thomas Anderson reported that after Crazy Horse died, "his body was placed in a coffin and sent early the next morning to his village. Then the Indians moved to the Missouri in the fall of 1877. They took his remains with them, over two hundred miles. The following year they were carried back, when the Tribe returned to their present location. They finally buried them with great secrecy somewhere near the mouth of White Clay Creek. But the exact spot no white man knows."

On December 3, 1877, the *Omaha Daily Bee* reported that "the start of the trip to the Missouri River was made from the Red Cloud Agency which was, at that time, on the White River north of the Spotted Tail Agency. Things were going smoothly until about 2,800 Indians joined the Red Cloud group from the Spotted Tail Agency which was to the south. They brought with them the body of the late Chief Crazy Horse which they buried near the mouth of White Clay Creek.

"The Indians from the Spotted Tail Agency did not appear very friendly towards those of the Red Cloud agency, and were bent upon mischief. They tried to burn the prairie on both sides of the marchers. They were not satisfied, and they began to leave us in large numbers, and go to the north. Touch the Clouds was sent out to bring them in, but he could do nothing. Out of the 2,800 that had joined the march, only 30 or 40 lodges stayed with the march."

If indeed Crazy Horse's parents did bury his body near White Clay Creek, it is easy to understand why they chose that area. In 1870, the Spotted Tail Agency had a winter camp at the mouth of White Clay Creek, so this was familiar ground for Crazy Horse's people.

In an interesting coincidence, sometime after 1878, No Water lived near the mouth of White Clay Creek. It had been No Water's wife that Crazy Horse had run off with for a few days, only to be followed by a jealous No Water who shot and wounded him in the face. The two had been long-time adversaries. It is interesting to consider that No Water would settle in the area where White Clay Creek runs into the White River, a place where the spirit of Crazy Horse might easily haunt him.

SIOUX LANDS BROKEN UP, 1889

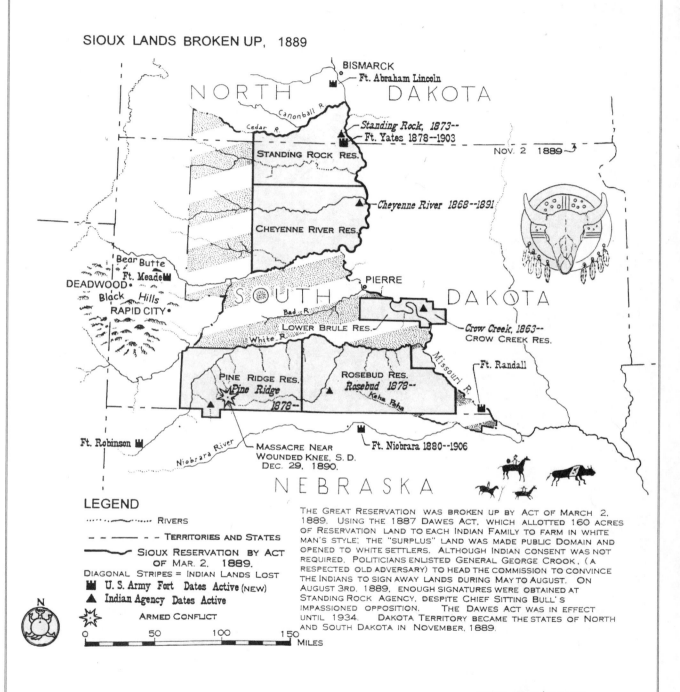

BISMARCK
Ft. Abraham Lincoln

N O R T H   D A K O T A

Canonball R.

Cedar R.

Standing Rock, 1873--
Ft. Yates 1878--1903

NOV. 2 1889

STANDING ROCK RES.

Cheyenne River 1868--1891

CHEYENNE RIVER RES.

Bear Butte
Ft. Meade
DEADWOOD•
Black Hills
RAPID CITY •

S O U T H   D A K O T A

PIERRE

Bad R.
LOWER BRULE RES.
White R.

Crow Creek, 1863--
CROW CREEK RES.

Ft. Randall

Missouri R.

PINE RIDGE RES.
Pine Ridge
1878--

ROSEBUD RES.
Rosebud 1878--

Kaha Paha

Ft. Robinson

Niobrara River

MASSACRE NEAR
WOUNDED KNEE, S.D.
DEC. 29, 1890.

Ft. Niobrara 1880--1906

N E B R A S K A

LEGEND

········· RIVERS

— ·· — ·· — TERRITORIES AND STATES

———— SIOUX RESERVATION BY ACT
OF MAR. 2. 1889.

DIAGONAL STRIPES = INDIAN LANDS LOST

▥ U. S. ARMY FORT DATES ACTIVE (NEW)

▲ Indian Agency DATES ACTIVE

✶ ARMED CONFLICT

N

0   50   100   150
MILES

THE GREAT RESERVATION WAS BROKEN UP BY ACT OF MARCH 2.
1889. USING THE 1887 DAWES ACT, WHICH ALLOTTED 160 ACRES
OF RESERVATION LAND TO EACH INDIAN FAMILY TO FARM IN WHITE
MAN'S STYLE; THE "SURPLUS" LAND WAS MADE PUBLIC DOMAIN AND
OPENED TO WHITE SETTLERS. ALTHOUGH INDIAN CONSENT WAS NOT
REQUIRED, POLITICIANS ENLISTED GENERAL GEORGE CROOK, (A
RESPECTED OLD ADVERSARY) TO HEAD THE COMMISSION TO CONVINCE
THE INDIANS TO SIGN AWAY LANDS DURING MAY TO AUGUST. ON
AUGUST 3RD, 1889, ENOUGH SIGNATURES WERE OBTAINED AT
STANDING ROCK AGENCY, DESPITE CHIEF SITTING BULL'S
IMPASSIONED OPPOSITION.   THE DAWES ACT WAS IN EFFECT
UNTIL 1934.   DAKOTA TERRITORY BECAME THE STATES OF NORTH
AND SOUTH DAKOTA IN NOVEMBER, 1889.

27

The Rosebud Reservation

It may have been that Crazy Horse's parents traveled with their son's body on a route that went from the Spotted Tail Agency near Camp Sheridan to the area that is now Manderson, South Dakota, and then on to the Rosebud area. Three theories have been proposed that put the burial site on, or near, the Rosebud Reservation.

West of the Rosebud

William J. Bordeaux, author of *Custer's Conqueror*, was the son of Louis Bordeaux, the official interpreter for the Spotted Tail Agency and Camp Sheridan. William was born in 1884 on the Rosebud Reservation and later married Wicakpi-Oumini, the great-granddaughter of Chief White Thunder. William's grandfather, James Bordeaux, was a native of France who emigrated to the Platte River area in Nebraska where he established a trading post. James later built an outpost from the main station near the town of Chadron, Nebraska, where he married the sister of Chief Swift Bear. William's father, Louis, had been allowed to stay with Crazy Horse the night he was mortally wounded. Louis was responsible for making hourly reports to General Jesse Lee. Louis Bordeaux was also present on Beaver Creek when Crazy Horse's body was brought back to be placed upon the branches of a sepulcher tree for a night and a day.

William Bordeaux questioned Crazy Horse's nearest of kin and his close associates as to where Crazy Horse's body had been buried. Those questioned were reluctant to reveal the location. According to William, one of the relatives he questioned was Crazy Horse's sister, Mrs. Joe Clown. Her home on the Cheyenne River Reservation was near the banks of the Morreau River in Dewey County, South Dakota. There was no doubt she knew the exact location of her brother's secret grave, but when questioned, she declared, "We buried him where no one will ever find him." She then handed William Bordeaux a letter she had received with a postmark from Wounded Knee, South Dakota. The letter, written in the Sioux language, stated that the grave of her brother had been discovered, and that she should come at her earliest convenience. After reading the letter, William asked her if the letter told the truth. She replied curtly, "No, my brother's grave is nowhere near, or in, the Pine Ridge area."

Information Bordeaux gathered from eye-witnesses' accounts of the eastward trek of the Sioux following Crazy Horse's death indicated that the warrior's remains were laid to rest somewhere in the western part of Todd County, South Dakota, in the area of Rosebud, South Dakota.

Lakota people who are familiar with Crazy Horse's genealogy tell me that Mrs. Joe Clown was probably a cousin to Crazy Horse, not his sister. Often, in Lakota, a term like "brother" may mean a blood cousin, or even a close friend. "Brother" speaks to a closely bonded relationship. Even today, a funeral director who serves the Lakota reservations of South Dakota told me it is often difficult to write obituaries and to establish who are true blood brothers and sisters.

Up Scabby Creek

The United States government decided to move the Oglala and Brulé bands out of the Camp Sheridan area in northwest Nebraska to a location 200 miles east, on the tributary of Ponca Creek which runs into the Missouri River near Niobrara, Nebraska. The story of this relocation was of great interest to me. The ranch land along Ponca Creek was where my father had practiced veterinary medicine. This was an area I knew well, where I'd grown up going on calls with my father to tend sick animals.

William Bordeaux reports that, on the eastward trek, a pony travois carrying the corpse of

Chief Swift Bear—he was at the killing of Crazy Horse.
Photo courtesy Nebraska State Historical Society.

Crazy Horse was seen bringing up the rear of the column, quite distant from the rest of the caravan. At a point west of the Little White River on Scabby Creek, the caravan made camp for the night. The following morning, when the journey was resumed, the travois was not in evidence, and it is the opinion of many Indians that the body was disposed of somewhere in the vicinity of Scabby Creek in Todd County. The exact location of this place still remains one of the secrets of the Sioux.

Near the end of July 2000, I was headed down the road with my wife, Mony, for a few days of relaxation. We had been planning a kayak trip on the Dismal River in the Sandhills. Since the afternoon was cool and cloudy with an occasional mist in the air, it did not seem like a day my wife would enjoy kayaking. I told her, "You know, I think I would like to head for the Buechel Memorial

Early tepee village on the Rosebud Reservation.

Lakota Museum at St. Francis on the Rosebud Reservation." This was about ninety miles north of our original destination.

"Mony," I said, "last year down at Crow Dog's Paradise when we stopped to watch a Sun Dance, remember the guy named Lloyd One Star who told us that it was at the St. Francis Museum that there were some things that belonged to Crazy Horse? He told us that they were on display at certain times of the year."

We headed for St. Francis and found the director of the museum, Charmayne Young, to be a hospitable host who was preserving, protecting and promoting Lakota ancestry. I noticed a calendar hanging in the museum explaining the rotation of the Lakota artifacts displayed in the collection. The building that houses these artifacts has increased in size four times under the direction of Charmayne. She told us that the Crazy Horse belongings were on display at the time and she showed us an eagle feather that Crazy Horse had given to Alex Water who kept it for thirty-eight years. The Battle Medicine Feather was given to Father Buechel in 1915.

Some of the other items that had belonged to Crazy Horse, which were now at the museum, were: a war whistle made from the wing bone of an eagle with a buckskin thong and eight hawk wing feathers attached to it, a stone club with a wooden handle encased in rawhide with sinew sewing that was given to Father Buechel in 1918, a charm buffalo horn that

Ceremonial lodge on Rosebud Reservation.

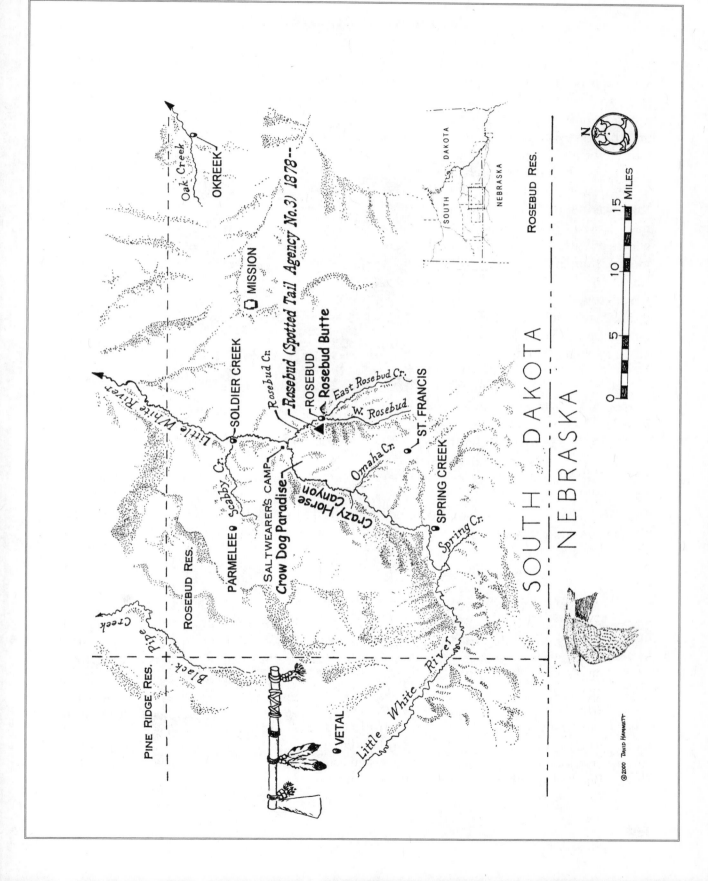

OKREEK

Oak Creek

MISSION

SOLDIER CREEK

Rosebud Cr.

Rosebud (Spotted Tail Agency No.3) 1878—

ROSEBUD

Rosebud Butte

East Rosebud Cr.

W. Rosebud

ST. FRANCIS

Little White River

PARMELEE

Scabby Cr.

SALTWEARER'S CAMP

Crow Dog Paradise

Omaha Cr.

SPRING CREEK

Crazy Horse Canyon

Spring Cr.

ROSEBUD RES.

PINE RIDGE RES.

Pipe Creek

Black

VETAL

Little White River

SOUTH DAKOTA

NEBRASKA

SOUTH DAKOTA

NEBRASKA

ROSEBUD RES.

N

0   5   10   15

MILES

© 2000 DAVID HAMMETT

hung around the horse of Crazy Horse while he was hunting buffalo, (used to make sure the horse was not afraid of the buffalo), an old saddle with the bow made of deer horn (wooden sideboards were on the saddle that were covered with buckskin), a horse necklace that hung around a horse's neck during battle (contained a sacred herb for the protection of the horse), and the horn of an antelope used as a medicine bag that was carried on the left side of the body. Crazy Horse had made this and given it to White Deer. Then Wooden Leg inherited it.

In 1915 Father Buechel received a war shirt made of muslin that was painted with designs in red, yellow, and green. It was adorned with birds and crescent moons, human hair locks and dyed horsehair locks with the ends wrapped with sinew and dyed red. Small eagle feathers were sewn along the sleeve seams. This was given to old man Red Sack by Crazy Horse who had worn it. The tufts of horsehair count the number of horses taken from enemies he killed.

Scabby Creek where the creek runs into the Little White River.

Charmayne told me that the story that had been handed down about this war shirt was that Crazy Horse was given this shirt by He Dog, Kicking Bear, and Short Bull after Crazy Horse lost his Shirt Wearers Shirt when he eloped with No Water's wife, Black Buffalo Woman. He Dog had been honored as a Shirt Wearer at the same time as Crazy Horse. He Dog said, "This honor was like becoming a chief." After Crazy Horse lost his shirt, these men felt for him and bestowed this new shirt on him because of his exemplary war leadership skills.

After Charmayne showed us the Crazy Horse sacred objects, my wife and I asked her and her husband to join us at the Rosebud Casino for dinner. She gladly accepted and we met that evening.

I had explained to Charmayne that I was interested in stories about Crazy Horse and what happened to him after he was killed at Camp Robinson. I had heard his parents were buried in the area. She told me that she lived west of the community of Soldier Creek, which is located in Crazy Horse Canyon west of Mission, South Dakota. One evening she was coming home from a night college class and as she approached home, a large orange globe rose in the sky just southwest of the Soldier Creek community, which is where the mouth of Scabby Creek is. Her daughter was with her and she did not want to startle her so she said nothing as she watched in silence, wondering if she was seeing something that she could not explain, or if maybe she was only seeing a reflection that no one else could see. A few minutes later her daughter asked, "Do stars go up? Do they move upwards?"

Scabby Creek.

A few days after the huge glowing ball disappeared, she heard from two individuals that the sound of someone singing in Lakota could be heard in the valley southwest of Soldier Creek. Charmayne said, "I remembered faintly hearing this singing that night, too. I could not say this was some supernatural occurrence. I had heard it. It was just unusual. I told my husband, Bruce, about this, and he related it to his stepfather, Louie Leader Charge Sr., whose grandfather was Chief Rain In the Face. Louie had practiced the complete avoidance of taboo with me, and I was not allowed to talk about the supernatural with him. It would be proper for me to talk with my husband about the singing and the glowing light, who could then discuss it with Louie. Louie told my husband that this is the canyon where Crazy Horse was buried and that is why these things happen." I asked Charmayne if she felt the spirit of Crazy Horse spoke to her that night when she saw the glowing ball. She said, "It would be unfair to say that his 'spirit speaks to us.' By doing so, we would allude to the thought that we would claim to have powers to communicate with those whose presence is missed today. If a spiritual leader would make that statement there would be great credibility. A spiritual leader is endowed with powers unknown to commoners such as myself."

From Omaha Creek to Rosebud Creek

In Mari Sandoz's chapter on the burial of Crazy Horse in her book, *Hostiles and Friendlies*, she quoted from the writings of Mrs. Susan Bettelyoun, born in 1857, the daughter of James Bordeaux, the French fur trapper, and Red Cormorant Woman, a Brulé Lakota of the Red Top Lodge band. Susan's uncle was Chief Swift Bear. Her brother was Louis, whose son, William, authored *Custer's Conqueror*.

Susan Bettelyoun was angered by the way white scholars had presented the times in which she had lived. She wrote, "I have read many books on Indian lore, none of which have entirely reflected the facts as I know them from my own observations and from statements made to me by my parents and other relatives. The reading of these books has stirred my ire, because of a lack of understanding of the Plains Indians by the authors." Susan was determined to set the record straight.

In September 1998, I stopped for the evening at the Rosebud Casino north of Valentine, Nebraska, and checked into the casino motel about 11:00 P.M. I told the women at the desk that I was working on a book about the possible burial sites of Crazy Horse. One of the women

On the way to Chief Iron Shell's grave, Doc Walstrom tells his wife and grandsons Woody and Wally about Chief Red Hill's grave that is five miles east of Carter, SD.

introduced herself as Johnna Bordeaux; her husband was a descendant of Susan Bordeaux Bettelyoun. She told me Susan had written a book titled, *With My Own Eyes*, and that I might find some information in it that would be of interest to me on the subject of Crazy Horse. She told me that Bettelyoun had also written about where Crazy Horse's parents were buried.

"You are just the gal I've been looking for," I told her. "My father and I always did wonder what happened to Crazy Horse's parents after their son died."

Johnna's father-in-law was Lionel Bordeaux, whose mother was an Iron Shell. It had been some of Chief Iron Shell's people who prepared and cared for the body of Crazy Horse. That night, it seemed like much more fun to visit with Johnna than to play blackjack at the casino.

I told Johnna that I'd visited Chief Iron Shell's grave in September 1993 with my father and mother, my sons, Woody and Wally, and my wife, Mony. We had accidentally turned onto the wrong fork in the road as we were traveling on the Rosebud Timber Reserve. We'd taken a left instead of a right and found ourselves on a

Chief Iron Shell's grave lies on a high plain above Omaha Creek.

dead-end path by a small lake in a deep canyon. The trail had taken us to a desolate, but very peaceful, place with tall pines all about us.

On the shore of the lake were two fellows drinking cans of Budweiser and beside them was a little green pickup with west coast license plates. One of the guys was probably in his twenties and the other I gauged to be in his fifties. Something in this picture did not look quite right. Maybe it was their steely eyes and the west coast plates that made me uneasy. One guy abruptly approached our vehicle, so I quickly got out and told him we'd taken a wrong turn and that we were looking for the Iron Shell Cemetery. He had no idea where it was either but he seemed quite relieved to find out what I wanted to know. They seemed like nice enough guys in their own state of harmony. I drove us away from the place in deep sand and as I gunned the accelerator up a steep grade, Mony said that she was glad to be on her way. I said I was sure I'd seen those two on *Unsolved Mysteries* two weeks ago. "They were jewel thieves," I said. I think the excitement of that idea prevented the boys from getting car sick.

Of all the Native American cemeteries we visited, the Iron Shell Cemetery was my father's favorite. He liked the tall pines and the deep canyon on the west end of the cemetery just a few feet from Chief Iron Shell's grave. When we were there, the grave was decorated with colored streamers. Johnna and the other night clerk at the Rosebud Casino Motel told me that yellow streamers on the grave represented the east, red the south, white the great north, black the west, blue the sky, and green stood for Mother Earth.

I told Johnna about my blackjack playing days when I was attending college in San Francisco. A schoolmate of mine, Jon Padden, now my business partner, and I would drive to Reno and we'd camp out, sleeping in the back of my little pickup. One time the country road we chose seemed to be rather busy. Later we discovered that we'd been camping very near the entrance to Mustang Ranch, the infamous brothel. It was a well-traveled road that didn't afford us much sleep. When we couldn't get to sleep, we drove back into Reno at about 3:00 A.M. where we played blackjack. We could hear sirens outside and the dealer told us that the bank across the street from the casino had just been robbed. Later we learned the robbers had gotten away with several million dollars.

The dealer was a lady I guessed to be in her late forties, with hair done up in a French-style bun. She had jade green fingernails and rings on each finger. She had the kind of eyelashes that seemed to disturb our playing cards when she blinked. I said something to our dealer that I meant as a compliment, and she replied tersely, "You have had it." This was back in the days when dealers put the discards from cards played under the deck of cards that had not been played—all held in the same hand, rather than dealing out of a container about the size of a shoe box. I lost thirty-three out of the next thirty-four hands dealt. I'd heard about card mechanics who could manipulate the deck to deal whatever they wished, and I thought I'd be able to tell if that's what was happening, but I couldn't detect anything unusual. In a normal night, using our blackjack system, we calculated we usually made about a dollar an hour, but not that night.

I told Johnna that, even though the Rosebud Casino deals from a box, I felt I'd probably have better luck visiting with her and the other clerk that night. Many white guys lose money at the tables, therefore helping the Indians get money to buy back their land. I think Crazy Horse would be delighted to know that! As it turned out, Johnna was quite knowledgeable, and she introduced me to a number of helpful people. I told her that when I'd helped my father with his book, he always found the most interesting information at the Lakota casinos, not in museums or archives.

When I read *With My Own Eyes*, it said that Crazy Horse's body had been given back to his old parents. Author Susan Bettelyoun wrote:

They sat on a hill opposite the garrison for two or three days. When orders came from the Department to move the Indians to the Ponca Agency so annuities could be issued to them, the journey was started. The soldiers escort went first and the Indians and their travois and the half-breed families in their wagons followed. The stops were made about every ten miles; it took about a month to reach the Ponca Agency. It was getting cold then.

Crazy Horse's niece, Mrs. De Noyer, told Susan that the body of Crazy Horse was hidden in the cliffs of Eagles Nest Butte. "The old father and others came with the rest of our people on the way back to Rosebud in the spring. They lived with the Salt Users who camped two miles northwest of the agency. It was here that the mother died two years after Crazy Horse's death and Old Man Crazy Horse died three years after his son's death. They were both buried there along the banks of the Rosebud Creek. It has been said the bones of Crazy Horse were brought back and buried beside his parents."

Johnna told me she had heard stories about Crazy Horse's parents being buried along the banks of the Little White River near where Rosebud Creek flows into the Little White. She also

Mouth of Rosebud Creek where it runs into the Little White River with Salt Users Camp in the background.

said she'd heard talk about Crazy Horse being buried close to his parents. Johnna had once lived close to the camp of the Salt Users. [*Historical literature often refers to the Salt Users, but the band was actually called the Wears the Salt Band. They were so named because, for ceremonies, they wore red paint, and when the one in charge of the ceremony mixed the bowl of red, he would add more salt instead of more red paint, and thus they were the Wears the Salt Band. Terry Gray at the Rosebud Archival Office told me the Lakota people traveled on a well-worn trail to New Mexico to find salt. The salt trade was recorded in the winter counts, which were simple pictures of the biggest events of the year that the tribal historian sketched on an animal skin. One skin would often record a hundred years of events or more.*]

In August 1999, I was attending a Sun Dance at Crow Dog's Paradise a few miles up from the mouth of Rosebud Creek. I was visiting with Lloyd One Star, a chief on the reservation. He is also a descendant of Chief Iron Tail, whose profile graces the Indian-head nickel. I asked Chief One Star if he had ever heard where Crazy Horse's parents were buried, and if it might be near the mouth of the Rosebud. He replied that the old-timers told him that the parents were buried on the banks of nearby Omaha Creek. Chief Iron Shell was buried on a cliff high above the canyon ridge of Omaha Creek.

Later that same day, I wandered in the area of many tents and tepees and struck up a conversation with Christine Red Bear. I found out that she was a sister of Chief Leonard Crow Dog, who was giving the Sun Dance. I told her I knew her sister, Dinah Crow Dog who had been very helpful in guiding my father in his work recording information on Sioux chiefs. The Iron Shell and Crazy Horse families had migrated together. It was the Iron Shell family that had helped to prepare the body of Crazy Horse for the death scaffold. She told me that after Crazy Horse was killed, while the parents were traveling to their new agency on the Missouri, they camped at a spring close by the area of this Sun Dance. Because of that, this canyon was called Crazy Horse Canyon.

Eagles Nest Butte

Eagles Nest Butte, where Crazy Horse's bones may have lain for a winter when his parents traveled east, is just south of Wanblee, South Dakota. The first time I tried to find that place was in August 1998 when it had been raining intermittently. It was a cool August late after-

noon; the clouds were thick and the ground was saturated. I could not find this butte. When I returned two months later, I saw it clearly from a distance, and I could not help but marvel over the fact that Mother Nature could so easily make this giant vanish from sight. On this trip, the spirits allowed me to see the awesome sight, visible from as far away as thirty miles.

Eagles Nest Butte is sacred to the Lakota. In his book, *The Sioux*, Sioux historian Royal B. Hassrick tells about a sacred ceremony performed on the butte:

Eagles Nest Butte.

> In the old days, Black Horse hiked to the summit and cleaned out a vision pit; a covered hole to the north, large enough for a man to rest in. The pit was lined with a bed of sage. His friend, Horn Chips, set up sticks with tobacco offerings and colored banners at the four sides. Around the perimeter of the pit many tiny tobacco offerings had been strung up to satisfy the gods, each tied in a bundle made of a bit of flesh from Black Horse's forearms and thighs. When the site was prepared, Horn Chips descended the butte leaving Black Horse standing alone holding the stem of his sacred pipe to the rising sun. All day he stood there looking for a vision. As the

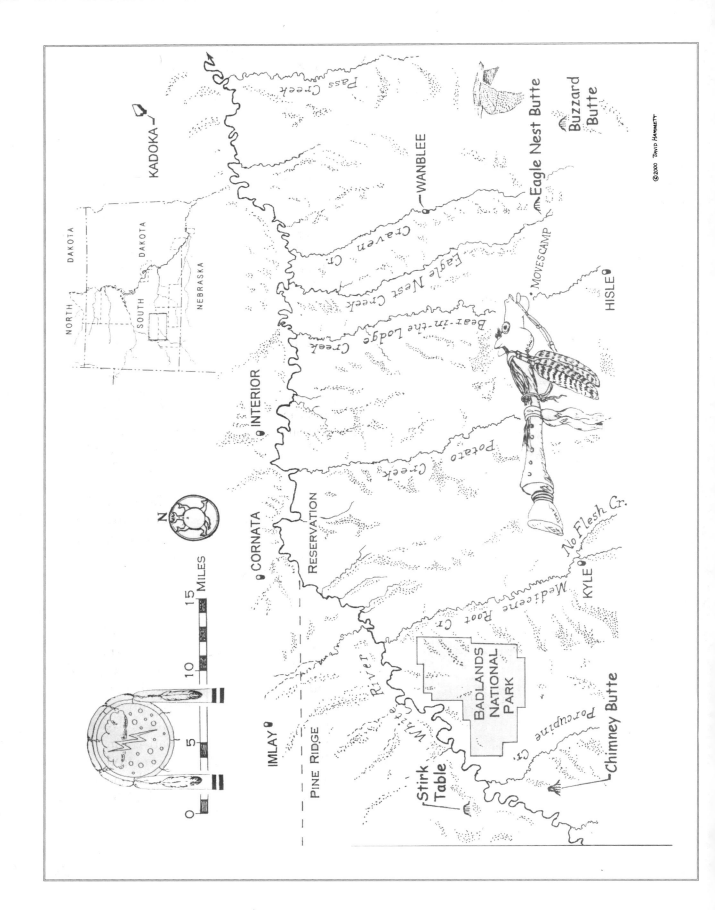

© 2000 DAVID HAMMETT

sun reached its high point, Black Horse slowly turned, raising the pipestem toward the sky. When the sun finally set in the west, Black Horse stood facing it with his pipestem lowered in its direction. When darkness came, he remained facing the west. The owls were hooting and the entire hill shook and voices called from the sky. When the moon was high, Black Horse entered the pit and lay on the bed of sage.

Long before dawn, Black Horse arose and faced the east, and a voice came to him from the sky, saying, "What is it you want, Black Horse? Why do you stand here like this?" Black Horse answered that he wanted to become a medicine man to cure his people. The voice replied, "You are going through the ceremony which not everyone can do. There are only a few men chosen."

When day began to break, Black Horse heard another voice calling to him, saying, "You have come to be a friend to nature's animals." As Black Horse looked up, there was an eagle above him to which he said, "Grandfather, I came here to be your servant." And the eagle said, "You have undertaken to live a life that is difficult." And with that, the eagle flew away.

Black Horse realized that he was in another world. He heard an aged voice from the north telling him, "Grandson, the birds and animals on earth will hear you when you ask anything of them. If you are calling from the depths of earth, your voice will be heard and your thoughts answered. Should you receive gifts from someone you have cured, you shall not keep them, but give them to someone else. Be kind to all men and animals and do nothing to harm your families. Now, return to earth."

Even today, offerings are made to the gods on this mound. When I hiked this butte, streamers and tobacco offerings were seen fluttering in the wind as the sun was resting in preparation for another day. On the east side of Eagles Nest Butte is a lone butte where spotted eagles once nested and is a site once used to catch eagles. Lore tells that the largest eagle ever seen by anyone was spotted in this place.

Bordeaux Family

Six months after I first visited with Johnna Bordeaux, she came to a lecture that I gave at Sinte Gleska University in Mission, South Dakota, where I described how my father and I gathered stories about the Sioux people. Johnna's father-in-law, Lionel Bordeaux, was the president of the university. That evening, Johnna and her husband, Brian, joined our family for dinner at the Rosebud Casino. My son Wally enjoyed listening to Brian who, with great affection, told about his ancestors who had come to this country from France in the early 1800s to make their way as fur trappers. The first Bordeaux brothers both married Native Americans.

In the course of the evening's conversation, Brian discovered that we were from Marysville, Kansas, and I noticed that his eyes became smaller and the skin on his handsome face became tight. He told me about his brother, Shawn, who, until recently, had lived near

Powhattan, Kansas, about an hour's drive from Marysville. Shawn's wife had been shot and killed in a drive-by shooting at their home on November 21, 1997.

Not two months later, when I was back at Sinte Gleska University, I met Shawn Bordeaux when I stopped at an office on campus trying to find some people I'd previously met there. I introduced myself before asking for directions, and quickly learned that the nice-looking man I was talking to was Shawn. He'd moved the four hundred miles from Powhattan back to the Rosebud to work at the college close to where he'd grown up. I asked him if he felt like telling me about his wife's tragic accident. I know that one never really gets over a loss of that sort, but I hoped that talking about what happened might help move his grieving toward healing, a process that often requires encouragement.

Johnna, Brian and Shawn Bordeaux.

Shawn told me that he had been working as head of operations at the Golden Eagle Casino, and that his wife, Jodie, supervised the slot machine department. He related the events of that evening in a letter he wrote me:

> It was shortly after midnight, and Jodie and I were sitting in the living room with our two dogs watching television. All of a sudden, I heard a popping noise coming from above and behind my head. I thought it was coming from the light bulb in the lamp behind my chair. There was a brief pause, and I turned to look at the lamp and winced as I saw what I thought was smoke coming from the lamp. I didn't know at the time that it was dust from the bullet that had come through the wall. The popping continued, sounding like someone had lit a twenty-pack of firecrackers. I kept expecting glass to fly from the bulb, so I turned away and ducked my head down. My dogs jumped and ran into the kitchen and dining room area. Jodie and I simultaneously stood up and looked at each other, then I followed the dogs to the kitchen and she ran into the bedroom. Once I got into the kitchen, my dogs began to turn in frantic circles. I opened the kitchen door and let them outside, then I proceeded back through the house calling to Jodie, asking if she was OK. I saw that she was lying in the bedroom near the doorway. She had been struck once in the top of her head. As I dialed 911, I noticed that the wall above the phone was riddled with bullet holes. Eleven shots had been fired into our home. Jodie was six-and-a-half months pregnant with our first baby girl who we had already named Jordan Shay. I lost my wife and child that night. It was a week before Thanksgiving.

Shawn and Jodie had been married for two years. Shawn had earned his masters degree from the University of Nebraska, and his work at the casino was his first professional job.

Two months earlier, when my family and I visited with Brian Bordeaux over dinner, Brian told me that his brother Shawn would call the Kansas Bureau of Investigation every so often, but that nothing seemed to be getting done to find who was responsible for such an atrocity. Brian had asked me if I knew any law enforcement people who could possibly find out more about the case in hopes of resolving his brother's grief—even if the responsible people were never brought to justice. "Jodie's parents are also having a very difficult time," Brian explained. "She was their only child."

I'd thought to myself about the young people I've helped make funeral arrangements for, and how I have tried to help guide their parents while they were trying to deal with terrible tragedy. It has to be the toughest time of any parent's life. I have always prayed that I could do more to help than just provide a funeral where friends and relatives come to grieve.

I told Brian that I knew a man at the Kansas Bureau of Investigation who might be of some help. Every once in awhile there is a homicide or an unusual death in my area where the KBI are called in to investigate. From these experiences, I have come to know some of the KBI personnel. I told Brian the story of one of my first experiences with the KBI.

My phone rang early one Saturday morning. It was our janitor at the mortuary on the line; he was distraught and needed my help. The KBI had been there interrogating him since 6:00 A.M. regarding the murder and whereabouts of a person who had been missing for more than a year. Raymond Vogelsburg had been our janitor and helped us around the mortuary for somewhat more than a year. I told Brian about the time Raymond came to interview for his job. He was dressed in a three-piece suit and was neatly groomed. I knew he'd had some trouble in his past, but I also knew he was working hard at turning his life around. He had joined a church and was seeking guidance and understanding from the Lord. I hired him and he proved to be a very capable employee. I'd only wondered about him on one occasion, and that was when he had driven several hundred miles to western Kansas to pick up a person who had died while on vacation away from Marysville. Raymond drove most of the way in a terrible January blizzard. The driving hours were long and treacherous. When Raymond turned in his time sheet, he had added a five-dollar charge to us for a candle. When I asked him about this, he told me that driving conditions near Hays, Kansas, had been very icy. He was afraid that something bad might happen, so he stopped at Cathedral of the Plains just east of Hays. This is a large historic limestone Catholic church that towers above the flat Kansas prairie. At the Stations of the Cross, Raymond lit a candle and said he'd asked for safe passage. I reimbursed Raymond for the five dollars and felt it was a good investment.

On this Saturday morning, Raymond had been desperate as he told me, "I did not kill her. You got to believe me. You've got to come help me." Of course, I was not sure what he was talking about, so he explained that some psychic from ten miles south in Blue Rapids, Kansas, had told the KBI that a person who had been missing from the area, and presumed drowned in the river, had been placed in a cistern in Home City, Kansas. The cistern happened to belong to Raymond; it was located on one of his rental properties.

I wondered how I could help Raymond without creating too much of a scene. As a mortician in the area, I had no intention of showing up at the cistern before the proper authorities notified a funeral director. I was apprehensive about driving the five miles east of Marysville to Home City and being recognized. This could be an embarrassing situation. Raymond was desperate, so I did drive out to Home City, contacted a person I knew, and explained the situation. He understood why I was uncomfortable and he was willing to go over and relay a message to the nearby KBI agent telling him that I wanted to see him. When my friend returned, he told me there were frogmen coming up out of the cistern. He'd heard from the frogmen that there was no evidence of a human body. Only some unusual albino bullheads were found swimming in the deep water.

An hour later, the KBI agent came by our funeral home in Marysville. I told him point-blank that I did not think Raymond was the one they were looking for. I said that Raymond had been doing good work here, and that he was worried that he might be blamed for this tragedy. The KBI agent told me that Raymond was not a suspect. He went on to say that they had only been checking out a tip that the body in question could be located in a deep cistern in Home City. Raymond, he assured me, should not be worried about any allegations.

I told Brian Bordeaux that the "cistern who done it" case was never solved. "It is a situation somewhat like your brother Shawn's wife's murder. When circumstances warrant, that same KBI agent's path has crossed mine. I'll make a special effort to call his attention to your brother's case. The spirit of truth surfaces in strange ways."

That night, after Brian and Johnna headed home, I reflected on the depth of his brother's grief. Not knowing who had done this to his wife and unborn child increased his grief and it extended to the rest of the family. I had difficulty sleeping that night, and when I finally saw the rays of the morning sun, I saw a reflection of Shawn and his family, and also the family of Crazy Horse, that bled deeply into the gullies of the vast western prairie.

28

The Missouri River

There are at least five historians who suggest that Crazy Horse's parents carried their son's body with them on the trek from the Rosebud to the Ponca Agency located on the Missouri River between Verdel and Niobrara, Nebraska: George Hyde, Lieutenant William Philo Clark, Charles P. Jordan, Carroll Friswold reporting stories from He Dog and Luther Standing Bear.

On the Trek to the Missouri

In his 1961 work, *Spotted Tail's Folk*, George Hyde wrote that in 1876, the chiefs at the agencies had been bullied and coaxed into signing an unusually-worded agreement that the government thought would effectively restrain the Sioux. Suddenly, it appeared that the Indians had broken the cords with which an upset Congress had bound them. The Indians did not want to live on the Missouri.

Spotted Tail was being directed to the Ponca Agency on the Missouri, and Red Cloud had been sent upriver, much farther north, above the Great Bend at the mouth of Yellow Medicine Creek. It was certainly easier for the supplies the government furnished for the Indians to be brought in by steamboat to these port agencies, but the Sioux were stubborn and refused to go near the Missouri. Red Cloud formed his winter camp near the forks of the White River, seventy miles west of the agency to which he had been ordered. Spotted Tail wintered with his main camp on Rosebud Creek, well over one hundred miles from the agency to which he had been ordered. Rations and supplies for those Indian camps had to be hauled from the Missouri River during the winter, forcing the government to pay shockingly high rates for wagon transportation.

Spotted Tail's people were divided by quarreling and therefore some left the winter camp and went on to the Ponca Agency. Spotted Tail struggled through the winter and spring to prevent his people from becoming violent, knowing that an uprising would enrage the whites and cause serious trouble. He was trying desperately to prevent the government from getting control of his tribe. At the Ponca Agency, buildings were being put up at great expense. Local

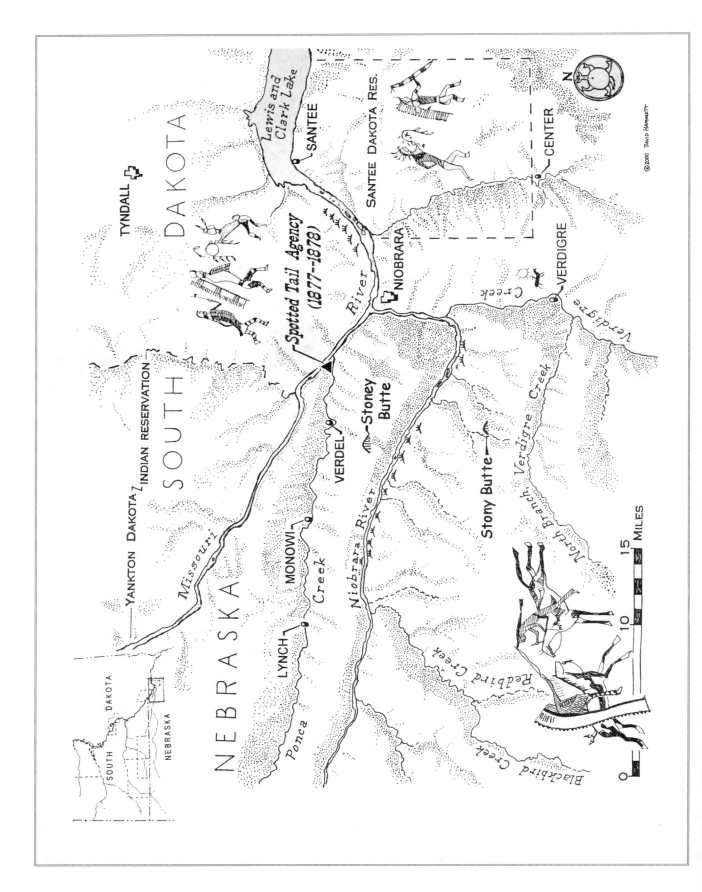

TYNDALL

Lewis and
Clark Lake

SANTEE

SANTEE DAKOTA RES.

CENTER

© 2000 DAVID HAMMETT

N

DAKOTA

SOUTH

Spotted Tail Agency
(1877–1878)

Missouri River

NIOBRARA

Verdigre Creek

VERDIGRE

YANKTON DAKOTA
INDIAN RESERVATION

Stoney
Butte

VERDEL

Stony Butte

MONOWI

Ponca Creek

Niobrara River

North Branch, Verdigre Creek

LYNCH

NEBRASKA

Redbird Creek

Blackbird Creek

SOUTH
DAKOTA

NEBRASKA

10   15   MILES

white men had been hired to cut wood and hay, since there were few Indians who would do or knew how to do that type of work. They had been hunters, not builders or farmers.

In George E. Hyde's *Red Cloud's Folk*, he states that groups of Brulé were slipping away from the camp at Rosebud Creek to go to the Missouri River near Ponca Creek. Spotted Tail did not wait for these groups to gain strength; he pulled up stakes on Rosebud Creek and

moved his big camp to Ponca Creek, closer to the agency. He ordered his soldiers to intimidate those who had left camp early. In June, he held a great Sun Dance on Ponca Creek to exhibit his power, which caused the disobedient faction to seek cover like small birds when the hawk is circling.

Lieutenant William Philo Clark also wrote an account of the Indians' movement to the Missouri. Clark was described as a very able officer who had the reputation of feeling and thinking like the Indians themselves. He was present at Fort Robinson when Crazy Horse went there

The site of the old Ponca Agency on Missouri River where Spotted Tail and his people came in 1878.

in May 1877. There had been much friction and backbiting among the Indians at that time. Rumors and innuendoes were everywhere, favoring one chief over another. Such things kept the Indians divided at a time when it would have been very difficult to deal with a united group. Clark had his share of dividing and conquering plans. He was known among the Indians as the Chief with the White Hat. He later wrote a book on Indian Sign Language.

In a letter dated November 7, 1877, Clark wrote to Carl Shurz, Secretary of the Interior:

Dear Sir:

    The movement of the two agencies can, I think, now be considered well started. Lt. Lee with Spotted Tail has without doubt passed the crossing of old Fort Randall Road at Wounded Knee Creek. I heard from him at the crossing of this road at Big White Clay—some of his Indians have joined us. As we came down stream we found at mouth of Beaver Creek over two hundred lodges mostly northern Indians— we call all Indians who came in last spring and surrendered and had never before lived at an Agency a northerner. They comprise Minneconjous, San Arc, Oglalas and some Brulé and number about two thousand people. These people are wild, stubborn, restless and still smarting under the bitter feelings engendered by the killing of Crazy Horse— whose remains they are I understand hauling along—so that even as a dead chief he exercises an influence for evil. Indian soldiers and scouts are watching them and I anticipate no particular trouble.

The head men here are working finely, particularly Young Man Afraid of His Horses who has great influence with both Agency and Northern Indians and used it only for good.

The Indians as a rule are poorly clad— old men and women and young children and sick people. Eight thousand people are congregated together make a march of this sort very trying and tedious. We have had very disagreeable weather, rain, sleet, snow and this has of course made wretched roads. You can imagine this column of savages eight miles long with its fifteen thousand ponies transporting this horde. When in camp a village of tepees a little over three miles long is made; and as we camp sometimes in this midst, and listen to their infernal drumming and singing late into the night, see their painted faces looking particularly savage and wild by the light of their camp fires civilization, and gentleness and kindness look very faint and far off.

I desire particularly to invite your attention to the fact that these Indians honestly believe they have only given away the Black Hills and that all the lands round them are still theirs. They claim and I think believe they were frightened and forced to give the Hills away. Again all the northern Indians claim that at the time the Black Hills were ceded they were in possession of this land, that it belonged to them, and as they express it, "Red Cloud or any other buffalo bulls who had been driven out of the herd had not right or authority to give away what did not belong to them." I have tried to explain this to them but find it worse than useless. One of my very best and most reliable Indian Scouts replied to me "I know this cannot be so the commissioners have lied about it. I was then a soldier on the Indian side and at that very Council I had one hundred young men there to see and know that nothing of the kind was done. We had ears and heard what was said."

I think everything is so well organized in the different bands that no lodges will leave us en route. The Agent and myself are working earnestly and will hurry up matters so much as possible but so large a body of Indians under such circumstances (many forced to walk) must from necessity move slowly but every effort will be made to reach some point near the new Red Cloud Agency as soon as possible.

I am Sir
With Great respect
Your obt. sv't
W.P. Clark
U.S.A.

A postscript was added by a government agent to explain part of Clark's letter:

The letter noted that the two agencies referred to are the Spotted Tail Agency being relocated on the old Ponca Reservation on the Missouri River ten miles west of Niobrara, and the Ponca Agency which had been relocated in Oklahoma during the summer of 1877. It must be that W. P. Clark and Jesse Lee both, I think, were escorting segments of Spotted Tails People independently. The Brulés straggled into Raymond Township, Knox County, from November to January.

It was exciting news to me to learn that Spotted Tail was leading his people to a site ten miles west of present-day Niobrara. This was close to where I'd grown up collecting turtles and tadpoles and raising many an orphaned raccoon along the Verdigre Creek. Nine miles downstream from Verdigre is the town of Niobrara.

In the late 1940s, my father had a ranch on bottomland along the Missouri ten miles west of Niobrara. I wondered if this was where Spotted Tail was headed and if Crazy Horse's parents were with this Brulé band.

That land my father owned had an old cabin on it that he used as a poker-playing retreat. I remember my mother decorating the place with trinkets that she hung from the ceiling. A big flood hit in the early 1950s leaving sandy deposits. Dad had to hire a Caterpillar and a ten-foot plow to bring up the rich dark soil that had settled under sand left when the flood receded. The Missouri River banks were cutting away the land so fast that Dad was afraid that within twenty years most of the ground would be gone.

He sold that land to a potato grower who needed a place to live. The guy who lived in that cabin had been an attorney. Dad told me the fellow had broken up with his girlfriend years earlier and wound up living like a hermit, hunting and fishing and growing vegetables. He would trap beaver and leave them lying, skinned, in his living room near his potbellied stove. His three dogs slept in the extra bedroom, going in and out of the bedroom window always left open for them. When we stopped by once a year, we'd still see the decorations my mom had put up for the poker games. I think they hung there for more than thirty years.

A duck club wanted to buy some of the potato farmer's land and in return, agreed to haul in rocks to stabilize the land from washing away at such an alarming rate. The potato grower made the deal with the duck club and rocks were hauled in to slow down the bank erosion. They also hauled in trailer homes for the duck club members. Today, there are at least fifty trailers that line the Missouri bank on the Nebraska side. It is unsightly. Visitors on the South Dakota side of the river were so repulsed by the view on the Nebraska side that they passed a law that there could be no trailer homes

Chief Spotted Tail.

along the banks of the Missouri. As yet, nothing has been done to beautify the Nebraska side of the river. Sometimes I have to wonder what Crazy Horse would have thought of all those aluminum, rubber-wheeled, weekend live-in boxes that white folks pulled down to the river's side.

Today, most of this bottom land, once the best farm ground in Knox County, is saturated with silt from Gavin's Point Dam, fifty miles downstream. When the dam was built in the 1950s, the reservoir was not supposed to back up to this area, but the Corps of Engineers did not calculate the sand the Niobrara River would bring from the Sandhills and dump into the Missouri at Niobrara. This pushed the water table up so high that the town of Niobrara had to be relocated in the mid-1970s. The present Niobrara golf course is where the town used to be situated. Golf games are periodically interrupted by high water. Instead of sand traps, there are water hazards. When that course was built, my brother-in-law, Bob Janovec, suggested naming the course Mosquito Flats. T-shirts depicting a mosquito attacking a golf ball were made up, but the local Chamber of Commerce didn't think it was a commercially appealing name, so it was dropped. Now, when locals hit the bar after a few rounds of golf, the talk is not so much about how their games went, but about the conditions of the hazards and what the slap count was at Mosquito Flats.

The state park at Niobrara also had to be relocated to a high hill that overlooks the Missouri River because of the result of the Corps of Engineers' miscalculation. Most of the farm ground where the old Ponca Agency once was—where Spotted Tail was sent—is no longer fit to be farmed or even camped on. The best camping spot now is in a cabin at the state park, high on a hill above the swamped campsite where Spotted Tail did not want to be. Or, there is also the Hill Top Motel in town which looks over the recently-constructed Standing Bear Bridge that spans the river east of Niobrara. The bridge was named for the great Ponca chief who had wanted to leave that area of the country because of Sioux harassment.

The Poncas had been requesting a move because of years of aggravation from the Sioux who lived up river. In 1876, a war party of about thirty or forty Sioux attacked the Ponca village, killing one Ponca and running off thirty head of ponies and three cattle. The Ponca were working in their corn and potato fields when the Sioux attacked. Summer war parties of Sioux were becoming more and more common. Ponca pony stealing was a big game to Brulé Sioux.

In Charles Mulhair's *The Ponca Agency*, he states that the small Ponca tribe had become content to live as farmers and they were always friendly with white settlers. Predictably, however, the residents of Niobrara were distressed by the frequent Sioux attacks on the Ponca and the other settlers on the Niobrara River, even though they wanted the Ponca to stay in order to increase their trade with the Indians. Governor Newton Edmunds of Yankton, South Dakota, was one of the commissioners who had made the original treaty with the Sioux in 1868. He instigated the removal of the Ponca, who at that time numbered 170, to Oklahoma. Whisky shops were being erected by nearby Yankton citizens to accommodate the much larger Spotted Tail band which was expected soon.

Since the Ponca Reservation was in Dakota Territory until the Nebraska-Dakota border was later changed, Dakota Governor Edmunds was also the superintendent of Indian Affairs in charge of the Ponca Reservation at the time. He was considering moving the Poncas and opening their lands for either white settlement or else the relocation of eight thousand to ten thousand Lakota, which would help the whisky shops of Yankton, South Dakota. The people of Niobrara and the local newspaper publisher and village attorney, Sol Draper, advised the

Ponca chiefs to stay near Niobrara, assuring them that they had title to their land. Governor Edmunds wanted them moved to Oklahoma. On March 31, 1877, Sol's newspaper editor, Ed Fry said, "These benevolent Yankton gentlemen want these outlaws (Spotted Tail's Sioux) settled upon our border that they may be able to have a big Indian trade."

Treaties in 1858 and 1865 greatly reduced the size of the original Ponca Reservation, yet the tribe remained peaceful. An 1868 error in the Treaty of Fort Laramie ceded Ponca lands to their enemy the Dakota Sioux, resulting in eight years of repeated raids against the Ponca and ending with the forced removal of the tribe to the new reservation.

In the spring of 1877, the Ponca left Niobrara and headed south across Nebraska. Every few days someone died of exposure or disease. Several children like White Buffalo Girl perished and were buried along their route that became known as the Ponca "Trail of Tears" (see map page 96). The people of Neligh, Nebraska, provided a Christian funeral for the child and an oak cross was erected at the gravesite. The father's last request was that the grave of his daughter would be honored and cared for by the people of the town.

In June, near the village of Milford, Chief Standing Bear's daughter, Prairie Flower, died of consumption. The townspeople gave her a Christian burial in the village cemetery. The Chief was so overwhelmed by the kindness of the ladies of Milford who had arranged the burial service he stated to those gathered at the grave that he wished to give up his Indian ways and become a Christian.

Later on the day of the funeral, the Ponca camp was devastated by a tornado that swept away supplies and wagon boxes. Some people were carried as much as three hundred feet through the air. When camp broke the following morning and the Ponca proceeded on their way, another child died. Remembering the kindness of the people of Milford, a tiny coffin was sent back to be interred in the grave with Prairie Flower.

In his book, *The Ponca Tribe*, James Howard states that ten days later the party reached Marysville, Kansas. More deaths had occurred along their way, and the dead were also all given Christian burials. Not far from Marysville, four families, homesick and discouraged, dropped out of the march and turned back toward Nebraska. When they were missed, Agent Howard rode back upriver to find them. By using patience and diplomacy, he succeeded in convincing them to rejoin the expedition and continue to the land reserved for Indians in the Oklahoma Indian Territory.

When Chief Standing Bear's people became destitute and starved in the Oklahoma Territory, the chief also wanted to return to the homeland. He and some thirty of his people started north to honor the dying wish of his oldest son who wanted to be buried in Nebraska. They were considered escapees by the army and were pursued. Eventually, they were arrested by General Crook for leaving the Indian Territory without permission and were taken to Omaha to stand trial.

Although Crook had been the arresting officer, he was sympathetic to Standing Bear, and secretly he hired Andrew Poppleton and J.L. Webster to act as Standing Bear's attorneys in a lawsuit against the federal government with regard to the Fourteenth Amendment—the rights of habeas corpus. Soon after, acting editor Thomas Tribbles, writing in the *Omaha Daily Herald*, took up the cause of the still-grieving father/chief.

On August 27, 1998, *The Niobrara Tribune* recalled:

> During the trial, Native Americans were established as persons under United States law. Judge Dandy, who presided over the trial, was won over when Standing Bear held out his hand and uttered these compelling words: "My hand is not the color of yours, but if I pierce it, I shall feel pain. The blood that will flow from mine will be the same color as yours. I am a man. The same God made us both." The arresting charges of being an escapee were dropped. Standing Bear was given liberty. Those words of Standing Bear's mark the first great statement of civil rights for Native Americans.

Chief Standing Bear of the Ponca with his wife and child.
Photo courtesy Nebraska State Historical Society.

After the charges were dropped, Standing Bear and most of his people went back to Niobrara, which is the homeland of the Ponca. Standing Bear died in the area and is buried high on a hill overlooking the mouth of the Niobrara.

In 1877, the land near Niobrara was where the United States government wanted Spotted Tail to establish his camp. Agency buildings were put up just a mile east of where my father's old poker cabin was later built. In *Spotted Tail's Folk*, George Hyde wrote that the chief set up camp within sight of the agency buildings. In some of my research I found evidence that my dad's old cabin just might have been one of those agency buildings. That land is now a duck hunter's paradise, and the backwater fishing is great. In the last one hundred years, the white man has first hunted deer there, then he has grown corn on the bottom land, and today the fish and ducks of the water-saturated land that was created by the downstream Gavins Point dam are his meals.

Charles Mulhair states that the Sioux were moved to this Niobrara area to facilitate the shipping of supplies by river, although Spotted Tail feared he could not control his people in a location so near the river because it gave them easy access to the steamboats with their plentiful supplies of firewater. If they agreed to spend the winter, the great white father promised to

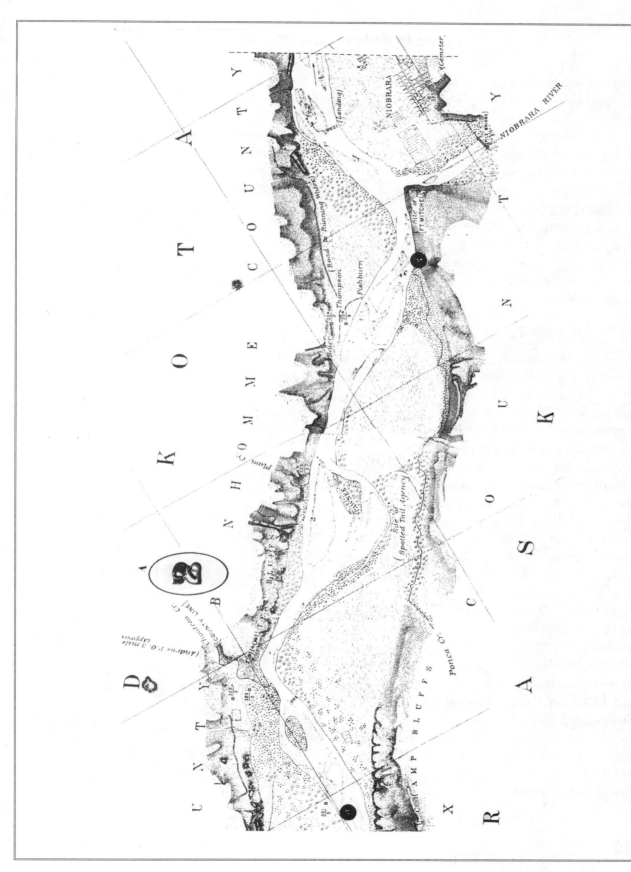

Original map sketched by J.N. Nicollet in 1839. Site of Spotted Tail Agency drawn on map after 1878.

consider another agency location for the Brulé Sioux that was more to their liking. Spotted Tail and his Sioux people stayed on the Niobrara Ponca land for the winter of 1877 and the spring of 1878.

In his article, "Killing of Crazy Horse," Thomas Anderson says it is possible that Crazy Horse's bones were taken to the Missouri River on this trek of Spotted Tail's people. Charles P. Jordan was a long-time licensed Indian goods trader from a post at the Rosebud Agency when Spotted Tail was chief. In 1877, he lived at the Red Cloud Agency. Jordan's mother, Nancy Blue Eyes, was full-blooded Oglala, and her eyes truly were blue.

In support of the notion that Crazy Horse's body was taken on the journey east to the Missouri, Jordan wrote to Doane Robinson in a letter dated June 26, 1902: "Crazy Horse was taken charge by the Indians and was put on a scaffold and guarded when the Indians were removed to the Missouri River in 1878. The body was carried along and I never learned nor could learn whatever became of it."

He Dog Recalls Times with Crazy Horse

From the edited collection of stories in *The Killing of Crazy Horse*, Carroll Friswold wrote about the friendship between Crazy Horse and He Dog. He Dog was reputed to have had a remarkable memory. Although he was a nephew of Red Cloud, he sided with Crazy Horse in the fighting in 1876. He belonged to the exclusive group of Shirt Wearers with Crazy Horse—a group of supreme men honored for their great deeds in war and their benevolence to the poor.

He Dog was elected a chief with Crazy Horse. To become a chief in the Lakota tribe, a man must possess these four attributes: bravery and outspokenness, ambition, honesty at all times, and kin to all creatures. Once elected, the chief is given buckskin clothing, an eagle feather, and a pipe with tobacco bags. Then one of the wise old men of the tribe gives the new chief a lecture about lessons that must be followed, along with oil from an animal to wash out the bad spirits if any of the lessons are broken.

According to Friswold's *The Killing of Crazy Horse*, the main points of the lecture to a new chief were: remembering that there are a lot of wasps and flies that sting, and being beware lest they sting and confuse him; remembering that there are a lot of dogs that will bark and defile his tent or place of dwelling, but he should not pay any attention to the dogs; re-

He Dog. Photo courtesy Nebraska State Historical Society.

membering that if one of his close kin is killed in battle, he must not stop to look lest he feel the need to retaliate (It is considered disgraceful for him to lose his temper); not being stingy with his food and feeding everyone who may visit him; offering tobacco to whomever visits him.

When Crazy Horse lay dying at Fort Robinson, Chief He Dog told William Philo Clark (White Hat), "You promised in a treaty that we both swore to, that nothing like this would happen again; that there would be no more blood shed." And with those words, He Dog slapped the officer across the face.

He Dog told his son, Eagle Hawk, that after Crazy Horse passed to the Happy Hunting Grounds, his people came for his body at the fort hospital. His father, his mother, and his wife put him on a travois hitched to a horse and started back to their camp. When they came to camp, Crazy Horse's parents held a sort of funeral service for him. All the Indian tribes had come together there. After this, the parents took their dead son with them to Chief Spotted Tail's camp. Later, a small frame house was built by the soldiers into which Crazy Horse's body was placed and guarded. This was the burial at Camp Sheridan.

These Indians (Crazy Horse's people) were to be taken to their reservation by groups. The tribe known as the Rosebud Sioux were to be taken along the Missouri River. When this tribe left, Crazy Horse's parents left with them, taking their dead son's body along. The Oglala Sioux left for Holy Butte at another location along the Missouri.

Friswold says, "Up until the present time, it has not been definitively proven that Crazy Horse was buried at Wounded Knee, Porcupine, White Clay, Eagles Nest Butte, or any one of several other places."

Ponca Valley near the Missouri

In his book, *My People the Sioux*, Luther Standing Bear, who was of no relation to Chief Standing Bear of the Ponca, wrote about the migration of the Sioux to the old Ponca Agency on the Missouri River. Standing Bear explained his relationship to Crazy Horse: "The father of Crazy Horse was a brother of my stepmother's mother. In Indian relationship, they were brother and sister." According to Luther's own account, Luther's father was one of those who persuaded Crazy Horse to surrender in 1877.

Luther's father had told him that "when Crazy Horse lay dying, his father and friends carried the body from the spot where he fell. Why had they tried to kill him? He had done no harm. They had invited him in, and then had stabbed him. When the father brought him out into the open, the old man said, 'If my son had known this was coming, the bayonet of the soldier would never have pierced his body, but he was taken unaware.'"

Chief Standing Bear, Luther's father, continued his story, "The Red Cloud and Spotted Tail people then stepped forward and, because they were jealous of him, they began to get ready to shoot at the dying body of Crazy Horse. But I stood over his body to protect him. I held my gun all ready to shoot any man who dared fire a shot, as that was a cowardly act. When they saw I meant to shoot one, they stopped. Then I wrapped Crazy Horse in a blanket and left him in the care of his father."

Luther was back at the Spotted Tail Agency near Camp Sheridan waiting for the body to be brought back.

Some of the friends of the Crazy Horse family remained loyal to their fallen leader. They did not run away with Sitting Bull into Canada, but moved along with the band that included the Oglala Sioux Standing Bear's family.

Luther Standing Bear recalled:

Chief Standing Bear of the Sioux with Victoria Standing Bear Conroy, Henry, Luther and Willard Standing Bear. Photo courtesy Crazy Horse Memorial.

We waited for them to lay the body away, but they did not build up a bier for him as had been done for other great chiefs. I think this was because they did not want their son touched by hands that were jealous of him.

I want you to remember that all the celebrated Indians who have big names in the white man's histories and stories were not the ones we considered important men. Their prominence was due either to getting into the show business, or to selling things that did not belong to them personally, or trading it to the white people for little money.

Crazy Horse was the greatest chief the Sioux ever had. I make that claim because he was a wonderful man. He was always in the front ranks when there was a fight.

In the Battle of the Little Bighorn, Crazy Horse rode to meet the soldiers first. He rode before them from one end of the line to the other. The soldiers were all in a line shooting at him, but they did not harm his body. Right after the killing of Long Hair [Custer], Crazy Horse took his band and ran away across the border to Canada [Buecker says Dakota not Canada].

Spotted Tail, Red Cloud, and my father [Chief Standing Bear] and other chiefs went up to Canada after Crazy Horse. They were bringing the pipe of peace with them, just for him. This was with the understanding that if Crazy Horse accepted and smoked the pipe, the United States government was to appoint him head chief over all the other chiefs of the Dakotas. They would then take him to Washington to see the Great White Father.

Luther Standing Bear. Photo courtesy Nebraska State Historical Society.

All the people of the Red Cloud and Spotted Tail agencies did not like this idea, especially Spotted Tail and Red Cloud. So they were against Crazy Horse, and he was in danger from both factions, but he did not know it. He trusted both sides and they killed him.

Soon after this we were compelled to move toward the Mud Water River, which the white people call the Missouri. The Spotted Tail Agency was located there. We were now supposed to go to the old Ponca Agency, which was located below the Yankton Agency on the west side of the river, the Yankton Agency being located on the east side. We heard the Red Cloud Agency was to be moved also. They were following the Big White River to the Missouri.

When we came to the Little White River, where the Rosebud Agency is now located, that country was full of game. The deer were so plentiful that they often ran right through our camp.

The idea of moving our band was because the Government had several men scheming to get our land away from us. If they could persuade enough of the Sioux to keep these two agencies on the west side of the Missouri River, from the mouth of Big White River down to the mouth of the Niobrara, then the Government would jump in with some sort of agreement to be signed. Then some of the crooked chiefs among our people who were standing in with the whites would be given some firewater, and promises, and after they were good and drunk they would sign off what did not belong to them alone. This would be done without the knowledge of the other chiefs. The agreement would be signed and the Sioux would lose their land. This happened more than once.

When we got to the Missouri River, we discovered that it was no place for us. Everything necessary for our comfort and needs grew wild in our land. Why move us here when there was nothing? We wanted plenty of game, wood, and water.

Now that we were at the Missouri River and found it was not the place for us to stay, we tried to be content for the winter. The parents of Crazy Horse moved away from us a short distance. They built up a tripod to which they fastened the body of their son, wrapped in a blanket and covered with a skin. In the old Indian days, a dead body was never allowed to touch the ground, but was fastened to a tripod. We wondered when they were going to put the body of Crazy Horse away, but we never asked questions. It was their son, and they had the right to do as they thought best with his body.

We stayed there for the winter.

The Poncas who had lived there had moved farther down the Missouri River, between Sioux City, Iowa, and Omaha, Nebraska. Some of these people settled in Nebraska and called themselves "Poncas." But they were all of the same tribe.

Crazy Horse's Bones Camped for a Winter on Land Near My Family's Old River Cabin

When I first came across the account from Luther Standing Bear, I was shocked. I had never seen or heard this version of the story before. To think that, in all the stories I had collected through the years about what happened to Crazy Horse after he was killed, he might have ended up spending that first winter on land near or even right where my father's poker cabin was. This haunted me. I wondered why his parents carried his bones with them for such a long time.

I presented this question to Steve and Jack Warner, a couple of kayaking buddies who are both clinical psychologists. The Warner boys, or the Walrus Brothers as fellow kayaker Varmit calls the former football linemen, are still in decent shape, in spite of Varmit's taunt. The Walrus Brothers grew up at the base of Chimney Rock. I'd been kayaking with them in the fall of 1998. With the stars out dancing and the campfire blazing, we talked about the things that might have gone through the minds of Crazy Horse's parents. They must have been suffering tremendous grief, and they must have been very proud of their son. Letting him go would have been as difficult for them as it would be for any parent. The Warner boys told me they had a colleague, Gary Coats, who'd grown up on the Pine Ridge and was a descendant of Chief Red Cloud. He'd been living in the Denver area, but could be found at that time visiting his parents near Martin, South Dakota.

Two days later, when I pulled into the town of Martin, I asked the Amoco station attendant for directions to Gary's parents' house and she told me she was a cousin of his and he had just been there at the station.

The Warner boys had alerted Gary that I might show up. Gary's ideas about why Crazy Horse's parents had carried his body around for so long were valuable, both because he was a clinical psychologist who had once worked for the tribe, and because he is a person knowledgeable about tribal history and tribal society. He noted that Crazy Horse's father, Worm, was regarded as a medicine man, although he may not have been especially high up in the society of the Lakota Sioux at that time. Gary was of the opinion that Worm's son, Crazy Horse, was revered—highly revered—and that his parents were very proud of his accomplishments. They did not want their son's bones to end up in a white man's museum, and so they kept the secret for only them to know. Their hope was that Crazy Horse's spirit could be felt forever and everywhere. Gary also told me that John Wayne, the western film star, is buried in an unmarked grave as it was his wish that his burial place not be made public. He preferred that people focus on the spiritual quality of his accomplishments and on what he stood for. Gary felt that John Wayne's way was also the way of Crazy Horse. It was the way his parents would have wanted it.

Gary spoke of Crazy Horse as a young warrior who fought the white infiltration until the very last, even when other chiefs and some of his people had given up. Crazy Horse was still young and full of fervor, and would not give up while there was still much fight in him. The older Red Cloud understood the white numbers, and had witnessed the power of the big guns. Red Cloud had been invited back to Washington, D.C. for negotiations of treaties involving land deals. And, although he was a war chief, he was now older. He had seen the cannons, the ships, and the vast number of people who would be pushing west, and he no longer had the fighting spirit in him that Crazy Horse did. Red Cloud knew he must negotiate or die. Crazy Horse would have nothing to do with this. He was a hunter of the Plains, invincible, an adventurer of the windswept land between the Rocky Mountains and the Missouri River. This was his land and his life to share with his people. He was prepared to fight to the bitter end. His parents, coming from a lower echelon in tribal society, were especially proud of what their son had achieved and were determined to keep his bones with them as long as they could.

In the Kadlecek's book, *To Kill an Eagle: Indian Views on the Last Days of Crazy Horse*, Standing Elk, Running Bear, and Fat Crane say "the story arose that Crazy Horse's parents took their son's body with them on their long trek, the descendant of Crazy Horse's followers—Standing Elk, Running Bear, and Fat Crane—denied that this was so. They did carry the spirit bundle with them, and this, however, may be the origin of the story."

According to Standing Elk, Running Bear, and Fat Crane, the parents observed the proper rituals on the trip and the year's vigil was completed in the fall when they arrived back on the Rosebud with Spotted Tail's people. Shortly after the return, the ceremony of Spirit Keeping was held. Before a gathering of people from the camp, the medicine man asked the blessings of the Great Spirit through the medium of the sacred pipe. Special food was prepared for the occasion. With careful ritual, the spirit within the bundle was released toward the south where, according to tradition, it entered the realm of Wakan Tanka.

Luther Standing Bear witnessed the event as a young boy, but did not understand it, write the Kadleceks. Luther Standing Bear was born in 1863, according to the *Pine Ridge Allotte No. 4644* and the 1932 federal census records, but Luther claims he was born in 1868, making him ten years old at the time of the Sioux camp on the Missouri in late 1878.

Perhaps Luther Standing Bear did not understand the spirit bundle ceremony, but, in his book, *My People the Sioux*, he wrote, "When we got back from the Missouri River to the place where Rosebud is now located, we learned that Spotted Tail was allowed to draw credits for fifty dollars from each store on the reservation. A short time later, the government built a two-story frame house for him to live in at the agency. The other Indians began to wonder how it was that Spotted Tail received all these favors, as nobody else was accorded such generous treatment, but they were kept in ignorance for some time." Because Spotted Tail was chief, the white government favored him with a form of payola because of the great influence he had with his people.

Luther Standing Bear went on to write, "When we arrived at our destination [Rosebud Creek (The Sioux left the Ponca Agency in the summer of 1878)], the parents of Crazy Horse still had the travois covered with the skin, but they did not build up a tripod at this time. One day, we heard that the parents had opened this bundle which was supposed to contain the body of their son, and there was nothing but rags inside! What had they done with the body and where was it buried? Nobody could tell. It was a secret of Crazy Horse's family. His body was put away without the knowledge of anybody, and where it now reposes no man knows. He was a great man, a good chief, and a wonderful leader. He never had a picture taken in all his life, and his burial place is unknown to anyone. Such was the end of one of the greatest men of our tribe."

Some of this may indeed have been a mystery to young Luther Standing Bear, but other people also made note that Crazy Horse's parents had the body with them at the old Ponca Agency on the Missouri, among them army personnel Regimental Adjutant Lee and Second Lieutenant Clark.

In 1999, Lillian Firethunder, whose great great-grandfather, Fast Thunder, was a subchief in the Crazy Horse Oglala band, told me that it was a common practice among the Sioux to carry the bones of a child with a parent for perhaps a year. After the body lay on a scaffold for a period of time, perhaps until the skin was gone and only bones were left, the remains were then put into a pouch and blessed.

In November 1998, I visited with Charlie Mulhair, who has written about Ponca Agency history, to see if he knew if Crazy Horse's parents had ever camped at the old Ponca campsite. Charlie is a historian who has spent much of his life in northeastern Nebraska. He taught Plains history at the Indian College at Santee, and conducted summer tours of the Little Bighorn Battlefield in Montana.

Stoney Butte north of the Niobrara River.

Charlie said, "Yes, I knew that Crazy Horse's parents camped at the old Ponca site, and when they left to go back to the Rosebud they had the body with them, but when they got to the Rosebud, they had disposed of the bones. What if they put those bones up on Stoney Butte, located about six miles southwest from the old Ponca agency? Now, I am not saying that they did, but what if they put them up there on the highest spot in this area to be buried? The Sioux liked to bury on the high points and this would be it. In the 1930s, the Workers Project Administration (WPA) quarried stones from that big butte and used the rock to help stabilize the banks on the Missouri. And if Crazy Horse was put up there, his bones may be scattered up and down the banks of the Missouri River." [*References to this place are spelled as both Stoney and Stony Butte. There are two Stoney Buttes in the area: one north of the Niobrara River and one south of it. The Stoney Butte location south of the Niobrara was a country school near an unnamed butte called Stony Butte School, spelled without an e.*]

Eighteen months later, a friend, Alan Feldhausen, called me at home because he was excited about a fellow he had encountered. Alan managed the electrical appliance store down the street from our mortuary. He had met Tony Arkeketa, a man from Oklahoma, who had a Ponca bloodline on his mother's side. His mother had come from the Niobrara area. Alan had arranged for Tony Arkeketa to come to Marysville to help dedicate the historic Trail Park on the west edge of town. Tony Arkeketah is the great-grandson of George Arkeketah, the Otoe Chief for whom the Marshall County, Kansas town of *Oketo* (derived from the combination of the words Otoe and Arkeketah) was named. Oketo is located a few miles north of Marysville on the Nebraska-Kansas border.

The Otoe people roamed the historic Otoe-Missouri-Kansas Trail along the Blue River from 1871 to 1881 looking for new lands in Indian Territory, but by 1882, the tribe was removed to reservations near Red Rock, Oklahoma. There are seven other historic trails that come together in Marysville: the California Trail, often associated with the 1849 Gold Rush; the St. Joe Road, coming from St. Joseph, Missouri; the Military Road, blazed from Fort Leavenworth to Fort Kearney in 1845; the Mormon Trail, which was traveled between 1847 and the completion of the transcontinental railroad in 1869; the Pony Express route, which ran through Marysville in 1860 to 1861; the Overland Stage route from Atchison, Kansas, to Denver, which provided five day service between Atchison and Denver; the Oregon Trail, which went from Missouri thru Marysville and on to Oregon from 1843 to 1869. Fur traders and gold seekers used this trail.

Alan, Tony and his daughter, and I sat down to eat at the local Wagon Wheel Breakfast Club. Alan commented on how lucky we were to get together. I thought to myself, yes, we were, and I told Tony that "our connection is one that did not happen randomly, but the spirits meant it to be," but I could not say why.

Tony's mother was Ponca, and married to an Otoe. Tony also told me about his mother's father, Ed Roy, who was born near Stoney Butte, about three miles south of Verdel, which is ten miles west of Niobrara.

I told him that I was familiar with Stoney Butte; one time our dog, Bugs, who always traveled with my father when he made his veterinary calls, got sick and his leg swelled. Doc had a call near the base of Stoney Butte to look at cows that might have had anthrax. Bugs was not feeling very well and my dad was not sure what was wrong. The rancher said, "Doc, you take good care of my cows, but even I can tell that your dog Bugs got bit by a rattlesnake." Bugs had been bitten when he went into a cellar at the old poker cabin down on the river. My father took Bugs to Verdel, a few miles north of Stoney Butte, to recuperate for a few days while lying on the bar at Joe's Place.

I also told Tony a few of the stories I have described in this chapter that supported the notion that the body of Crazy Horse and his parents had spent the winter in that area.

We talked about the rivalry of the Ponca and the Sioux. Tony had spent much time researching family history around Niobrara and had been looking for an old camp of the Ponca called Smells the Fish, or in Ponca, Who-B'thon. He thought it might be on the Niobrara River near the more recent Ponca Agency. Fish Smells was talked about in a tribal song. The song told of a Lakota blowing his flute whistle on a hill overlooking Fish Smells Camp. A Ponca warrior sneaked around behind the flute player and took the wooden whistle away from the Lakota. Since Tony was interested in traditional American Indian songs, he wanted to know more about this area.

I told him I was familiar with this area near the old Ponca Agency which had also been the headquarters for Chief Spotted Tail of the Sioux for that one winter in 1877. At a big bend in the Missouri River, the water became shallow in late summer, leaving fish stranded in pools that soon dried up. I told Tony that talking about this area jogged my memory about a time I was with a friend, Jim Frederick, in the early 1970s when we put his little yellow inflatable army surplus raft in the Missouri River a few miles above this spot. We were out for a leisurely trip down the "Big MO."

Jim and I had heard the stories about rattlesnakes swimming in the river, so I carried a long knife with us for protection. My ten-inch knife would surely keep the strike of a rattlesnake at bay. This knife was sheathed in a tough leather holster that was quickly softened from splashing river water. We soon noticed that our raft seemed to be getting smaller with each stroke of the oars. Jim kept pumping up the raft with air; I kept stroking. Somewhere in the tubes, we were losing air. We looked carefully but could not find the leak. I continued stroking and Jim continued pumping to keep the air chambers full. I suddenly glanced down beside me to see maybe forty or fifty pinholes in the yellow neoprene canvas very near my knife holster. We headed quickly into the shore, but could no longer keep our ship afloat, and walked out in waist-deep mud in those backwater pools. The smell of dead carp filled the air. At one point, we waded past the Sherman brother's campsite, consisting of a hut on a sandbar draped with fishing nets that functioned a bit like camouflage. The Sherman boys were true river rats; they could not read or write, but knew the river better than the highly educated people and curious muskrats. One of the boys was squatting like a chimpanzee with his long limbs dangling, a weed protruding from his lantern jaw. He told us we were in the Fish Smell Slough.

When we reached the bank, we managed to catch a ride with a farmer in a pickup who was checking his hay meadow. He took us the several miles upriver to our put-in to retrieve our vehicle—my cross-eyed fifty-dollar 1946 Ford. At a party down in Niobrara the week before, somebody had creased my front fender, causing the headlight beams to intersect at night.

Tony told me that in the early 1970s he had been on a vacation with his family on a trip to the Crow Agency of Montana. They were returning through the Black Hills of South Dakota when they stopped at the east end of Niobrara to reflect upon the old Ponca people. His grandmother, Running Over Water, had told him stories about a spring on the east edge of Niobrara. When he got out of the car he noticed a spring and a stand of cottonwood trees. Here he had a lonely feeling, but yet something drew him to the spring. He had the feeling the water here was special and remembered that his grandmother had told him the water at this spring is like what Holy water is to a Christian. He offered a blessing to his family, and as he drove away, a song came to him in the Ponca way but he was unsure of the meaning.

The next morning back in Oklahoma, he went to his grandmother and sang this unusual Native American chant to her. She had never heard it and did not know its meaning. She told him to go give tobacco, meat and corn as an offering and, "ask your other Grandpa Simon Eagle about this song—he will tell you."

Simon Eagle told him, "The spirits of the old Ponca people still abound and sometimes one of the spirits takes pity on you, but they come in a good way. Hang on to this song and you will find a purpose. It is a good song and it came in a good way at the springs of your ancestors."

Time went on and many people passed away including Simon Eagle. Tony began singing with a group around the drum, and a friend suggested they needed a song that has some meaning to be their theme song. Tony related to the group the song that came to him at the spring. In the Ponca language, the words of the song were "Non On Ki-Tha Thay tho thau non Zhi Wakonda Gah-q- bay." The English translation was "You are causing yourself to be heard, here where you stand, God made it this way." This song inspired Tony and his Red Land Singers to travel and to share the culture of the Native American way.

Silently, I thought of Crazy Horse and how he wanted to preserve the prairie, the buffalo, and his people's way of life. He wanted to "cause himself to be heard," but few listened.

Tony was also a dancer and he told me that the Ponca incorporated the Lakota Sioux Sun Dance into their grass dance ceremonies. He related a story told by his elders from the Niobrara River country a few miles over the hills and south of Smells Fish Bend. One day, some Ponca were overtaken by a Sioux war party. The Ponca thought they were in trouble; the band of Sioux looked tough and aggressive. On the hilltop overlooking the Sioux war party, the Ponca, clothed with grass dress and ornaments, danced in appreciation of nature. Their dance emulated the wind dancing with the tall prairie grass. The Sioux were impressed and moved by this performance. Their differences were set aside and ever since, the Sioux have honored the ways of the Ponca by using the grass dance in their own ceremonies.

I told Tony that I understood the way of the grass dance, and told him a story told to me by Tom Janis, my Schwan's food delivery man. Tom Janis and his son-in-law, Mike, had lived on the Pine Ridge Reservation. (Coincidentally, their great-uncle, Antoine Janis, was reported to have settled down the Sioux after Crazy Horse was killed. The incident is described in

Chapter 13). The Schwan's guys stopped every couple of weeks, and had gotten to know me pretty well.

On one occasion, I had been out in my barn shooting baskets. The Schwan's guys wandered out to the barn to check on my food needs. I'm in charge of breakfast around our house, and they help me with my menus. Since they saw that basketball was an interest of mine, they told me about SuAnne Big Crow, a champion basketball player from the Pine Ridge. In the late 1980s, the Pine Ridge girls' basketball team had been invited to play at Lead, South Dakota, in the heart of the Black Hills. This is gold mining territory; the world's largest gold mine, Homesake, is in Lead. Inevitably, the Pine Ridge team got harassed when they went there. Lead's hometown fans were fanatic, and they taunted the Pine Ridge girls' team by waving food stamps and making "woo woo" sounds with their hands over their mouths in fake Indian cries. They called the girls "squaws" and "moccasin feet," and some of the girls waiting to take the court were pretty scared. It was SuAnne, a small freshman player, who volunteered to lead them out onto the court for warm-ups, promising that she would not embarrass them.

The noise of the crowd got considerably louder as she led her team onto the court. SuAnne halted mid-court, took off her warm-up jacket, draped it over her shoulders, and began a Lakota dance on the court. The crowd grew silent. She'd been dancing at pow wows since she was small. She was graceful and she moved in beautiful rhythm, singing in Lakota. As

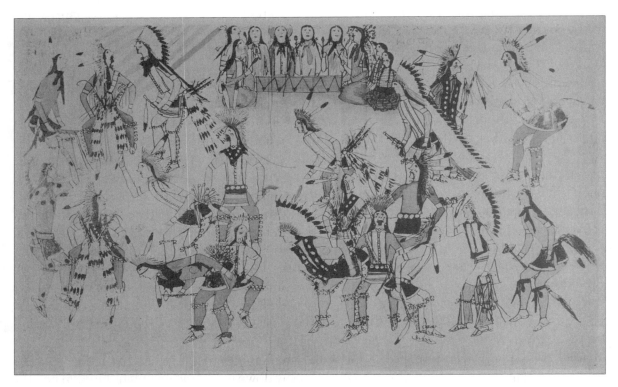

Grass Dance of the Sioux by Amos Bad Heart Bull.

with the Ponca grass dance, SuAnne turned the hostility to respect. Pine Ridge also won the basketball game.

SuAnne Big Crow became one of the greatest basketball players in South Dakota, leading her team to a state championship in her senior year. She was nominated for South Dakota Basketball Player of the Year. It was on her way to Huron, where the awards would be presented, that SuAnne fell asleep at the wheel and rolled the car in which she and her mother were riding. She was killed and her mother received minor injuries. Only a few days earlier, SuAnne had told her teammates on a bus ride to a game how much she had admired a teacher who had died suddenly of a heart attack. He had been, she believed, a good influence on many people. She hoped that if she died, that many people would come to her funeral to pay their respects, and she told them that she wanted a white casket because she was pure and untouched. The Janis guys told me that the cars formed a funeral procession several miles long, and that SuAnne was buried in a white casket.

SuAnne died in early February 1992, and in February 2000, the Janis guys told me that every year on the anniversary of her death, South Dakota radio stations play music in her memory for a week. They had been up on the Pine Ridge the week before and the radio station KILI had been playing SuAnne's songs.

I told Tony Arkeketa that the accident that killed SuAnne happened not far from where Crazy Horse may have been born, and where he may have been buried. As we parted from the breakfast table at the Wagon Wheel that morning, the look in Tony's eyes told me that the spirits of a war leader and a basketball warrior have moved many people.

The story of SuAnne Big Crow is one that I have heard others tell. While the story is true, it has grown. I later found out that SuAnne and her Pine Ridge basketball teammates did endure some racial epithets, mocking Indian music, and many other insults. However, they apparently were not nearly as intense or dramatic as are often reported. Each telling becomes a bit more dramatic, like the story I tell from my old football days when I broke six tackles and knocked three guys unconscious running for a touchdown; at least that is the story my sons hear and it's been told that way enough times that even I believe it now. I'm sure SuAnne was much like Crazy Horse—some of the stories about them may have grown larger as they were retold, although no rewrite of history is necessary to make a hero of either of them.

A month after Tom Janis and his son-in-law, Mike, told me this story, I read about it in *On the Rez*, by Ian Frazier. His telling includes much more detail about SuAnne and what she meant to basketball and to her people. It is a really cool basketball story. Frazier's book portrays the Pine Ridge Reservation at both the turn of the nineteenth century and today, and describes the regard the Lakota Sioux still have for Crazy Horse.

After Tony left to be part of the Indian Trail dedication on the west side of Marysville, I went to help make funeral arrangements with some girls who had lost their father. Tony and I had wanted to continue visiting, but we both had commitments to keep. As I walked out of the Wagon Wheel and drew a breath of fresh air, I remembered that, when my father sold his poker cabin land because the land was washing away down the Missouri River, he then bought ten acres of land three miles south of Verdel. My father and I were going to build a cabin there, but we never did, choosing to keep it a natural sanctuary. There was a small stream with clear water on the west end of the land. My father showed me several lilac bushes that were on it. Old-timers told him those flowers marked Ponca graves. The shadow of an eagle floated in the updrafts and then circled as I walked out of the Wagon Wheel to head home. It was then I realized that the land where Tony's home place had been was the same place on my father's land where the Ponca graves were. The next morning, I called Tony, who had driven back home to Oklahoma, to tell him about this connection. The spirits of Tony's people and my people seemed to have connected.

A couple of days after Tony left Marysville to head back to Oklahoma, a lady from rural Marysville called me. She had an interesting story to tell me about Tony Arkeketa's ancestors. She had heard Tony speak in town at the trails dedication. Mrs. Marjorie Chase Musil had relatives that owned land northeast of Marysville, and family history said that there was an old Indian burial ground on this land. When Marjorie was nine years old she got to ride in a farm wagon to the field southwest of the family's large house. Her papa would tell her what rows of corn to help shuck. It was on this outing that her papa, Joseph Chase, said that his grandfather Joseph Thoman had settled the land in 1857. Thoman was using an ox to plow a patch of ground with a sodbuster plow when he saw a tall Indian walk out of the woods toward him and spread his arms to show he had no weapons. Wondering what the Indian wanted, he stopped the ox. Then the young Indian began to talk brokenly, "That hill," and he pointed to the east, "Big Chief Arka-Keter sent me to tell no plow that hill, no plow ever; our people buried there. No plow."

Joseph thought, "If my people were buried there and I had to leave my land, I would say the same thing. So I put my hand over my heart to promise, and then I will shake his hand so that he understands, so it is done."

Marjorie said that to this day the family has never plowed the land and the wishes of the Otoe people have been kept. Marjorie knew that I did dowsing for gravesites and asked if I would come out to check the ground and offer an opinion if graves were there. The next day I walked the ground covered with one hundred-year-old cedar trees and my rod indicators told me there were a least twenty-five graves in the area. I told Marjorie there is no way of really knowing for sure unless we dig down. Indian burials should not be disturbed unless tribe members have asked the spirits for such an examination.

That evening I was able to contact Tony Arkeketa by phone and relay this story about the burial ground to him. Tony was delighted to hear the news of the burial ground of his people. He told me he wanted to pray with his people to seek a name for this ground. In the near future he would like the people of the area to join in a ceremony of dedication and erect a marker commemorating the ground.

The Curse of the Poncas

I knew the hills around the Niobrara and the Missouri River Valley well. I'd spent my early years in that country on veterinary calls with my father. One of the ranchers, Danny

Liska, published a book about the Ponca people he called *Ponca Curse*. Rancher/author Liska told about a band of Ponca Indians camping down river from Niobrara who:

>...were preparing to turn in for the night when soldiers, about fifteen in number, rode into their camp. Brandishing knives and pistols, the drunken soldiers demanded that the Ponca females be made available to them. Expecting to find a squaw to satisfy his lust, one of the soldiers jerked off a blanket only to discover that it was the young man, Wah-kuh-hung-gah. By taking advantage of a sudden burst of drunken mirth, the Ponca fled into the nearby willows.
>
>The next day, the thwarted soldiers tracked down the Ponca band, which had fled to where the Verdigre Creek runs into the Niobrara River. The soldiers killed four and wounded three—all females. The young man, Wah-kuh-hung-gah, with pistol balls whizzing by him, ran out onto the river and jumped into a hole in the ice where he remained submerged for as long as he could. Each time the youth raised his head, the soldiers would fire at him, but they never hit their mark. They either grew tired of their game or thought they had hit the boy, and they left. The youth climbed out onto the ice, fled across the river, and headed toward the agency to report what had happened.
>
>It was well-known in the town of Niobrara that the men involved were with Captain Wilcox's company. The night before the massacre, they had been paid their wages and became drunk but they were never charged with the murders. As a result of this incident, the Ponca shamans and an old Xube squaw sorceress cast a curse on all the whites in the valley.

Danny was interested in tracking down all the stories about tragic events which subsequently befouled the beautiful Niobrara Valley. He sought my help locating the graves of the Indian women who were killed in that massacre. My father had helped him find a grave or two and Danny knew I was experimenting with the dowsing method using L-shaped rods to locate buried objects. Danny thought I might want to help him investigate this period of Ponca history.

My son Woody was quite good at dowsing. When Woody was in second grade, for show and tell, he took four cups with him to school. When it came his turn to tell a story, he told the teacher to put each cup in a corner after he left the room. One cup had no peanuts in it, one was filled halfway, one was full, and one had just one peanut in it. He returned and, sitting in the center of the room, he used an L-shaped instrument as his dowsing instrument to locate the cups and identify what was in each of them. He correctly identified the contents of all four cups. After school that day, the teacher called us to ask what the trick was. There was no trick, we told her, it's a dowsing method similar to what dowsers use for finding water. "Oh," she said. She seemed not to believe me and never asked me again about how Woody located the peanuts.

Woody came along with me to the area of where Danny's story had occurred. It was good to have him along as he seemed to be much better at directional dowsing than I was. We set off across the hills to try to locate the graves of the Ponca who were massacred.

Woody told us he visualized an area of about ten square feet along a hillside with a depression where he thought the Ponca people might be buried. Danny, who had come with us, asked Woody to lead us to the place because he too had a vision of where the grave might be. Following Woody, we hiked through pasture land for more than a mile. We went up and down steep hills roaming for forty minutes or more until Woody came to a spot and declared that this was it. Danny told Woody he had been to this same place before, and that he felt this could be the place. I guess Woody picked up Danny's mental image because it was amazing that they both found the same depression in the grassland on that faraway hillside.

The next day, we came back to this spot with a hand auger to see if we could locate any sign of bones or clues to the spot we thought were the graves of the Ponca women. We only went about three feet deep because we felt going further would be a violation of a sacred place. Nothing was found. Woody has been apprehensive about dowsing ever since that time. My own dowsing reactions told me that the bodies may have been carried off across the Niobrara for burial. Once in a while, dowsing brings success, but there are also failures or misinterpretations.

I told Danny of many strange accidents that I knew had occurred in the area the shaman was said to have cursed. We talked about the place where people said that the old sorceress had lived. This is the same spot where my father totaled two brand new cars when deer jumped out in front of his vehicles. (In one instance, the fact that he was going 120 miles per hour checking out his new Oldsmobile rocket engine may have been a factor.) Later on, his good friend, Alvin Fosterman, had been killed in that very spot when his tractor upset and crushed him. My father and I came upon Alvin shortly after his accident.

Once, on a trail ride with my neighbor, Jack Jensen, our pack horse collapsed and would neither cross nor go near this same spot. We left our horse in a nearby rancher's corral and rode on to camp at Niobrara State Park. Two years later, that same rancher was killed by a truck that hit him as he was returning from the field. The fatal accident occurred in the same spot where our horse had collapsed. Jamie Kotrous and I used to shoot baskets at rims hung in our hay mow. Jamie later drove his car into the Niobrara River and drowned not far from this spot.

A new highway was being built near this area to smooth out a steep grade. After its completion, the new road surface broke up and slid toward the river. A hole developed in the roadway and the State of Nebraska highway crew had to fill in the hole daily with blacktop for years until the road was redesigned again. There were many strange things that I encountered in the area where the Verdigre Creek ran into the Niobrara River, where the Shaman was said to have stayed for many summers after the killing of the four Ponca.

Spotted Tail Leaves the Ponca Creek Country

When we were hiking with Danny Liska looking for the graves of those Ponca women killed by drunken soldiers in 1863, Danny told us a story about Spotted Tail as he was traveling down the Niobrara River. The Sioux were camped about fifteen miles upstream when an earthquake—a rare occurrence in this part of the country—shook the Niobrara Valley, scaring folks and knocking glassware off store shelves. The tremor was felt as far east as Sioux City. [*Historian John T. Prouty who lived in the area and who wrote for the* Nebraska Farmer *first reported this story.*]

The earthquake sounded like a cannon, and deafening rushing water roared down the Niobrara. At the same time, a long-extinct volcano erupted upstream. Lava began flowing and hissing into the Niobrara, discoloring the water and releasing the stench of sulfur. [*It has been documented that an earthquake occurred in this area in 1877 but it is doubtful that a volcano erupted.*] Considering this a bad omen, Spotted Tail ordered his people to break camp and they moved on down river to the Ponca Reservation where they set up camp at the mouth of Ponca Creek over on the Missouri River.

Things got worse for Spotted Tail. Doc Middleton, Kid Wade, and their band of horse thieves raided Spotted Tail's pony herds, driving the horses southward to be sold along the Elkhorn River. This was no laughing matter—Middleton's gang stole as many as 3,000 head of horses during 1878 and 1879, and 665 were pruned from Spotted Tail's tribal stock. The raiders lost nearly half of the stolen ponies from Spotted Tail's herd as they tried to escape across the partially frozen Niobrara River.

The very best way to aggravate an Indian was to steal his horses and Spotted Tail was furious. He submitted a depredation claim to Washington demanding $10,000 compensation for his pony loss. Back east, no one took his claim very seriously and by the spring of 1878, he was fit to be tied. The chief was convinced that the government had conned him into moving to the Niobrara area so that his annuities could be delivered more conveniently by steamboat. His people were hunters, not farmers, and the fertile soil of Ponca land meant little to him. Commissioner E.C. Hayt came to council with Spotted Tail in the spring of 1878, where Spotted Tail said, "We have the promise of the Great White Father that we shall be moved to an agency more to our liking in the spring. We will wait ten days longer, and then, if the word of the Great Father is not redeemed, I will bring my young men here, burn these buildings, and move ourselves. I have selected a place for our future home; we are going there, and it is useless for you to say that we shall not go."

In *The Ponca Curse,* author Danny Liska says that when the ten-day period expired and he still had received no word from Washington, Spotted Tail made good his threat. He burned down most of the agency buildings. In defiance of the government order, he moved his people westward to the Rosebud Creek area in southwestern South Dakota. Here, the chief and his people would be far away from Doc Middleton and Kid Wade's horse-thieving gangs.

In four short years, Spotted Tail would die at the hands of an assassin. A.G. Shaw told Eli Ricker in an interview in 1907 that Shaw asked Crow Dog why he killed Spotted Tail. Crow

Crow Dog shot and killed rival Chief Spotted Tail in 1881 as a result of a feud over tribal politics. He then drove voluntarily with his wife sitting beside him, in his buggy over 100 miles to Deadwood, SD where he was to be hanged. After his arrival in Deadwood, Crow Dog became famous when the Supreme Court ordered him to be freed because the Federal Government had no jurisdiction over Indian reservations and because it was not a crime for one Indian to kill another. Photo courtesy Nebraska State Historical Society.

Dog told him, "When Crazy Horse was killed, Spotted Tail became a great chief, so we thought that if Spot was out of the way, there would be a chance for some other Indians." Shaw understood Crow Dog to plainly mean he would have a chance to become chief if he killed Spotted Tail. Crow Dog justified his act with a family feud where a long time before, Spotted Tail's grandfather had killed a member of the Crow Dog family. According to Indian law, Crow Dog was justified in avenging himself on Spotted Tail. He could do this with no injury to his political or social standing.

Shaw had warned Spotted Tail to beware of Crow Dog only a day or two before the chief's death. Spotted Tail, in his complacent manner, disregarded Shaw's warning, saying with a soft and assuring smile, "I am not afraid. He is not brave and he has never killed anybody; he will not kill anybody now."

On the same day that Spotted Tail was to start at noon on a journey to Washington where he would head a delegation of Rosebud chiefs, the Brulé held a council about one mile from the Rosebud Agency. According to Shaw, Spotted Tail's home was about a quarter of a mile off the road between the agency and the place where the council was held. Crow Dog had stopped at the agency with his wife while driving home from White River. He met Spotted Tail about a quarter mile from the Brulé camp. There he halted his team, gave the reins over to his wife, jumped out of the wagon, crouched onto one knee, and shot Spotted Tail with his rifle, who fell from his horse, dead. The bullet passed through his heart.

Horse Thief Name Surfaces in an Eagles Club

In the summer of 1998, I was summoned to Crete, Nebraska, to pick up the body of Elmer Kruse, a truck driver from Marysville who had been unloading hogs at a meat processing plant outside of town and suffered a fatal heart attack. His body had been moved to the local funeral home, and I had called ahead to tell them that I would arrive in Crete at about 6:00 P.M. that evening. It was about an hour's drive to Crete and I had some errands to run in Marysville before I headed north. I arrived early in Crete, about 5:30, and there was no one around the funeral home when I got there. I did not have my cell phone with me, but I noticed an Eagles Club across the street, so I walked over to call someone. I was dressed in funeral home attire, including a white shirt and tie. It appeared that everyone had just gotten off work because the place was rather crowded. Most of them seemed to be acquainted, a closely-knit group of hard working laborers enjoying a beer after work. When I walked in to use the phone, the conversation quieted and finally fell silent. I walked to the end of the bar and, because it was a warm afternoon, I ordered a 7-Up. A couple of guys looked at me oddly since no one else was drinking pop. I asked the bartender if I could use the phone and she directed me to the northeast corner of the club. I got the funeral home director at his home and he told me he'd be there to help me in about thirty minutes. I told him not to hurry.

When I returned to the bar, two fellows sitting there glanced over at me and one said to the other, "Well, I guess I'd better go mow my lawn." The older one, maybe in his late fifties, said, "You know, my grass is getting pretty tall. I should probably go mow my lawn, too." I was starting to feel kind of bad that my white shirt and tie might be chasing these guys away. Since I was trying to kill time and start some conversation, I made a bold move. I knew this was Nebraska football country, so I said in a loud voice, "I'll bet anybody in here any amount of money that Kansas State's football team will beat Nebraska's this fall." The younger of the two guys, who was sitting two bar stools down from me and wearing a Husker's cap, proclaimed something about national championships and pushed his beer a bit farther away from himself. I could see his hands tense up when he said, "You know, I haven't met anybody with as much balls as you have since I heard stories about a horse thief called Kid Wade." I said, with a grin, because I knew the subject needed to be changed now, "You know, I know about a Kid Wade and Doc Middleton who used to steal horses from the Sioux up in northern Nebraska. My old neighbor tells a story about the Kid who used to live near where I grew up on the Verdigre Creek, south of the Niobrara River."

To the guys who were set to go mow their lawns I said, "There was a creek about five miles north of where I grew up called Bingham Creek. Kid Wade worked for a guy there doing odd jobs like building fences, and he also kept ponies on the guy's land that had been stolen from the Sioux. At night he shipped the ponies to auctions in central Nebraska. The guy Kid worked for had no milk cows, so he would send the Kid down to a neighbor's place to milk their cow. Kid was cocky, a showman, if not an exhibitionist, at heart. He could hang a bucketful of milk from somewhere you don't want to know about." I told the guys at the bar that I even had a picture of that stunt. One of them remarked, "Well, you couldn't have. They never had picture cameras back then." I told them that, no, it was a drawing featured in a book, *River Rat Town*, written by my old neighbor, Danny Liska. It showed Kid Wade standing with his back to the viewer looking at a milk cow with the bucket full hanging from his lower torso.

The younger guy at the bar said that he liked to hunt up on the Niobrara. A relative of his had a cabin along the river that he said used to belong to Kid Wade, and it was still standing.

I told the guys that after Kid Wade had been stealing horses for years, a Holt County sheriff took custody of him out in Long Pine, Nebraska. They planned to ride to Bassett and then take a train to O'Neill. The posse arrived after the train had left, so the group stayed in a hotel in Bassett. The sheriff and two associates stayed in one room with Kid Wade. About midnight, masked men disarmed the sheriff and sprung Wade. The masked men took Wade in a wagon east of town and hung him from a whistle post along the railroad track. Next morning, passengers saw the dangling body from the train windows.

Many decades after the hanging, stories circulated that a man dug up the Kid's grave and the bones were given to the members of the Odd Fellows Lodge in Bassett for use in rituals. That skeleton is no longer in the Odd Fellows lodge, nor is it in the Bassett Cemetery. The story goes that in the 1960s a very old woman who, as a small girl had admired Kid Wade, came to Bassett and asked for the skeleton. Lodge members, apparently anxious to be rid of the thing, gave it to her and she supposedly buried it in her family's plot in northern Holt County.

My father told me he knew that Kid Wade's mother is buried in the Highland Cemetery north of Lynch, Nebraska, west of the Ponca River. This is about twenty miles from Spotted Tail's old agency at the mouth of the Ponca where it flows into the Missouri. Danny Liska and I went to investigate her grave in 1989. Her stone bears the simple inscription: Debora Wade/1836-1921/Rest in Peace. There are no other tombstones or identifiable graves in that part of the cemetery. Our dowsing rods indicated that there might be a body in an unmarked grave about three feet south of Debora's tombstone. Upon a close examination, it became apparent that the sod over the spot had been turned over at some time. Walking over such a grave, it is usually rough to the feet. It is not smooth and there is a deviation in the flow of the ground.

If, indeed, Kid Wade is resting there, it would be a fitting end to the wild career of a young man whose capers of horse stealing from the Sioux were, ironically, much less heinous than the crimes of those who participated in his hanging. The spirit of Spotted Tail is probably smiling that Kid Wade's thieving bones are at rest in an unmarked grave near the place the chief never wanted to be: Lynch, Nebraska.

I excused myself from the bar. About a half hour had passed rather quickly, and I knew that a couple of those guys needed to get home to mow their grass. I explained that I was a mortician from Marysville who had come to pick up the body of a man who had had a heart attack out at the pork plant. The older guy at the bar told me he worked out there and that it had happened right by the unloading dock where he was working. "It was a shock to all of us," he said.

They told me to come back after Big Red Nebraska whipped Kansas State and I could buy them a few rounds of beer. I said, "Not a chance. But I might be back and you can put a 7-Up on the counter for me and I may just bring some beer-drinking buddies with me." A week later, the bar stool guys tracked me down and wanted a copy of Danny Liska's book about Kid Wade and his capers.

When the Kruse family came in for funeral arrangements, I told his brother, Butch, about the incident I'd had at the Eagles Club in Crete. "The guy who saw your brother collapse on the loading dock felt bad for your family," I told him. I also told him about the bet I'd made that Nebraska would lose the football game with K State. Since we are close to the Kansas-Nebraska border, there is plenty of rivalry here.

The Missouri River

A month later when Butch came in to pay for his brother's funeral, he told me stories about his brother Elmer. Probably to get his mind off his brother's death, he also said, "Say, I've been up in Nebraska making bets like you did on that Nebraska-K State game, and it sure starts a good session of talk going, doesn't it?" By the time October came around and Kansas State beat Nebraska for the first time in thirty years, we both felt better. I worked at the game that day selling hot dogs. My neighbor, Bruce Wehling, had gotten me the job. It was some of the best working conditions I've ever had and by the end of the day I was almost out of red catsup.

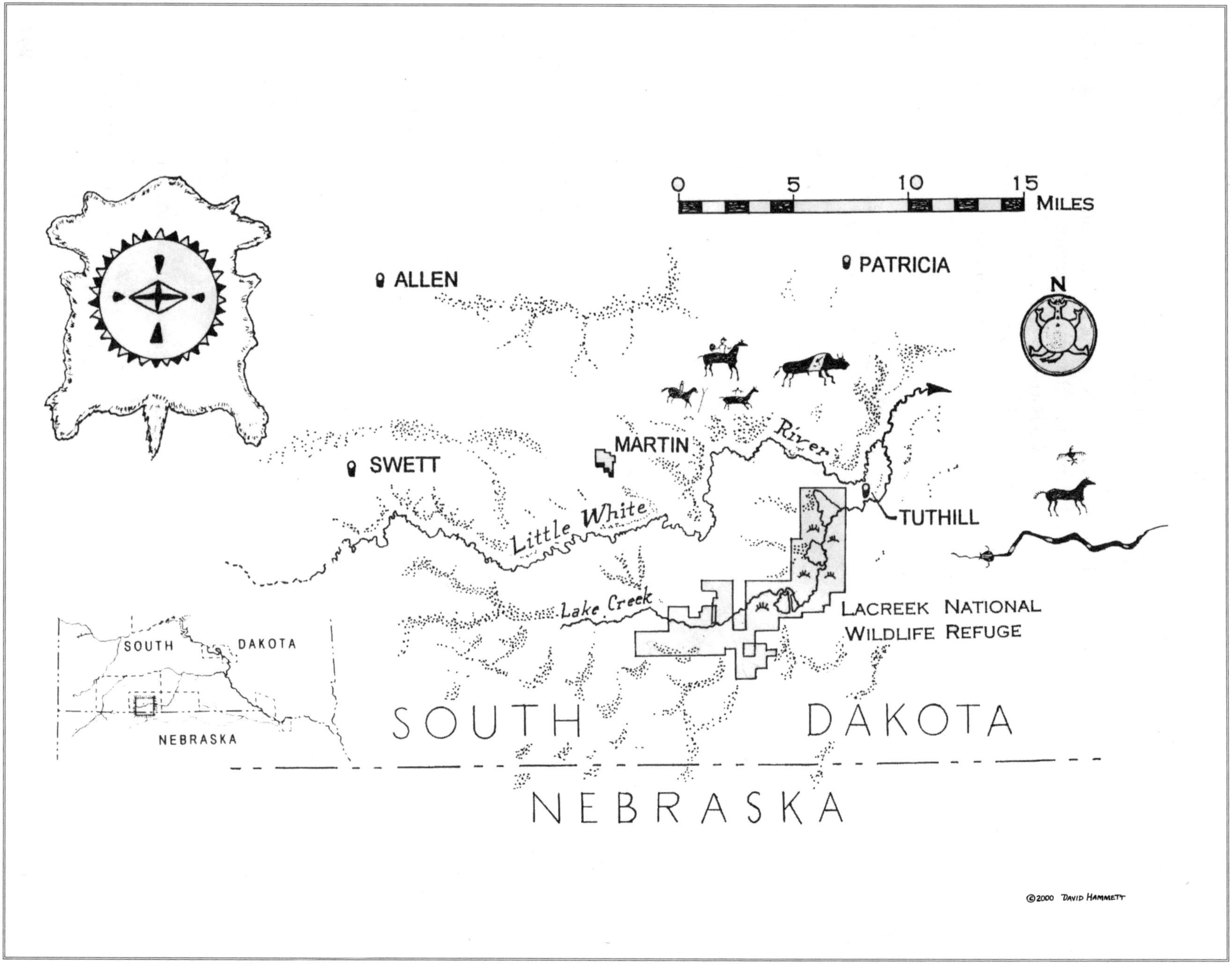

MILES

0   5   10   15

N

PATRICIA

ALLEN

MARTIN

SWETT

TUTHILL

Little White

River

Lake Creek

LACREEK NATIONAL
WILDLIFE REFUGE

SOUTH DAKOTA

NEBRASKA

SOUTH DAKOTA

NEBRASKA

©2000 DAVID HAMMETT

29

Basketball on the Rez and the Chicken Coop Diaries

There is much evidence that Crazy Horse's parents did, indeed, make the trip to the old Ponca Agency near Niobrara after their son's death. Whether the body of their son made the trip as well is a point of controversy. If the bones of Crazy Horse did go to the Ponca Agency, they most likely were returned to the Pine Ridge or Rosebud area because his parents went back to this area, presumably to be near their son.

Richard Hardorff has written much about the history of Crazy Horse in his book, *The Oglala Lakota Crazy Horse*. In that book, Hardorff analyzes a letter which was dictated by Victoria Conroy, the granddaughter of the sister of Crazy Horse's father, Worm. Victoria's grandmother, Big Woman, also known as Rattle Stone Woman or Rattling Stone, was related to Luther Standing Bear, who wrote *My People the Sioux*, from which I shared some of his reports of the Sioux trek to the Ponca Agency on the Missouri (see genealogy tree page viii).

Victoria's letter, written to Mr. McGregor, the superintendent at Pine Ridge, South Dakota, on December 18, 1934, contained the following excerpts that explain some relationships to Crazy Horse:

> My grandmother's name was Tunkanawin, marriage name was One Horse. When Crazy Horse was killed at Fort Robinson, he was laid near Beaver Creek. From here the department ordered the Indians to the Missouri River at the Ponca Agency at Nebraska. So they all moved.
>
> Old man Crazy Horse had two wives ([one was a] stepmother) to young Crazy Horse. My grandmother and (young) Crazy Horse's wife, (Black Shawl) who was Red Feather's sister. These five traveled together carrying the body of Crazy Horse, traveling in the rear of the procession of travois. These secretly buried his body between the Porcupine and Wounded Knee Creeks.
>
> When they returned from Ponca where they had camped through the winter, Crazy Horse and his two wives and Mrs. One Horse my Grandmother, went back without Mrs. Crazy Horse Jr. (whom they were afraid would marry again and reveal

the burial place). The four went back and buried him in another place, which this place is a secret.

Crazy Horse married Red Feather's sister, they lived together many years. Crazy Horse took Miss Laravere [*sic*] for a concubine wife, but he was a childless man so there were no offspring. He only had Miss Laravere a month or so when he was killed.

After his death she (Laravere) continued to present the ration ticket of Crazy Horse to draw rations with, when she remarried, the name was still carried on the rolls without any change. Her new man had a name but he was called Crazy Horse just the same. From this new man Miss Laravere had several children, enrolled as Crazy Horse children, but they were not related to the Chief Crazy Horse who was killed.

There are many who claim to know where Crazy Horse is buried, but I do not believe they know, because the last one who moved him died years ago.

All this information was given to me by mother and grandmother. It was familiar history to me, as my folks and Crazy Horse were in the same band and always camped together after our return from Ponca, Nebraska near the Missouri River. I was eleven years old at the time of Crazy Horse's death and could remember the trouble and the long journey we made in travois and the winter camp at Ponca Neb.

I am sending the names of those who could verify my statement: Mrs. John Dillon, Julian Whistle, and Henry Standing Bear. I hope this will help clear up the lineage of Crazy Horse of which there is so much confusion.

Very Respectfully[,]

Mrs. Victoria Conroy

This letter was dictated to Mrs. J.F. Waggoner of Hot Springs, South Dakota, when Victoria Conroy was sixty-eight years old. Victoria was a half sister to Luther Standing Bear who had a different story about the location of Crazy Horse's grave, which was discussed in Chapter 28. The trail of what happened to Crazy Horse's remains has many forks in the road.

In a 1999 interview with Conroy family members, the Runnels brothers, Jack and Victor, told me that the first burial spot mentioned in the letter could be in the Porcupine Butte area. As I was visiting with them in the Golden Eagle Casino near Horton,

Between Porcupine Creek and Wounded Knee Creek.

Sandhills near Conroy property.

Kansas, a mother was pushing a baby carriage by us with year-old twins pulling at each other's hair. The scene reminded the Runnels brothers that old family members had recalled that Indians had the first disposable diapers. The inside fluff of a cattail was used for the absorbent material. When soiled, it was then thrown out of the papoose and new fluff replaced it. Powder from the puffball mushroom was used to keep the baby's skin dry.

The Runnels also spoke of old relatives who used to talk about hunting trips to Canada where the bills of ducks were stuffed with government commodity maple syrup, wrapped, and brought back to the Plains for kids to suck on. Jack then told me I should contact his cousin Jean Hammond of Martin, South Dakota, who had knowledge of Crazy Horse that she received from her grandmother Victoria Conroy.

A few weeks later, I was in contact with Jean Hammond at her home. Jean lives south of Martin on the same farm where her grandmother Victoria once lived. A week before Thanksgiving 1999, I was in Valentine, Nebraska, not far from Martin, SD, to attend the graveside funeral services of Ralph Shaw, the father of my brother-in-law Larry. Ralph's father was Amberson G. Shaw, a photographer in the Valentine area from the 1880s until just after the turn of the century. Larry has shared with me some of Amberson's photographs that were of interest to my Native American research.

In Amberson's diaries, he claimed to have joined up with Buffalo Bill to work for the Union Pacific Railroad, which, at the time, had been built as far north as North Platte, Nebraska. Amberson wrote that "Bill had excellent horses but they were too high strung for the work of hunting buffalo and I could always manage to kill two buffalo to his one as my horses were what were known as the regular buffalo ponies. These ponies had one ear split as a mark of identification and would always run alongside of the buffalo until the rider shot. He would then swerve off to one side in order to avoid the horns of the beast as it fell. Bill's horses would invariably run faster when the shot was fired. I have often seen a buffalo horn his horse, but never caught him."

The same week that Larry Shaw's father died, I was also invited to participate in an Indian basketball tournament in Mission, South Dakota, about thirty miles north of Valentine. My trip north would include a visit with the Shaw family, a basketball outing, and, hopefully, an opportunity to visit with Jean Hammond.

Indian basketball is a big event on the reservations that host the tournaments. The weekend events rotate between the reservations; it might be on Pine Ridge the first weekend, then it would be on Rosebud the next, and the following weekend it would be up in Standing Rock.

The winners of the annual tournament usually get from $1,000 to $1,500 which increases the interest. Once in a while they let a few white guys play. My nephew Mitch Slusarski from Rapid City knew I would be in the area and asked me to fill in, as their team was short some players. Mitch is the assistant basketball coach of South Dakota Tech—where he previously played, held school records in assists, and led the team in free shots—and during the day he is a stock broker. They had won the tournament the year before.

I got into Mission on Friday afternoon and had lunch at the Antelope Café which seemed to be the meeting place for many locals. The sandwich I had was really good. The waitress asked what I was doing in town and I told her I'd come to play basketball in the big tournament. I didn't mention that I also hoped to collect a story or two and see Jean Hammond the next morning fifty miles west of Mission.

The waitress told me that three tall guys had been in earlier looking for the rest of their teammates. They had gone out driving around and would probably be back. I was sitting by a window of the café finishing my roast beef sandwich when a little car pulled up and three tall black guys in green warm-ups squeezed out from this little box with wheels. The waitress directed them over to me, and they came over to see if I'd seen two of their other buddies. One guy was close to seven feet tall and the other two were about six inches shorter. I asked them what time they were to play that night. They told me around 8:00 P.M., and I said, "You know, that is when we play, and I'll bet we're playing you. Now, I want you all to know that I am the oldest, toughest, meanest point guard around." I had noticed they had a college emblem stitched onto their warm-ups. I asked if they were in college and they said, yes, they were. I came back with, "You know this is a professional tournament, not for college kids. This one is for pros."

They smiled and said, "We are pros."

I smiled back and replied, "You will probably be guarding me tonight and you will probably have to let me shoot because I don't think the rules of the NCAA allow college guys to play in these pro games."

They laughed and said, "Oh, we don't want to be turned in. You can shoot all you want."

At 8:00 P.M. that night I was at the gym getting loose. The three guys had found their other two players, but the seven-footer had sprained his ankle going for a lay-up during warm ups. They forfeited. Management found us another team to play. That was tough on me because I hardly had any open shots. My con game had backfired.

If you have ever watched Native Americans play basketball, you know they can shoot from almost half-court and connect. They have great touch and flow with the ball. I suppose all the years of Sun Dancing and being steady hunters with arrows laid the groundwork for these great outside shooters. I saw one guy from lower Brulé bank a shot in from within five feet of the half-court line. The second half of the game he did the long distance bank shot into the bucket five more times. If these guys start building golf courses with their casino money, with their great touch and eye sight they will rule the sport of golf. Competitions of "pasture pool" learned on the prairie will belong to the Lakota. Mitch's basketball team went on to win the tournament without their forty-eight-year-old mean, tough, and very stiff point guard.

The next morning I was able to meet with Jean Hammond at Geo's Coffee Shop in Martin. Jean talked with a soft, soothing voice that made me feel very comfortable. Her daughter, Patricia, and her daughter's child, Alexandria, were with her. I was awestruck by Alexandria. She looked much like my son Woody had as a child, with a similar dark complexion, brown eyes, short nose, and the attractive features inherited from their mothers. I told Patricia that if my wife had been with me, she would have called Alexandria a cutie pie. I explained to them that Woody's mom is a redhead and since I am light complected, it made it a tough sell to compare Woody to a Native American in looks, but half of his grandparents were dark complected.

Jean shared a story about her son and an Indian healing rattle he had found in the attic. When Jean's son was learning to Sun Dance, he was having a hard time learning the rhythm. He used the rattle for spiritual guidance and from it came a new and exciting aesthetic movement to his dance.

In 1996, Jean found a cardboard box in the corner of a chicken coop on the family farmland. Jean had grown up on the place and had recently returned from California to live in her Grandmother Victoria's house. In the box were old letters, diaries, and photographs compiled by her father, Harry Conroy, and his mother, Victoria. Jean said that the notes were written on tablet paper like the red Big Chief writing tablets they'd done their homework on in Indian school. In the first line of one of the notebooks Victoria wrote that "someday, people will want to know about this family."

Victoria's stories, written in Lakota and requiring careful translation, were about her famous relative, Crazy Horse. The family is descended from his father, Worm. Worm's sister was Rattling Stone (also known as Big Woman) who was Jean Hammond's great great-grandmother. The diaries contain a story about Worm's father, White Rabbit, who was killed during an expedition to capture horses for his daughter Rattling Stone from a rival tribe, and also a note about Crazy Horse's mother killing herself when Crazy Horse was young. Worm remarried and his two wives reared the young warrior. Jean said that "the reason for the suicide is something the family does not talk about. People have whispered that Crazy Horse's father was white, and that his mother was violated by a white man, but that is not the story that was passed down in our family. It was much worse. But a white man was not involved. It would change the course of family history and so it is kept in the family."

A brief note was included about Crazy Horse's affair with Black Buffalo Woman, the wife of No Water. Harry Conroy wrote, "The wife of No Water came to Chief Crazy Horse's tepi one night and stayed with him. It was because of this No Water shot Crazy Horse in the cheek. No children from this contact."

Victoria had been eleven years old when Crazy Horse was killed in 1877. Jean Hammond said it appears that "Victoria wanted to recapture the feeling of knowing the great man by writing down what she remembered about him and how he continued to inspire her life."

The letters and diaries have not yet been completely translated, but one passage from Victoria does say that "Crazy Horse was a good man and good to look at. He wasn't fat; he wasn't skinny. His nose wasn't big; it wasn't crooked. "He had pity for many people and he wasn't jealous. He respected everyone. You can follow in his steps and that's why I respected him. He was a friend to everyone."

Jean Hammond works in Kyle as a mental health worker and plans to retire in a couple of years to work on translating the rest of the notes from the chicken coop. Jean told me that Victoria had been born as Yellow Bird in 1867, and later her name was Christianized to Victoria. Her father was the Lakota Standing Bear. Before the death of Crazy Horse, her people were nomadic in their ways, traveling around the Midwest as far south as the Republican River in Kansas. They would move in a clockwise fashion going from Kansas to Canada. Their people and the circle they traveled knew no boundaries. Victoria died in 1966 and is buried in the cemetery in Allen, South Dakota. "The death of Crazy Horse brought a great change to the Lakota people," Jean explained. "The stress of the family being moved from agency to agency with tight boundaries, while they were trying to understand the concept of land ownership, was very difficult for our people. There was great fear at this time. There was a great void."

Victoria attended school at the Carlisle Indian School back in Pennsylvania. There she met and married Frank Conroy. Frank's mother, Spotted Horse Woman (later Eulala) was the daughter of old Chief Smoke. Victoria and Frank had a son, Harry, who also attended Carlisle and who was a classmate of the great Indian Olympic athlete, Jim Thorpe. Victoria and Frank had both been good students, and their son, Harry, later earned a degree from Valparaiso University.

Frank and Victoria settled south of Martin, South Dakota, where they farmed. They adapted well to the white ways of agriculture, although they modified their lifestyle somewhat. They had two separate farmhouses; Victoria's was near Martin, and Frank's was a few miles to the southwest where the Sandhills start in the Lake Creek district. At times they lived together at Victoria's house, and at other times they would move together over to Frank's place. Such was the way of the nomadic, independent Lakota.

Lake Creek near Conroy land.

Victoria was a hard-working woman who chopped wood for the winter fires. She was a prolific beader who made a dress that weighed fifty pounds that can be seen in a museum in Colorado. Jean said that her Grandmother Victoria would put herself into an alpha state and "see" designs for her beading work revealed to her in her head. She never drew her designs out on paper.

Victoria also told stories of how Lakota leaders were selected for the tribe. One person was designated as an observer of the potential leaders to see how they cared for their families and if they treated others with respect and kindness. Those scenes were absorbed by the observer who would study and guide each person. Teaching was done by the entire tribe. A meaningful relationship was developed among the entire community of people. If a candidate developed according to the values and guidelines of the community, they were chosen to be the leader for their people. Native Americans once defined politics as a polite and humane process in the development and selection of leaders.

Jean noted that her people on the reservation were moving back to the more traditional ways of government, the ways Crazy Horse had tried to show them. I asked her if the spirit of Crazy Horse had ever visited her. She told me that she had been on her way to view a film that Turner Broadcasting made about Crazy Horse a few years ago. She said that the movie script was erroneous in its depiction of the facts about Crazy Horse and the writers acknowledged this. Jean felt that the commercialization of Crazy Horse was not right and that the way the film portrayed Chief Red Cloud was not in good taste. Later, the Turner people planned to use this film to teach children about Crazy Horse even though the errors were not corrected in the script. On her way to see the film, black clouds formed above her and maybe three or four eagles played in the clouds. She took this as a sign that she should protest the accuracy of the film.

She was told that only four people knew of the last burial site of Crazy Horse. One was Crazy Horse's father, the second and third were his two wives, and the fourth was Mrs. Joe One Horse, or Rattle Stone Woman, later Christianized Hannah. The family also remembered that Victoria had once owned a prized cavalry horse that she learned had been offered to the one who could kill Crazy Horse years before.

I told Jean that I have heard stories of various prizes relating to Crazy Horse. An old-timer from the Porcupine area told me that it had been passed down in his family that Crazy Horse had been buried with a fist-sized ball made of gold. My informant did not want his name revealed since he did not want to be responsible for instigating a lot of digging in the hills.

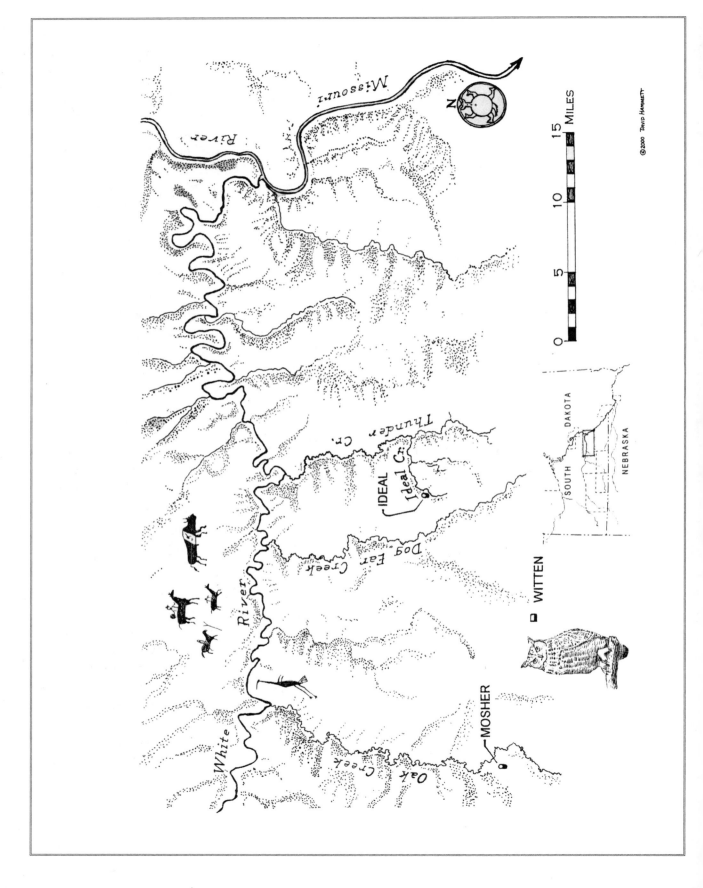

©2000 DAVID HAMMETT

30

South Central South Dakota

There is evidence that Crazy Horse's bones were brought back to south central South Dakota somewhere near the present day Rosebud Reservation, but it is only conjecture as to whether his body made the journey back there before or after his parents went to the Ponca Agency near Niobrara in the fall of 1877. Here are three more interesting theories about this topic.

The Ideal Spot?

Chief Lame Deer said that the Indians decided to hold a pow wow in Ideal, South Dakota, in August 1961 "because there are many conflicting stories concerning Chief Crazy Horse's life and place of burial." I found the following information about the pow wow in Mari Sandoz's notes. She had gotten it from an article in the *Omaha World-Herald*, dated August 27, 1961, right before the pow wow.

The Indian story that Chief Lame Deer, who also went by the name of John Fire, told is that two aunts brought Crazy Horse's body to Tripp County after he was killed near Wounded Knee by a soldier who stabbed him in the back. They traveled with the body to west of Wanblee, a site near Kadoka, and from there the body was moved to near White River. An unconfirmed story says it was then reburied below Ideal Creek in an Indian cemetery.

Chief Lame Deer told the *Omaha World-Herald* that the old men at the pow wow would explain that Crazy Horse is buried near an oak tree in northern Tripp County. That article also stated that Crazy Horse was Sitting Bull's war chief. According to Indian legend, Sitting Bull's medicine chief gave the war chief a secret talisman possessing bullet proof medicine. Old braves told long ago how Crazy Horse paraded in front of United States troops who fired on him and that he remained unharmed.

This pow wow in Ideal, South Dakota, was part of the state's centennial observance, and it was featured in an article in the *Omaha World-Herald* newspaper. It sounded as if the locals of Ideal were drumming up some excitement to promote their pow wow.

Ideal, SD.

In the spring of 1999, I was passing through Wanblee, South Dakota, and I remembered that tribal judge Mario Gonzalez had told me if I ever had the chance, I should stop and visit with Bernice Milk who lived up there. Bernice is the daughter of Chief Lame Deer who had organized the pow wow in Ideal in 1961, and I wanted to ask Bernice about that event.

My son Woody and I pulled up to the Milk's home and saw a spry man coming down the steps. It was Bernice's husband, Jasper. He had keen, lively eyes. I found out that Jasper's great-grandfather had been Chief Milk. I told him I had visited Chief Milk's gravesite south of Herrick, South Dakota, with my father five years earlier. We were invited inside. Bernice spoke English with a heavy Lakota accent. She did not know much about the pow wow called by her father over in Ideal. She did say, "My grandfather was a medicine man for Crazy Horse. His name was Turtle Ribs. It was told in our family that he helped bury Crazy Horse on the old Turtle Rib allotment down on Spring Creek near St. Francis." Spring Creek is located in the southwestern area of the Rosebud Reservation.

I asked her about the medicine man Chips, the one who had given Crazy Horse protection in battle. Bernice said she'd known of Chips and that Crazy Horse had probably had several medicine men he consulted. She told us that Crazy Horse went many times to Turtle Ribs for his medicine.

I was told by a Lakota authority on genealogy that Turtle Ribs was most likely the medicine man for Crazy Horse's father, Worm, who is probably the Crazy Horse that was buried on Spring Creek near Rosebud Creek. Worm once had the name Crazy Horse, but when his son was in his early teens, he bestowed it upon him and took the new name of Worm.

The town of Ideal, South Dakota, which was the site of the pow wow, is no longer on the Rosebud Reservation. The boundaries of the reservation have changed several times. Ideal is a few miles north of Winner, South Dakota.

In January 2001, I was reading the obituaries in the *Lakota Journal* and I noticed that a man named Chief Archie Fire Lame Deer had died. He had worked on ranches in South Dakota, also had a brief stint as a rattlesnake exterminator, and then worked as a drug and alcohol counselor. In later years he traveled the world teaching Lakota spiritual beliefs and ways of life. His father was Chief John Fire Lame Deer, the man who had organized the pow wow in Ideal, South Dakota. The obituary stated that a son, John Fire of Sturgis, South Dakota, survived. I was able to contact John Fire by telephone and ask him for insight about the Ideal Pow Wow. He told me the family would not reveal the Crazy Horse burial. "Keep the strength with the tribe, that is the wishes of the family and it should be respected. If they found Crazy Horse, it would be too much disruption."

Pass Creek

A tomahawk pipe that was said to be scavenged from the grave of Crazy Horse came up for sale at an auction in San Francisco in the summer of 1993. It was cast in brass with a hand-worked engraving of an Indian head on one side and a horse's head on the other. Tomahawk pipes are a combination of pipe and tomahawk heads; they were manufactured for the Indian trade. Just the hatchet heads, without the pipe bowls, were traded to the Plains Indians first, but by 1750, the metal pipe bowl types were available. The hatchet head was basically an English blade that looked like a straight axe. The Indian artisans decorated the tomahawks with beading, carving, fur, and painted handles. The tomahawk pipe was a symbol both of war and peace.

Near mouth of Pass Creek.

Author Thomas E. Mails says the Plains Indians that met to arrange treaties often buried the head of the tomahawk in the ground to show peaceful intent (as in "bury the hatchet"), or smoked the pipe end together to express the same thing. Tomahawk pipes eventually became highly ornamental and few wanted to damage such a beautiful work in battle.

Jim Hass, a department manager for the Butterfield and Butterfield auction house in San Francisco that was selling the artifact, said he questioned whether the tomahawk pipe belonged to Crazy Horse, but that it still had both historical and aesthetic value. Speaking about the authenticity of the object, Hass said, "I wondered about that right from the very beginning, but we typically sell them because collectors see beautiful historic examples of Native American art. We never just sell on star appeal. In this case, I expressed serious doubt about it. Even if there may be inaccuracies, it still has great international appeal. As of 1929, someone believed it was so. Whether it was a charade or fac-

Pass Creek Valley.

tual, whether the details got twisted or hidden, I can't verify. We will present the documentation that says so. I can't go back and dispute history. I have to go by the documentation we have. It takes a leap of faith." Hass would not reveal who now owns this artifact.

The Office of Indian Affairs in the United States Department of the Interior provided a history of the metalwork on the pipe tomahawk. It reads:

> Pipe belonged to Chief Crazy Horse, a chief who took a principal part in General George Armstrong Custer's last fight on the Little Bighorn Valley in Wyoming on June 26, 1876.
>
> Pipe was found by a grandson of Big Elk on July 16, 1929, on the old burial ground of Chief Crazy Horse and his family at the mouth of Pass Creek near the United States Rosebud Indian Reservation in South Dakota, fourteen miles south of Kadoka, South Dakota.

The history also states that the pipe was taken from the grave by Chief Big Elk and witnessed by Mr. and Mrs. Wallace Woodlock. Mr. Woodlock was the son of a government doctor, W.C. Woodlock, who was stationed at Wanblee, South Dakota, along with young George Bad Cob, the son of famous old Chief Bad Cob. The history is signed with the elaborate signatures of Chief Big Elk and Princess Pretty Woman, his wife.

On June 9, 1993, *Indian Country Today* said it was people from the Nebraska State Historical Society who spotted the ad for the sale of the tomahawk pipe in the National Rifle Association's magazine. It seemed unusual that family members would try to sell artifacts from Crazy Horse's grave as it would be viewed as desecration and violation of the sacred Lakota spirits.

Terry Gray, who works with Sinte Gleska University in the archive section at the Rosebud Reservation, talked with me in 1999 about the respect for Indian graves and artifacts from graves that his Lakota people have. Terry is in charge of enforcing the Native American Graves Protection and Repatriation Act. A federal law was passed in 1990 prohibiting the trade, transport, or sale of American Indian remains and artifacts and requiring museums to report their inventories of sacred objects and burial items. Terry worked with archeologists for the Smithsonian Institute.

"Burial customs and beliefs about the dead vary among the more than seven hundred tribes, but one common factor links all people," Terry explained. "Native Americans have definite ideas about what is appropriate and what should not be done with the dead. The Lakota people believe that the soul does not rest until the physical remains are brought back to their own land. The spirits are then free to make their journey back to the spirit world."

Terry told me that University of Nebraska archaeology students had collected remains of Native Americans years ago. Recently, a medicine man had been invited to pray for the return of the bones to the native lands. The medicine man, Ronald Little Owl of North Dakota, had a vision the night before the ceremony was to take place at the University in which he saw a little round chimney coming from a campus building. He saw that the remains had been burned in an incinerator and dumped on campus ground outside this building.

After an investigation, it was found that between 1965 and 1967, an unknown number of American Indian bones were loaded into the trunk of a car, transported, and incinerated along with the remains of diseased animals. The ashes were scattered on the campus lawn overlooking the student union on East Campus near the Speech Pathology Department where my wife, Mony, graduated with her masters degree in 1977. The medicine man showed the University people the exact location where the ashes were dumped, explaining that the soil was softer in this location because of the ash that had been dumped. Few students would have been aware that, for more than thirty years, the captured spirits, seeking release to the four directions, danced nearby as the students pored over their textbooks.

This memorial states that an unknown number of Native American remains had been taken from their graves for inclusion in the University of Nebraska's archaeological collections. In the mid-1960s, those remains were incinerated in a facility located near this site, in a manner totally inconsistent with the beliefs and practices of the tribes of the Great Plains. In 1998, UNL Chancellor James Moeser and tribal representatives agreed to set aside this site as a memorial to honor these Native Americans and to remind future generations of this cultural injustice. Memory of these events must be more than symbolic, for people who forget the past are bound to repeat its mistakes. May we learn from this and treat all persons with honor and respect.

Terry Gray was invited to a special ceremony on the East Campus at the University of Nebraska in which the remains were prayed for and a cedar purification process was offered. University Chancellor James Moeser made an apology on behalf of the University for the insensitive and grievous treatment of the physical remains of Native Americans done in past decades in the name of science. He noted that the anger and hurt that Native Americans felt as a result of this were certainly understandable.

At the request of my son Woody, I was in Lincoln, Nebraska, in the late fall of 2002 to pick up information for him about the University of Nebraska's graduate school. I was on East Campus visiting with the head of the water resource department, Robert Kuzelka, when I asked him if he knew anything about the story of the Native Americans who were cremated. He told me to walk one hundred feet east of his office and I would find a special rock telling of the episode.

We can also understand the fears Crazy Horse's parents must have had when they thought white men would dig up their son's body. They did not want the spiritual connection between the dead and the living world interrupted. They felt that the way human remains are treated is important, for it affects the spirits of the people on the other side. If human remains are disturbed, the Lakota people believe this distressing effect on the dead can lead to adverse consequences for the living. The remains belong to Mother Earth. The spirits are restless if the body is not buried in the homeland.

From Wanblee toward the Rising Sun

In April 1999, I was sitting in the conference room of the Rosebud Casino discussing water rights with Fremont Fallis who is the Tribal Utility Commissioner. Fremont was waiting for people from the Army Corps of Engineers to show up for a meeting on water rights along the Missouri River. An early spring storm was hitting the region to the west. The Corps' engineers were late. I told Fremont that they were hard folks to get a response from. I related to Fremont an incident about the Corps that occurred back in the 1970s.

The upper Missouri River region had a fair amount of snow that year. The Corps was letting an extreme amount of water out of Fort Randall Dam and holding a fair amount of water back on the reservoir below at Gavin's Point, near Yankton, South Dakota, causing the water to flow needlessly over the banks of the Missouri around the Niobrara, Nebraska, area.

Many residents who lived near the Missouri in what was called the Lazy River Acres were upset that the Corps was not better controlling the flow. These inhabitants were in danger of losing their homes and cabins. This was within a half mile of the old Spotted Tail Agency where the parents of Crazy Horse camped until the spring of 1878.

In the early 1970s, a medical doctor from nearby Plainview built a round house on a pedestal near the river. Dr. Kopp was a good friend of my father's and he invited us to stop in one afternoon to show how the river was cutting away at the banks and how that was endangering his cabin, a situation my father had encountered twenty years earlier when the river was washing away the land where his poker cabin stood a mile upstream. Dr. Kopp tried but had gotten no response from the Corps when he called their offices. That afternoon, my father and Dr. Kopp decided to call Paul Harvey's news program and air their concerns. I remember them telling Mr. Harvey that the Army Corps of Engineers are higher up than the CIA, and you sure can't get through to them. One of the Corps must have heard the broadcast because the water level around the old Spotted Tail Agency began to drop soon after that.

Fremont said, "The Corps may not show up today, either. They are still hard to talk to." It was on this occasion that I first learned about Mario Gonzalez. Fremont said, "You know, you ought to visit with a guy down in your area by the name of Mario Gonzalez. He knows a lot about Crazy Horse. He is now Tribal Attorney General for the Kickapoo tribe in Kansas, and he lives in Horton. He's originally from over in the Pine Ridge area."

"That's not far from Marysville. Thanks," I told him.

Mario Gonzalez wrote a book, *The Politics of Hallowed Ground*, about the Black Hills land claim. Mario is a champion for the return of United States Forest Service lands in the Black Hills to the eight Sioux tribes that held title to the land through the 1851 and 1868 treaties. In 1981, the Indian Claims Commission rejected a government offer of 100 million dollars as payment for the Black Hills, citing the religious sanctity of the Black Hills and the need for the protection of the future of Sioux culture, sovereignty, and economic self-sufficiency. They felt

220

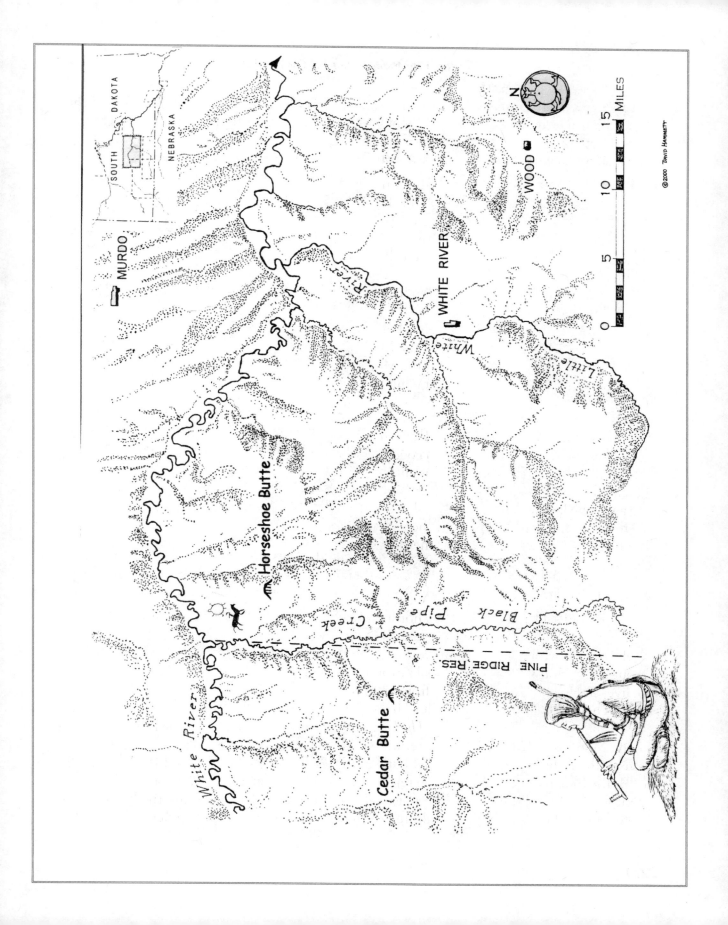

SOUTH DAKOTA

NEBRASKA

MURDO

WHITE RIVER

WOOD

White River

White River

Little

Horseshoe Butte

Cedar Butte

Black Pipe Creek

Pipe Creek

PINE RIDGE RES.

N

0   5   10   15
MILES

© 2000 DAVID HAMMETT

that money could not make amends for the loss of the land, and that if they accepted the money, the land that is sacred to the Lakota would be forever lost to them. The Lakota people are still hoping for better terms; they want the land.

Mario was amazed that some white guy from northern Kansas was so familiar with the people from Pine Ridge and Rosebud. He seemed to be delighted to visit about Crazy Horse and the people he knew. We were far from his homeland on the Pine Ridge, but he was comfortable and excited about sharing his knowledge of Crazy Horse.

As tribal attorney, Mario also studied old tribal claims where Congress appropriated money to pay for Sioux horses lost to white men. Over dinner in May 1999, Mario told me it would be necessary to prove to the Secretary of the Interior who the heirs of deceased claimants were in order to be rewarded money. There was still controversy over the estate of Crazy Horse for the amount awarded by the United States government for one pony claim. It was unsure whether the pony claim belonged to Chief Crazy Horse's father Waglula (also known as Worm or Crazy Horse the Elder), who had married two of Chief Spotted Tail's sisters, or the man who married Chief Crazy Horse's half-blood wife, Nellie Larrabee (also spelled as *Laravere, Laravie, Larivee, Larivier,* and more) after the Chief was killed, and then assumed Crazy Horse's name so he could use his ration card.

Mario had claim documents filed in the 1930s of a man called Making Coffee who said he was an heir of Crazy Horse, the warrior, son of Worm, making claim for the loss of two horses in 1877 on the Niobrara River. I told Mario that Coffee was the name of the man Darlene Rosane told me had been the caretaker of the Crazy Horse grave for many years. Mario thought that made sense, because the sworn horse claim indicates that Coffee was a relative of Crazy Horse.

Mario had also heard that Coffee often visited the grave of Crazy Horse. Mario told me he had always heard stories about Crazy Horse being buried in the Manderson and Wounded Knee area, but he was told by Robert Dillon, a son of Emily Standing Bear-Dillon, that his remains were moved several times and the final burial site is east of Wanblee. The Standing Bears were relatives of Chief Crazy Horse's father. Dillon said he had heard Robert Burnette, a Sicangu politician of the 1960s and 1970s, tell about a man named Coffee being related to Crazy Horse and how he would visit the gravesite. But when he went, he would never tell anyone where he went, and he would not let anyone follow him. Burnette said Coffee would head out walking, go north toward Norris from the community of Spring Creek on the Rosebud Reservation, and return the next day.

The Dillon family had a ranch a few miles north of Wanblee, and Robert said his parents would travel east by wagon in one day to the burial site of Crazy Horse. A one-day journey by wagon would be about thirty or forty miles.

Mario told me how I could get in contact with Robert Dillon's son, Gene, who lives in the Rapid City area. In August 1999, I was able to visit with Gene and he told me that the family would go east from their home allotment to Black Pipe Creek to visit the grave. Gene knew where there were graves because he studied the ants. Ants bring artifacts to the surface in areas where a grave would be. Gene said, "The visits occurred between 1920 and 1930. This was a special area that the Plains Indians would visit because there is a black rock located here that was used for ceremonial pipes. This was good rock, and one would not have to travel all the way to Minnesota for the pipestone that so many revered. Black bowl pipes are used for healing, and Crazy Horse was a healer. The pipe is used to open the gates and release powers and then it becomes the channel through which the great powers flow. It travels in the six directions and blesses the person and blesses the rest of the Mother Earth."

Black Pipe Creek, so named because the Lakota used a black rock from this area to make their pipe bowls.

Gene told me Crazy Horse wore two Red Tail Hawk feathers. It had been told in his family that he wore those feathers rather than the traditional eagle feather because Crazy Horse regarded himself as fast and maneuverable, like the Red Tail Hawk who could strike quickly. Crazy Horse had a philosophy that we should let our dreams soar like a bird. Gene said the family felt there was some deception in the stories about Crazy Horse's burial. This was done to protect his bones from grave robbers. "Crazy Horse is my hero," said Gene, "and I am my own hero. Let the spiritness speak for yourself."

Gene related the following to me in a letter:

A hero is regarded as a person who was above everyone else in physique and intellect and, therefore, was above reproach. But our family history says Crazy Horse was just a regular person. According to my family's knowledge and other reflections of his tiyospe, Crazy Horse was an individual for absolutely carrying out orders and directions from various chiefs. He did not institute any skirmish unless it was to protect. He obeyed instructions with maximum diligence. He maintained himself and immediate family as much as other members of the band and did all this in a very humble, unassuming, but responsible, manner.

Crazy Horse would be remembered today in that he is honored by family and others of the clan in a quiet and dignified manner by the way they live, giving grace and courage to all ages of persons around them, seeing the spiritual blessing of each. Honoring all aspects of this world and its total purpose in our daily lives. Crazy Horse realized his blessings and carried them out with a great intensity. He never attempted to prove himself, but conducted his life with a demeanor of honor and duty to all....

My father, Robert Dillon, would visit the Marshall family in Martin, South Dakota. From there he would venture silently and solemnly to seek Victoria (Standing Bear) Conroy, where he would leave me with her while he continued on his own to carry out traditional prayers. This would be in the area of the tributaries leading into the creek before the La Creek Refuge area as it is named today. This is located primarily southwest of Martin, South Dakota. This was a special place for Crazy Horse to be remembered; his resting place may have been here or in the Black Pipe Creek area, a long way from Martin, South Dakota. During the night after my father returned from his prayer vigil, my aunt Vic would serve traditional foods and would talk in Lakota with my father.

Gene was the second generation descendent of the Standing Bear brothers, Luther, Henry, and Ellis, who are classified as his great-uncles. He talked about them for a bit.

"They all shared the knowledge of the burial of Crazy Horse. It was of their integrity they maintained the secrecy of the burial site and included with them that secret which went with them on their journey via the Milky Way to the next life."

Gene said he could not discount the knowledge of his grandmother, Unci, who had been a child of six at the encampment of the Battle of the Little Bighorn, who personified Crazy Horse as the individual who almost single-handedly won the battle, well beyond just encouraging the others to fight well.

"My great-uncles and my Unci and other members of the clan continued their prayer life in the Eagles Nest Butte Area where they made trips to the Hisle, Wanblee, and Black Pipe Creek areas offering prayers and memorials with a sense that they were in the Power Area as they remembered all souls gone before and prepared themselves for their journey into the next life with their band which included Crazy Horse's family.

"Most of the Band of the Eagles Nest Butte area and the Hole-in-the-Wall protectors had similar attitudes of Crazy Horse in a historical sense, and have perpetuated the attitudes of his by wanting to continue the old ways of prayer and life which dictates the numbers of success in all aspects of life from the remainder of the nineteenth century to today. All of these people carry the folkways of Crazy Horse with great intensity as they also had family members at various skirmishes before boundaries of reservations had been established. This intensity in the spiritual realm was provided to me in my prayers and Hunblaca (hillside sacrifice) at Eagles Nest Butte and Bear-in-the-Lodge Creek where I received guidance and strength to conduct myself as a spiritual being. Many of the spiritual procedures were shown to me by my father, Robert H. Dillon, and my Unci Emily (Standing Bear) Dillon when I was five and six. I make it a habit to return frequently for confirmation."

Gene's family showed him a few possible areas where the burial site might be located, but he had an understanding with them that he would not tell where they were in order to perpetuate the intensity he had as member of the tiyospe regarding that site. Gene said, "The majority of his family live in a responsible manner insuring for many generations of hope, desire, and perseverance to continue life's processes to obtain admission to the next realm."

Mario Gonzalez knew a man by the name of Ray Martinez, from Kyle, South Dakota, who was related to Crazy Horse. Over breakfast one morning, Ray told Mario that the reason Chief Crazy Horse's parents moved his body so much is that they were afraid the soldiers were going to cut off his head and take it back east as a trophy. Mario knew the soldiers had been cutting off the heads of Indian warriors in the 1870s so scientists could study the size of Indian skulls to determine if Indians were intellectually inferior to non-Indians. The Smithsonian Institute has the skulls of many warriors taken from battles with the United States Army for such study.

White River north of Wanblee, SD.

After our visit over dinner, Mario said, "Storytelling sessions like this are happenings that most of us, in our busy lives, are only rarely party to. To many people, the Indians are just wanderers or simply berry pickers who follow the herd. Those are the worst stereotypes. The Sioux are people with sophisticated notions about cultures and historical legacies."

A month after I met Mario, I was visiting with my brother-in-law, Jerry Mlinar, who lives in central Nebraska. We were talking on the phone about the possible Crazy Horse burial sites. Jerry worked for us while he was a college student attending the University of Nebraska; while there, he competed for the quarterback position on the football team. Now Jerry is a stockbroker and raises cattle. He was telling me he had a family taking care of his cattle on pasture west of White River, South Dakota. I told him Mario's story about the Dillon family traveling northeast of Wanblee to visit the grave of Crazy Horse near the place where his cattle were grazing. Jerry put me in contact with the Mednansky family who were tending his cattle. He really liked the care his cattle were getting. The family, he told me, was good caretakers of the land.

Looking northeast toward the White River from high on Horseshoe Butte.

I stopped to visit Mrs. Oleta Mednansky in Mission, South Dakota, where she was working on her business degree—a four year degree she would complete in three years. It turned out Oleta and Mario shared the same grandfather, Harry Quiver. Oleta was also related to the Crazy Horse family on her mother's side through Nellie Larvie, one of Crazy Horse's wives. Oleta's parents, Ansel and Mary

225

Woodenknife, had told her when she was a young girl that Crazy Horse was buried in Mellette County. The grave was on a hill near a lone cedar tree that overlooked the White River. She did not know the exact site, but had feelings for where it might be.

My son Woody was with me the day I visited with Oleta. Later, we spent some time driving the back roads of Mellette County, meandering up and down the White River Valley just to get a feel for the area. We saw several lonesome cedar trees on high hills as we wandered. We also saw that the White River is filled with milky water colored by the light clay soil. I wondered to myself if that was the same clay that Crazy Horse used when he made the white lightening stripes and hail spots on his cheeks before he went to deal death to those who invaded his people's land.

31

The Circle of Life: From Birth to Death

At the visitor's center at Bear Butte, there is an explanation by the Okute (Teton Sioux) of the significance of the circle to the Indians: "The power of the circle is a strong force within their culture. All things in nature are interrelated, and any unusual disturbance can throw the circle out of balance. Although the names differ—sacred circle, medicine wheel, sacred hoop, circle of life—the underlying belief remains that all life revolves in a circle, an endless loop bound to the natural and spiritual world."

Black Elk said that "the sky is round, and I have also heard that the earth is round like a ball and so are all the stars. The moon does the same [orbit], and both are round."

Near the end of March 2000, Terry Gray of the Rosebud Reservation invited me to sit with him at a tribal meeting of leaders from all the Lakota Nation reservations to discuss their positions on the National Historic Preservation Act. I was the only white person there listening to Lakota leaders tell about sacred ground that the government was defiling with roads and other projects that they called "progress." After the meeting, I quietly went to one of the tribal leaders who had spoken and mentioned to him that white men find it difficult to understand why ground and animals may be sacred to the Lakota. I told him we needed to be educated as to the importance of this ground to the Lakota people. It seems that they were saying that this is sacred, and that over there is sacred, and that all is sacred. The whites seek an understanding of specifics. The Lakota lecturer nodded his head.

That day I was told by Tim Mentz that a new school building in Pierre, South Dakota, was being built over a graveyard, and that a child had been choked by a spirit that was bothered by this action. Tim was diligently working to enforce the Preservation Act so that building would stop and the tribe had called in spiritual leaders for help. Tim said that sacred sites such as te-pee rings need to be protected from government construction. Leaders were reluctant to tell all of the sacred stories of why they were so important, but the people of the Standing Rock Reservation knew they must help the white government understand. Lakota people are afraid to reveal many important facts about these issues for fear of retribution from the spirits that have whispered to the people not to speak too much of the Lakota sacred ways. Tim told me that in

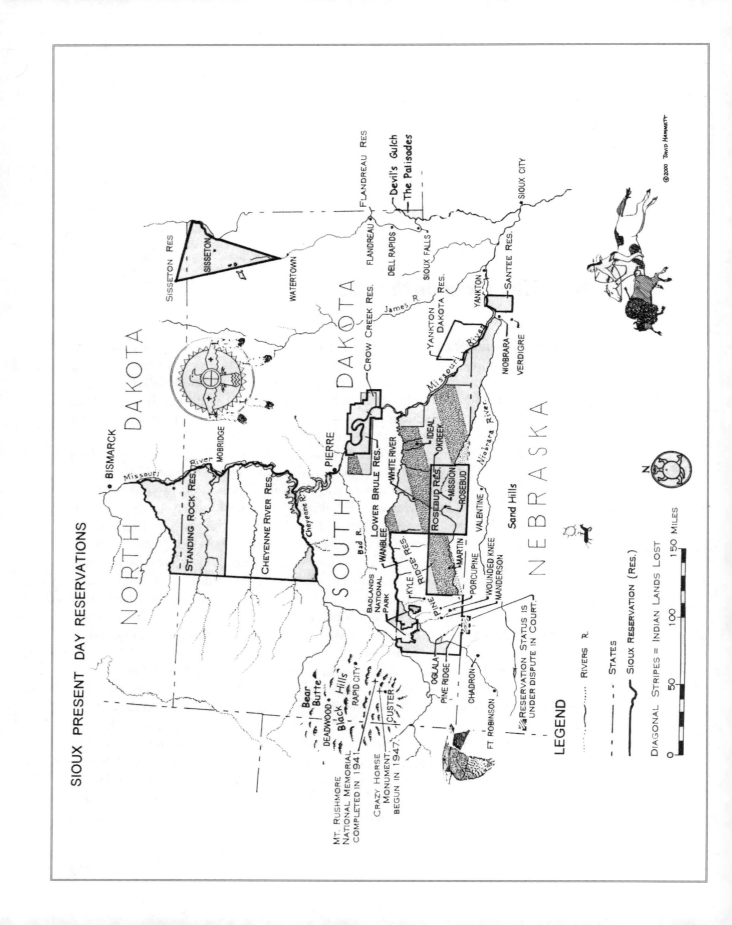

SIOUX PRESENT DAY RESERVATIONS

©2000 David Hammett

NORTH DAKOTA

SOUTH DAKOTA

NEBRASKA

Bismarck

SISSETON RES.
SISSETON

WATERTOWN

FLANDREAU RES
FLANDREAU
DELL RAPIDS
SIOUX FALLS

Devil's Gulch
The Palisades

SIOUX CITY

CROW CREEK RES.

James R.

SANTEE RES.

YANKTON DAKOTA RES.
YANKTON

NIOBRARA
VERDIGRE

Missouri River

STANDING ROCK RES.

MOBRIDGE

Missouri River

CHEYENNE RIVER RES.

Cheyenne R.

PIERRE

Bad R.

LOWER BRULE RES.

WHITE RIVER

IDEAL
OKREEK

ROSEBUD RES.
MISSION
ROSEBUD

Niobrara River

VALENTINE

Sand Hills

WANBLEE

BADLANDS NATIONAL PARK

KYLE
PINE RIDGE RES.
PINE RIDGE
MARTIN
PORCUPINE
WOUNDED KNEE
MANDERSON
OGLALA
CHADRON

FT ROBINSON

Bear Butte
Black Hills
DEADWOOD
RAPID CITY
CUSTER

MT. RUSHMORE
NATIONAL MEMORIAL
COMPLETED IN 1941.

CRAZY HORSE
MONUMENT
BEGUN IN 1947.

RESERVATION STATUS IS
UNDER DISPUTE IN COURT.

LEGEND

. . . . RIVERS R.

– – – – STATES

⌇⌇⌇ SIOUX RESERVATION (RES.)

DIAGONAL STRIPES = INDIAN LANDS LOST

0   50   100   150 MILES

N

the future leaders would be debating what should be revealed and by whom. He told me an older man may do this, but that as a man in his forties, he was not yet willing to risk the possible spiritual consequences.

Tepee rings predate 1870; after that time, stakes were used. This much about sacred rings was shared: to hold tepees down from strong winds, rocks were placed at the base of the tepees; these circles of rocks are the tepee rings. When the tribe moved, these tepee stones were left behind and used as burial markers. For example, where a circle of tepee stones would lie, there might be a straight line of stones outside the circle that would mark a point away from the circle toward the east to show a burial spot, perhaps as much as a quarter of a mile away. Crystals were put on the grave and they would emit an energy that helped communicate with the dead. A Lakota authority on tepee rings told me that wherever Crazy Horse is buried, there would probably be circles of crystals.

Crazy Horse carried a white crystal with him. White spots which represented hail were painted upon his neck and shoulders, and on the flanks of the horse he rode and a forked lightning strike appeared on his face. These were death dealing agents that showed no mercy and were part of Crazy Horse's medicine and also of the Thunder Cult to which Crazy Horse belonged.

Reggie Cedarface, an anthropologist from the Pine Ridge Reservation who is part of the Crazy Horse tiyospe, told me that the circle is part of nature; a bird makes a round nest and a dog circles before lying down. Reggie also told me to be sure to tell people that the first-born is given a pair of moccasins at birth, and that when that person dies, those moccasins are buried with them but not on their feet. Instead, another pair is worn by the deceased. If this does not happen, it is believed that the individual will not walk a spiritual journey. Reggie also told me that Louie Pablo's grandmother left offerings at the Crazy Horse burial site near Manderson, South Dakota.

At the same time I was visiting with Reggie, I was putting together our annual Blue River Jolly Jogathon Track Meet that has been held in Marysville for more than twenty years. Each year we honor outstanding track and field athletes. This year, Don Holst was to be honored. He was a former track coach from Marysville who now lives in Chadron, Nebraska, and was coming down to compete in the Master Age bracket competition. Don coached at Chadron State College and was also the 1968 Olympic jumps coach. I told Reggie that Don was trying to talk Joe American Horse and Joe Swift Bird, both great runners from Pine Ridge, to come down to our meet. Reggie said that Joe American Horse beat Billy Mills, the Olympic 10,000 meter Gold medal winner, in almost every race they'd run.

There is a tradition among Native Americans that the remains of the dead be brought back to be buried near the land where they were born. Not surprisingly, in addition to the many possible locations of Crazy Horse's burial site, there are also several theories about where Crazy Horse's circle of life began. William Bordeaux reported that Mrs. Joe Clown told him Crazy Horse was born somewhere near the mouth of the Laramie River in southeastern Wyoming. Mrs. Clown and her husband agreed that Crazy Horse's birth was in the spring of the year that Left Hand Nose was killed by Shoshone. Bordeaux traced back on an Oglala Wintercount

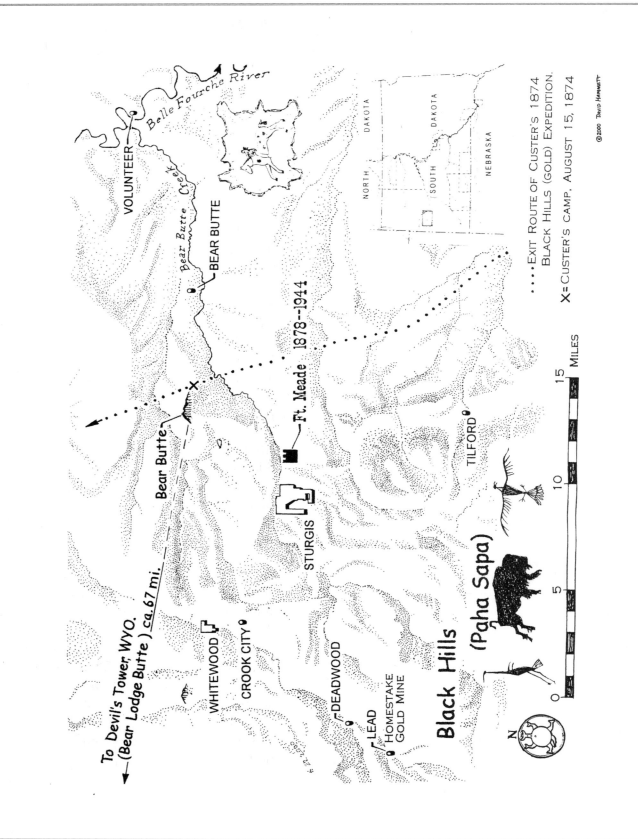

Belle Fourche River

VOLUNTEER

BEAR BUTTE

Bear Butte Creek

Ft. Meade 1878–1944

Bear Butte

To Devil's Tower, Wyo.
(Bear Lodge Butte) ca. 67 mi.

X

NORTH DAKOTA

SOUTH DAKOTA

NEBRASKA

©2000 David Hammett

·····Exit Route of Custer's 1874
Black Hills (Gold) Expedition.

X= Custer's camp, August 15, 1874

WHITEWOOD

CROOK CITY

DEADWOOD

LEAD

HOMESTAKE
GOLD MINE

STURGIS

TILFORD

Black Hills
(Paha Sapa)

N

0   5   10   15 MILES

from the time of his death and discovered that this would place his birth in 1839. [*Wintercounts are calendars drawn or painted on tanned skins. The most important events of the year were depicted. History was preserved by the Lakota people in this manner. One hide would tell the events of many years.*]

The medicine man Chips had reported that Crazy Horse was born on a small butte near Bear Butte. There are a couple of different theories as to whether his body was returned to where he began his life or to some other place.

Bear Butte

In the summer of 1998, David Kadlecek received a letter from a man named David Hajny, from Hastings, Nebraska. Hajny had read the Kadlecek's book, *To Kill an Eagle: Indian Views on the Last Days of Crazy Horse*, which mentioned a possible burial site of Crazy Horse on Beaver Creek north of Hay Springs, Nebraska. Hajny thought Kadlecek might be interested in hearing about another possible burial spot for Crazy Horse.

In 1991, Hajny visited with Chuck Rambow who was working at the visitor's center at Bear Butte. Rambow told Hajny that Crazy Horse was disinterred three or four times and the remains of Crazy Horse ended up at Bear Butte. Hajny had a lengthy conversation about Native American history with this man. Rambow said the burial spot was about a mile southeast of the visitor center on private property. It is in a little ravine marked by four rocks in the pattern of a rectangle. Hajny was told that many old people come up from the reservation to pay their respects at this spot.

Chuck Rambow was a hard guy to catch up with. I located his wife by telephone. She told me they were divorced and if I found him I should let her know. "He might be sleeping with somebody in a trailer near the base of Bear Butte," she suggested and then started to laugh. I said I guessed it had been an amiable divorce. She said they'd been apart for five years and that only in the last year had she been able to laugh about it. She had a nice phone manner and I thanked her for her help. I finally located Chuck and interviewed him at Bear Butte in August 1999.

Chuck had grown up around Sturgis, South Dakota, and taught high school there for many years. He was presently teaching Native American History at Black Hills State College and he gives tours of the Bear Butte as a government employee. He told me he liked being at Bear Butte so much that it had probably interfered with his marriage.

In the 1960s, a fellow named Fred Brown told Chuck a story about Bear Butte. Brown shod horses for a rancher during the 1920s and 1930s, just below Bear Butte. During that time, Lakota people used to come to Bear Butte to pray. Those same people would stop at the base of the mountain and pay their respects to someone who must have been very special to them. The special place was in a ravine at the base of Bear Butte which Chuck and Fred had marked with four rocks. Chuck told me that the mountain itself is not a place for burials, but is a place of mystery, power, and promise. For the Cheyenne and Lakota, it is a spiritual place that is most powerful. Fred had gotten indications from the Lakota who visited that this may be where Crazy Horse's remains lie.

It was also here that a young Cheyenne, Sweet Water, received the Four Laws given by Maheo (God) to guide the Cheyenne and Lakota lives. The laws told that no one must kill, steal, commit adultery, or marry into their own family.

The Lakota people were allies of the Cheyenne, and both prayed here. Chuck told me that in 1857, this was where the father of Crazy Horse announced that his son had a sacred vision that he had the power to be safe from harm in battle. Chuck said Black Elk had said, "Crazy Horse saw people in bugs (cars); he saw flu epidemics; he saw the desperation of his people." With the gift he was given, Crazy Horse would lead the defense of the Lakota territory. The father then took the name Worm for the remainder of his life. Many believe that Crazy Horse is buried at the base of the mountain. Chuck said, "The spirit voice of Crazy Horse is sought today when many arrive at the sacred mountain to speak with the spirits of the past. Prayers are also offered for peace and healing and respect of all people and animals on earth."

Bear Butte Creek Valley.

Chips was the medicine man who gave Crazy Horse his special guiding medicine that consisted of two tail feathers from a spotted eagle. It was said that one feather was worn upside down in the loose hair, while the other one was tied to a strip of rawhide that also covered the little round stone. In 1910, Chips told Walter Camp that Crazy Horse was born near Bear Butte Creek, which is a tributary of the Cheyenne River, close to Bear Butte.

In *Fool's Crow*, Mails says, "Bear Butte has been described as the most awesome vision-questing place in the Black Hills." For several centuries, great Indian leaders made their vision quests that would last four days on this mountain; it was also here the revered medicine man, Fools Crow, received the secret medicine that he would use to help his people through sickness with the help of herbs. He could only apply that medicine at night. It was here he was warned that, as a medicine man, he could not engage in war or in personal fighting. He could never hate anyone or indulge in jealousy or revenge. He could never accept payment for his treatment of the sick.

Chuck Rambow told me Fools Crow wanted to have Crazy Horse's peace pipe on display at Bear Butte, but that it had been stolen by some kids who broke into Fools Crow's home shortly before he died.

Bear Butte.

Fools Crow was a good friend of Chuck's. Chuck had been given a wristwatch with Lakota beading on the band as a gift from Fools Crow for his work on reconstructing the ceremonial grounds at Bear Butte. Chuck was flattered by this, and gave his own personal watch to Fools Crow.

Bear Butte is sacred for other reasons, too.

Barbara Adams, the archivist at Lakota College near Kyle, South Dakota, told me her parents had gone to Bear Butte for the ritual of conception. Barbara is related to the Black Elk family that was related to Crazy Horse. The old volcano on Bear Butte is believed to be the source of all souls. A man and woman would come here to stay until the woman became pregnant. Barbara's parents came here in hopes they would capture a good soul for their first-born child. Barbara said that following her birth, her parents returned to Bear Butte and placed a flat rock in the fork of a tree as an offer of thanksgiving.

Bear Butte is a holy mountain where sage and cherry branches are used to mark vision questing spots. Prayers are offered here by Lakota wearing buffalo robes for warmth and for sacred power. In recent years, a court case made it a point of law that jet planes from nearby Ellsworth Air Force base are not allowed to fly over and disturb the air space at Bear Butte.

A creek valley below Bear Butte where Crazy Horse may lie.

The sacred White Buffalo Calf Pipe is the central pipe of Lakota ceremony, used in sweat lodges, rites, Sun Dances, and healing. Fools Crow said it has been handed down through the generations since sometime between AD 1200 and 1500. Arvol Looking Horse, the keeper of the sacred White Buffalo Calf Pipe, said, "The Great Spirit gave us the sacred bundles and the sacred sites and the sacred knowledge of the stars. To our people, the Black Hills is a sacred place, so we pray there, and we follow the buffalo there and, sometimes, we live there."

Victor Douville, who teaches Lakota studies at Sinte Gleska University on the Rosebud, told me that "the Lakota people believe that the Black Hills is where the Pte people, forefathers to the Lakota, came out of the earth. Here is where their ancestors are buried, and where they go for prayer."

Victor told me about *Lakota Star Knowledge*, published in 1990 by Sinte Gleska University. It tells of the Lakota belief that the stars mirror the earth. That belief has been handed down through oral tradition and was also kept on two tanned hides. On one hide is a star map and the map on the other hide is of the earth. Wakan Tanka placed the stars in such a manner so that what is in the heavens is on earth, and what is on earth is in the heavens. As the sun journeys counter-clockwise through the constellations, the Lakota travel clockwise through the Black Hills from one ceremonial site to another. The people mirror the sun's path on the Plains similarly to what the buffalo did when they followed the sun in their seasonal migrations.

Bear Butte is but one sacred site, but it is an important one. The Creator gave the sacred instructions to the Lakota people on Bear Butte, much like the Ten Commandments were given to Moses. The Sacred White Buffalo Calf Pipe and Bear Butte hold the secrets to the past, present, and future of the Lakota people and their life cycles.

In September 1998, Darlene Rosane told me that Wankan Tanka told Crazy Horse to go to Bear Butte to fast for four days. It was here he fasted to cleanse his body and then fight the temptations that his people would encounter. While fasting on this big butte, his warriors guarded him from other tribes who, at times, were trying to hunt him down. Crazy Horse sang that night to the gods while he was nestled in the rocks. Then he disappeared; he was gone. His people thought he was resting, but they searched the area and could not find him. Later he was located on faraway Devil's Tower where he then fasted for three days. Here he saw evidence of the two children that had been saved from a chasing bear when the earth was raised up and the tower was formed to save the children from the encroaching bear. The children evidently lived to adulthood on this tower. Crazy Horse now saw the adult skeletons of the grown children. He knew that they had lived off snakes and rats because he also saw skeletons of those animals. It was here that he received a warning that it was evil for him to fast at Bear Butte. The spirits picked him up and carried him back to Bear Butte to tell his people that this was not a place to fast.

Darlene told me that, when coming down from the butte, medicine men and helpers burned the flag colors of the four directions and the tobacco ties. This was done so the Great Spirit would recognize the rising smoke. Sage was also burned to keep away any contamination from evil. Crazy Horse's relatives kept this smoke message to the gods to themselves.

Many people think Crazy Horse got his power and medicine here on Bear Butte, but this was not so; there was no one place where he acquired his power. Instead, it was gathered during visits to a combination of different hills in the Sandhill region and probably other areas. Darlene says that today people still fast and seek vision quests here, but none of those closely related to Crazy Horse's people do so.

Victor Douville said that when the summer solstice occurs, there are eight stars in Gemini that correlate to the sacred site of Bear Butte. Plains tribes held Sun Dances here during the solstice. Victor told me that Devil's Tower is what whites call the place that the Lakota call Bear Lodge Butte. There are many versions of the legend about the creation of this place. One legend, very similar to the story of Crazy Horse's vision that Darlene Rosane told me, was about a brother and sister who were chased by bears. A voice directed them to climb a hill that was nearby. The bears closed in on the children and surrounded them. A sacred god named Fallen Star commanded the earth to rise up, well out of reach of the bears that clawed at the hillside as it rose. The clawed hill became known as Devil's Tower. Later an eagle carried the children back to Mother Earth and to safety.

After listening to the various opinions about Bear Butte, I wondered how at ease his spirit would be if Crazy Horse really was buried there. It is safe to say, however, that he would always have water from the spring runoff on the sacred mountain, and there would be no noise from Air Force jets.

Oak Creek

Black Elk asked readers in *Black Elk Speaks*:

> Is not the south the source of life and does not the flowering stick truly come from there? And does not man advance from there toward the setting sun of his life? Then does he not approach the colder north where white hairs are? And does he not then arrive, if he lives at the source of light and understanding which is east? Then does he not return to where he began, to his childhood, there to give back his life to all life and his flesh to the earth whence it came?

Darlene Rosane told me that Crazy Horse was not born near the base of Bear Butte, but that he was born in a camp near Oak Creek. She said this was not the town of Okreek, South Dakota, but somewhere on the creek called Oak Creek which begins west of that town. When I was traveling around with my father, the residents of Okreek told us that when the people applied for a post office, the government postal department declared that it would not accept any town name which consisted of two words. Oak Creek was out. The townspeople suggested Okreek, and it was accepted.

A well-respected Lakota woman educator from the Manderson, South Dakota area told me that Crazy Horse's father was not Worm, but a white man. I asked Darlene Rosane about

Oak Creek Valley near the mouth of Oak Creek.

235

this and she said that what she considered full-blooded Native Americans in her family sometimes had light hair and light-colored eyes.

My wife and I visited Okreek shortly after Christmas 1998. We were near the mouth of Oak Creek when a spotted eagle descended from the sky. The eagle rode the updrafts smoothly, hardly ever stroking its large wings. The floating bird glided in a circle over the mouth of Oak Creek for half an hour. It was difficult not to regard this as some sort of sign. Perhaps if Crazy Horse had been born here, he might have been brought back here to be buried in this place.

In 1999, our mortuary prepared the funeral of Harry Gausphol who had grown up on a farm northeast of Marysville. After high school, he moved away to work in the Chicago area, but I remembered him from twenty-two years earlier. Harry's wife died in 1977, and he had her brought back to be buried in Marysville, even though Elizabeth had never lived in the area. This was his home, and he knew that one day he would be brought back to be by her side. Harry wanted to come home for his final rest. Many people choose to return to their early homes, and this always touches me. Harry must have had very fond memories of the farm he'd grown up on and the family ties

White River just above the mouth of Oak Creek. My wife Mony wanted to stop and watch an eagle ride the up draft.

he'd had. He was buried in the Catholic cemetery just down the road from the place where he had been born.

I told Harry's surviving daughters that I had remembered their father. I told them how most Native Americans want to be buried where they were born; that it was a tradition. I shared with them the mystery of Crazy Horse's burial.

Thinking back to that December morning with my wife, I remember looking to the east over Oak Creek and on toward the morning sun where I witnessed a true vision. It was that eagle, circling over the mouth of Oak Creek, bringing a sense of light to a place where the spirit of Crazy Horse might be searching for a place of rest.

32

Where the Spirit Rests

The trails that lead to where Crazy Horse's body might have been carried are many and divided. We have followed the paths of Crazy Horse after his death at Fort Robinson, then on to the Spotted Tail Agency and Camp Sheridan. From there, the parents went to the Manderson, South Dakota, area and closely followed the White River down to the old Ponca Agency near Niobrara, Nebraska, where the body of Crazy Horse may have accompanied them. We have seen that the parents went back to the Rosebud Reservation to live—and then die—in that area. We have briefly peeked into the past of his blood mother.

Crazy Horse could be buried in any number of places, and perhaps, like the remains of his adversary, General George Custer, he may be buried in several places. Black Elk knew that it did not matter where Crazy Horse's body lies, "for it is grass. But where his spirit is, it will be good." I have followed his spirit and it has taken me on a journey of understanding that I never had before.

Could Dowsing Find Crazy Horse's Grave?

In 1999, I spoke to a Lakota studies class on the Rosebud Reservation about recording history and writing about oral traditions that have been handed down for so many generations. We talked about Lakota Sioux heritage and about gravesites my father located while working on his book. One of the fellows in the class had done some archeological work using dowsing instruments to locate graves. He asked me about this method.

Even though dowsing has often been viewed as a questionable activity, I've used it to find water, lost possessions, and even burial sites. I've seen my father dowse with astonishing results. Earlier in this book I described how he predicted that water could be found 42 feet underground, and it was found 42.5 feet below the surface, startling the skeptical well-driller. I've spoken of the dowsing at Little Bighorn that may shed more light on the historical view of that battle, and of my own experiences dowsing for gravesites. I related to the class the following stories.

A much-respected Marshall County historian, Ray Ellenbecker, was interested in dowsing. Through the years, we had traded many stories, with me mostly listening. Ray handled our printing for the mortuary in Marysville until he was in his nineties, when his health no longer permitted him to work. When I first moved to Marysville in 1976, he had asked me where I came from and I told him Verdigre, in northern Nebraska, adding that it was a town he'd probably never heard of. "Verdigre," he'd said. "Well, I just came from there yesterday. I'd been there to visit that old mill they have." I told Ray that my father had been instrumental in restoring that mill after it had been moved from west of town. It sat on my father's land for a year before the foundation was ready for exhibit in town.

Ray and I hit it off right away, and most people would agree that his memory for historical facts was phenomenal. He knew I was interested in dowsing, and he wondered about its effectiveness. He told me about the Twin Mounds located about twenty miles south of Marysville, close to the California-Independence branch of the Oregon Trail. Explorer Lieutenant John Fremont had stopped at the mounds and noted the beauty of the valley in 1842. It had been rumored for years that there were gravesites on the tops of the mounds. There was an old legend of a great battle atop those mounds, and that the graves of the slain were located beneath the stony cairns that impart an aura of mystery to the place.

Oretha Ruetti, reporter for the *Marysville Advocate*, shared information about this battle in an article she wrote on November 3, 1977. A farmer, Grant Ewing, who lived in the area, reported that in 1842 a three-day battle began between three hundred white men and fifteen hundred Indians. The white men had muzzle loading rifles and a few Indians had rifles and the rest had spears. The white men climbed the Twin Mounds so they could see a long distance and shoot the Indians when they tried to climb the hill. Supposedly, there were fourteen white men killed, and more than one hundred Indians died. After the battle, the white men buried their dead partners, seven on the center of each mound.

Ray wanted me to give an opinion on the possibility of gravesites on Twin Mounds, and he asked the land owner for permission to hike to the mounds. The day I was able to go, Ray had a leg bothering him. He told me to go alone, but I passed.

A few months later, a man named Dick Russell, who had lived near the mounds at one time, stopped by and I asked him to come hiking to the mounds with my boys and me. Dick has written articles about the arrest of Leonard Peltier at Pine Ridge after the shoot-out with FBI agents occurred in the 1970s. He was also working on a book about the Kennedy assassination. Dick was staying in the area visiting relatives of the Midwestern Plains artist, Thomas Hart Benton.

I showed Dick the method of dowsing I use, holding L-shaped rods in my hands. The dowser must focus on what he is trying to locate—in our case, graves—and, if the rods cross while walking, there may be a grave there. He just shook his head. I said that it was okay, that it was just something with which I was experimenting.

On the pinnacle of the west mound, the rods crossed three different times indicating that there may be three graves. There was no crossing of the rods on the other mound and probably no graves.

I once was asked to move a baby's grave from Axtell, Kansas, to Summerfield, Kansas, a few miles away. There was a stone that marked the spot of the grave in the cemetery at Axtell, but my dowsing showed that the stone was not over the body; it was off by a full two feet. Was the stone off or was my dowsing wrong? When it was exhumed, the wooden casket was right where the dowsing said it would be.

On another occasion, I was called by a funeral director to find the grave of a Native American medicine man, supposedly buried under the railroad tracks that ran past the town of Paxico, Kansas. The medicine man's name was Pasqua. Local residents had been told that Pasqua was buried under the tracks and wanted to know if it was true. They were hoping for a boost in tourism, but they had been told by authorities that unearthing the grave would result in a $20,000 fine. The solution was to dowse for the grave. I told them that dowsing wouldn't conclude who was buried there—dowsing should be regarded only as an opinion and not fact, unless you dig down and find human remains. The results of the dowsing were negative, although I was able to determine that someone was buried atop a nearby hill. Without digging, there was no way to tell if it was the medicine man.

Another time, I was called to the Marys-ville, Kansas, cemetery by a sexton named Kent Nester. He recounted a story first printed in a newspaper in 1884 reporting that a man named John Pennington and his wife may have been murdered. A neighbor at the time reported seeing a door ajar, and told his wife something was wrong at the Pennington's. The next day, that neighbor found the body of John Pennington. He was lying by a corn crib in a pool of blood, a bullet hole in the head. His pants pockets were turned inside out. It appeared that he died without a struggle, which led investigators to conclude he had been murdered by an acquaintance.

His wife was found dead in the barn. By the position of the body and her clothing, it was determined that she had been sexually assaulted. The Pennington's sorrel mare was missing. One person also conspicuously missing was the family's hired man. Nobody knew his name, but a description was given to authorities.

A report came back from Beatrice, Nebraska, that a man fitting the description of the Pennington's hired man had sold a sorrel

Hanging of Sam Frayer for the brutal murder of Mr. and Mrs. John Pennington on the Spring Creek Bridge near Marysville, Kansas.

239

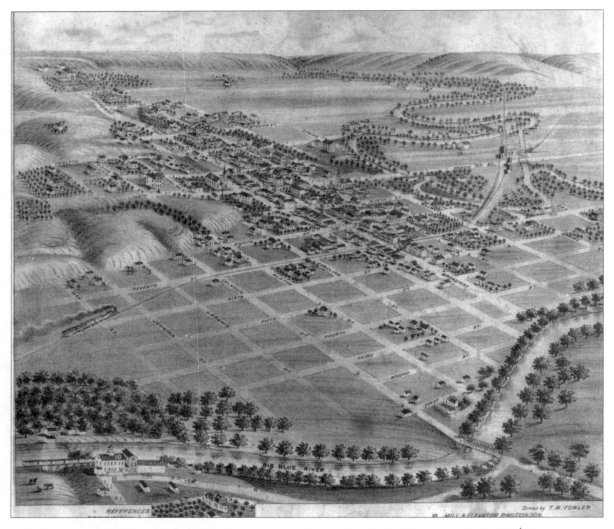

A bird's eye view of Marysville in 1879 looking east toward Spring Creek which flows into the Big Blue River.

mare in town. The man was arrested in Seward, Nebraska, where he had just been hired on as a farm hand.

He was taken to Marysville, where he was tried and convicted in a four-day trial. Following the conviction, a lynch mob stormed the sheriff's office and forced the deputy to turn over the keys to the cell. The man, identified as eighteen-year-old Samuel Frayer, was taken to a bridge over the Spring Creek and was hanged.

The location where Frayer's body was buried had long been a source of speculation. Some said it was in a field near that bridge, others say he was buried in the northeast corner of the Marysville cemetery. Kent Nester, the cemetery sexton, asked me to dowse that area of the cemetery.

The area I was asked to dowse was about the size of three square blocks. On the first pass, the dowsing rods gave no indication that a body was to be found. I made several passes to be sure. After an hour of searching, no response. I asked Kent to move the pick-up, and I dowsed there. My rods crossed. Indications were that the body lay north-south, while all the other bodies in the cemetery were east-west, which would indicate that the body was purposely disrespected when it was buried.

Like the burial site of Pasqua, the remains believed to be those of Frayer were never unearthed. Dowsing simply indicated that there was a body there.

Another problem I was called upon to help with was when a worried lady called our mortuary insisting her husband, George Farrell, had been buried in the wrong grave plot in the cemetery. Widow LaVonne Farrel was distraught, wanting an explanation of why her husband was not in the precise spot she told the sexton to place the body. According to the placement of the headstone, the body was placed about two spaces further south than it should have been.

It was of great concern to LaVonne because when her time came, she was to be buried between her husband and their young son, Tim, who died in a farm accident. Now she wasn't sure that would happen and it was causing her great anxiety.

The cemetery caretaker explained that upon measuring the family plot, they found the stone marker for the son was located in the walkway, not where it should have been. The sexton felt the boy was not buried by the stone, but one grave space to the south. He said there was a depression several feet south of the stone; this, he concluded, was where the boy had been laid to rest. I called LaVonne and explained the situation to her and it seemed to calm her anxiety for the time being.

LaVonne's daughter had been doing some investigating on her own, and talked to the man who had actually dug the grave twenty-seven years earlier. I'm not sure what LaVonne's daughter was told by the gravedigger, but when I got that final call from LaVonne, deeply disturbed by the situation, I went to visit her.

I had planned to go see Sheila Reiter in a Lincoln, Nebraska, hospital that day. Sheila was a professor at Doane College and had been working with me on this manuscript in its early development. She was suffering in the late stages of cancer.

I met LaVonne and her daughter at the cemetery and explained to them how dowsing worked. Digging down was the only way to know for certain, but dowsing would leave the family plot untouched by shovel. LaVonne was inquisitive about the process, so I taught her to dowse. We began by dowsing over the freshly dug grave of her husband. She knew there was a body there, and it worked for her. The rods crossed when held over the grave of her husband.

I instructed LaVonne to walk to the north, toward her son's grave. The rods crossed before she got to the headstone. She gasped, "The headstone *is* in the wrong place!"

LaVonne's daughter wanted to try dowsing. Geneva got the same results as LaVonne. At this point, I again explained that the only way to be sure was to dig. They were satisfied with the results, and chose not to disturb the family plot.

But as I was about to leave the cemetery to drive north to visit Sheila, I noticed an unusual license plate on the front of Geneva's vehicle. It looked like a scene of an Indian warrior in solitude on a horse. [*Kansas does not have a state requirement that a vehicle needs to be identified on the front, only the back.*] The horse's head was bent down as if it might be taking one last drink before it resumed another journey across the earth. Geneva told me the license plate symbolized the end of the trail. Her family identifies with the Native American ways. I told her that I knew a Lakota family in Lincoln by the name of Fire Thunder whose son paints that same symbol on drums. To them, it is the symbol of Crazy Horse coming to a point in the trail where he is seeking guidance from the Great Spirit.

That mid-August afternoon as I approached the hospital in Lincoln, Nebraska, something told me to stop and see the Fire Thunder family before I went to visit Sheila. I was greeted warmly by Lillian Fire Thunder, a woman who had been a great help in my learning about the Lakota way of life. I explained to Lillian that I had come to Lincoln because Sheila was not doing well and was in the hospital just down the street from the Fire Thunder home. Lillian gave me some sage to burn for Sheila to cleanse her spirits. She also had a small drum to give to Sheila that her son had created. It was painted with red, gold and black colors and the picture was of a warrior seeking guidance. It looked just like the warrior I had seen on Geneva's vehicle earlier that day in the cemetery.

Sheila was delighted with the gifts from the Fire Thunder family; it brightened her day to know Native American people were thinking of her.

Sheila was a lovely person to work with on this book and she also reminded me of my father, as both liked the color white. White clothing, white cars, white carpets where they lived. Sheila Reiter once said to someone, "I do not need to put color in my life; you put color in my life."

Sheila died two weeks later. She offered guidance on the trail of life...and the journey into death. This teacher who rode in white was there for us to follow through the valleys, past the yucca plants, and over the hills beside the clear streams. Thoughts of her resting peacefully, free from the pain of the illness that took her life, have led me to conclude that another great soul ought to have the same sort of peace...Chief Crazy Horse.

The students at Sinte Gleska wanted to know if dowsing could be successful in finding Crazy Horse. I believe in dowsing.

I've seen it work for others, and I've seen the results of my own dowsing. I told them I believe that dowsing is a tool that could possibly help us identify the final resting place of Chief Crazy Horse...but there are ethical questions that must be considered.

My feeling is that Crazy Horse was different from other warriors in his life. He had not sought recognition for his accomplishments and would probably not want to be commemorated at one specific gravesite. While some of his descendants may think they know where he lies, his spirit would not want the body to be found by the general public. If one's spirit does not want the body to be found, it is difficult, if not impossible, to zero in on an area using dowsing as a locator. I respected what I believe his spirit desires and told the students that we should focus on what he stood for instead.

The spirit of Crazy Horse and what he meant to the Sioux doesn't lie with him in his burial site. His spirit is soaring with the eagle, alive within the Sioux Nation. Historians might like to find the site for the sake of putting closure to the story. Others would like to erect a great monument, and I have no doubt that somebody would like to make money off the gravesite, which is the one thing that bothers me most.

If somebody dowses for that site, it won't be me. Even if I tried, I believe that his spirit would not let me find it. Let Crazy Horse rest in peace, and let the story end with a devoted people keeping their greatest secret for all eternity…

Where "His Horse Is Crazy" Rides

In the late winter of 1999, I was introduced to Seth Big Crow by Terry Gray. We all had lunch together at the Antelope Inn in Mission, South Dakota. Seth explained that he was related to Crazy Horse through Rattle Blanket Woman who had two sisters, Looks After and Good Looking Woman. Seth's blood lineage came from Good Looking Woman. His family had kept the Crazy Horse family tree hung on their porch for many years. Brian Bordeaux told me he'd seen this family tree on Seth's porch in April of that same year when he was doing some carpentry work at Seth's house. It had been a family tradition not to speak of Crazy Horse because he is so revered. Not until a beer company named their product Crazy Horse Beer did Seth ask permission to step out of the circle of silence.

The family protested the beer name and filed suit against the beer company, seeking damages because alcohol was something of which Crazy Horse did not approve. Seth is the spokesperson for the family in the fight to have the name of Crazy Horse removed from the beer can.

Since 1992, Seth is the only family member to have stepped forward. He said, "In a way, I am an outcast in my family, since I have broken the circle of silence." Seth introduced me to his brother who had just walked by our table. Seth told me that his brother remains inside the circle of silence and will not speak of being related to Crazy Horse.

I told Seth that I was not privileged to know where Crazy Horse was buried, but I knew that even people from the game show *Jeopardy* wanted to know about the chief that was killed at Fort Robinson. However, I understood that the burial place was to be respected as a family place. I asked if he could share something with me about Crazy Horse for my story. He told me that a medicine man, Leslie Fool Bull, the son-in-law of Seth's grandfather, Henry Big Crow, had been the caretaker of the grave. Fool Bull died with the secret of its whereabouts in 1998. Seth said that even he had never visited the grave, but he knew about the general vicinity where it was, and that it was not on any reservation of today.

We talked about the Crazy Horse mountain sculpture, which many Lakota people are against, believing it goes against nature to take a mountain God made and change it into a sculpture. "The spirit of Crazy Horse is working against them," a Lakota spiritual man said, according to an article published in *Indian Country Today* on July 2, 1996. Seth said that, personally, he was glad it is there. "The Lakota people may never claim the Black Hills, but this is the best symbol to leave behind. It will be better than the four faces. The mystery of Crazy Horse will reign. White men cannot have the body of Crazy Horse, but one thing the Lakota will have that cannot be taken away is the monument of Crazy Horse." When we parted with smiles and a firm handshake, he said, "Wasta." Terry Gray translated, "Good."

From the White Cliffs of Manderson, South Dakota, through the Sandhills of Nebraska, I traveled in a white Grand Prix along the dusty backroads for years with my father in search of Crazy Horse and an understanding of the spirit world in which he lived. As the trails wove around big buttes and vast, wide-open spaces with sagebrush as well as a mix of tall and short prairie grass, the land of Crazy Horse kept calling. We circled Lakota country more than once. There were no dead ends; most every person we asked had a story where the great warrior might have been laid to rest.

The spirit of Crazy Horse seemed to toy with me more than the Dismal River raccoon that, one cold night, unzipped my tent four times. I threw it out each time until, as a last resort, I looked it in the eye and said, "If you want in here then go to sleep." I couldn't believe it when it circled around my sleeping bag and crawled in! We kept each other warm until the sun came up. I thought raccoons were creatures of the night, but that next morning we went crawdad hunting together. Walking up and down the river it dawned on me that both Crazy Horse and that rowdy raccoon yearned for the wide-open spaces, but once in a while they would stop in to tease a white man.

I honestly did not grasp some of the deeper significance of the continuing mystery of Crazy Horse's burial spot until a couple of years after the death of my father. It haunted me that some of the Lakota people wanted his spirit to go into another world.

My son Woody and I had just left Verdigre, Nebraska, and were headed west through the lands where Crazy Horse's people had roamed. In a few minutes we were driving beside familiar pastures that overlooked the Missouri River. That sight triggered memories of the time I helped my father try to hunt down a family of three buffalo that had escaped from an enclosed pen on a ranch near the Devil's Nest, thirty miles from Verdigre. The snow had drifted above the top of the fence and the buffalo just walked out and ran loose in the hills of Knox County for many months, destroying ranching fences wherever they roamed. Their ancestors had always roamed free and this buffalo family did not understand the white man's barbed wire. The ranchers decided that they had to be captured, and they banded together for a buffalo hunt. Even the highway patrol got involved. Unfortunately, the bull and calf were killed in the hunt, but the cow escaped and no one could find her.

Several weeks after the death of the two buffalo, a rancher came into my dad's veterinary office and I overheard him telling my father that the lone remaining cow buffalo was living in a heavily wooded ravine on his land. My dad asked me to go with him to check on the buffalo. We drove out to a huge pasture on the ranch where we found a little spring creek that ran year round surrounded by a thickly wooded area. I stared through the tree cover just beyond the stream and saw what looked like the shadow of a buffalo but then it disappeared. Months later the rancher told us that the buffalo was still living in that hideout.

For years I did not know what happened to that buffalo; all I knew was that it fought hard for freedom from the small pen that it once was in. It was not until after my father died that I found tape recorded notes he made pertaining to that buffalo cow:

> The buffalo had stayed in the pasture of the rancher from north of Verdigre for about a year. He would give me an occasional report on the animal and one day he came into my office and told me it was standing by itself, looking over the fence line, staring. The rancher took me to the spot and I was able to use my tranquilizer gun on the animal. We loaded the buffalo on a hay wagon, the kind of wagon used to haul big haystacks, and hauled it to the rancher's corral near his big barn. I drove out and injected dextrose into the buffalo's vein everyday for a week, but it died of stasis of the lungs.

> A couple of years after this I was invited to St. Louis, Missouri, to move animals from Anheuser Busch's farm on down to his new Busch Gardens in Tampa, Florida. A chemist by the name of Dr. Palmer, who invented the tranquilizer gun, asked me to help him. I told him I would accept on one condition and that was if my young son could go along. We flew to St. Louis and the Busch people had a helicopter at the airport to transport us the next few miles to the animal preserve. After a couple of days of tracking down red deer and elk, he asked me to tranquilize a buffalo with his gun. I shot a dart at a buffalo and in a few minutes it hit the ground. After about ten minutes it got up and ran away. He told me that he used a new tranquilizing agent called succinylcholine. It really worked well. He related to me that the old drug nicotine sulfate caused many problems in its use on buffalo. He told me with nicotine you could use 100 drops on cattle or deer but one drop will cause problems or death to a buffalo. Usually it affects the lungs. Although I realized that the buffalo was not quite 100 percent healthy before it received the dart, I also knew right then that nicotine may have played a part in the death of the buffalo cow that roamed the hills between Verdigre and the Missouri River.

> Right after the buffalo cow died, the rancher whose property the animal died on asked me what to do with the animal. I told him to bury the animal down by the Verdigre Creek and put up a great big cross. We used a big telephone pole and part of another one.

> A year later people would come up to me and say they had seen the buffalo cow roaming the hills around Verdigre. I knew differently but I never said anything.

I told Woody that a year or two later, I went with my dad to treat some sick buffalo that were contained in a small pasture surrounded by barbed wire. I was a little kid but I can recall him saying, "Oh heck, confinement of these animals causes disease. These animals really don't need my medicine; they just need a bigger grassland." Years later, as I began to understand the passion that Crazy Horse felt for freedom and a land without boundaries for his people and the animals, I would understand that my father seemed to have been voicing those same thoughts back then.

Woody and I had been on a long drive that day and I felt tight, so I stopped and got out of my white pick-up truck to stretch my muscles. A breeze came up, and I felt relaxed and cooled. I looked out over the horizon and I thought about how Crazy Horse was buried in an unmarked grave in one spot and my father in another. Even though they were separated by a couple of generations, they had both cherished the same land. They both mourned the loss of freedom for the animals and native people that had been brought about by the growth of the white man's civilization. I wondered if their spirits had ever met; maybe even at that very moment they were moving around a campfire somewhere in the Sandhills, talking about buffalo hunts and vast herds of free-roaming horses.

That day we made our way to near the foot of Eagle's Nest Butte, to the home of Richard Moves Camp, the descendant of Crazy Horse's medicine man, Chips. We asked Richard about Crazy Horse's desire that, after his death, his body was to be placed in a stream for four days so that his spirit would come back stronger than ever. I told Richard that the Lakota oral history passed to the American Horse family told that the people of Crazy Horse wished that he go on to another world since there had been enough war and killing. His body was not placed in the stream. But if he was *not* placed in the stream, why do we still feel him so strongly? Richard declared, "He was a great warrior and we should remember his deeds and what he stood for. The warrior belongs to the earth and the grass. Mystery is what he believed in; he is in the spirit world and let that spirit be. It has a life of its own. Let it carry on."

Sioux Indian Village at dusk.

References

Adams, Barbara Means. Personal interviews. July 1998. June 1999.

Adams, Barbara Means. *Prayers of Smoke*. Berkeley: Celestial Arts, 1990.

Albers, Kelly Jo. Personal interview. 30 July 1998.

Anadarko Oklahoma Daily News. 15 Aug. 1954.

Ambrose, Stephen E. *Crazy Horse and Custer*. New York: Doubleday Publishing, 1975.

American Horse, Joe. Telephone interview. 6 June 2000.

Anderson, Thomas M. "Killing of Crazy Horse." Unpublished. Anderson Folder. Fort Robinson Archives. Fort Robinson, NE, 1890.

Arkeketa, Tony. Personal interview. April 2000.

Bark, Leveda. Personal interview. 28 July 1998.

Belt, Mary. Personal interview. 28 July 1998.

Bettelyoun, Susan Bordeaux, with Josephine Waggoner. *With My Own Eyes*. Lincoln: U of Nebraska Press, 1998.

Big Crow, Seth. Personal interview. 4 Feb. 1999.

Blevins, Win. *Stone Song*. New York: Tom Doherty Associates, 1995.

Bordeaux, Johnna. Personal interview. 15 Sept. 1998.

Bordeaux, Shawn. Letter to author. n.d.

Bordeaux, William J. *Custer's Conqueror*. Sioux Falls: Smith and Company.

Bourke, James G. Diary entry. Aug. 1878. Fort Robinson Archives. Fort Robinson, SD.

Bourke, John Gregory. *On the Border with Crook*. n.p.: Time Life, 1982.

Brininstool, E.A. "Chief Crazy Horse: His Career and Death." *Nebraska History*. Jan.-Mar. 1929.

Buchan, Robert. Personal interview. 27 July 1998.

Buchan, Robert, and Father Joseph Karol. "Crazy Horse Site." Presented at Plains Conference. Lawrence, KS, 1969.

References

Buecker, Thomas R. "History of Camp Sheridan, Nebraska." *Journal of America's Military Past.* 1995.

_____. Personal interviews. June 1996. July 1998.

_____. "The Search for the Elusive (and Improbable) Photo of the Famous Oglala Chief Crazy Horse." *Greasy Grass.* 14 May 1998.

_____. *Fort Robinson and the American West.* Lincoln: Nebraska State Historical Society, 1999.

Buffalo, Short. Interview with Eleanor Hinman. 13 July 1930. Nebraska State Historical Society.

Camp, Walter Manson. Manuscripts. Brigham Young University Archives. Provo, UT.

Capper's Weekly. "Grave of Crazy Horse Found." 5-12 Aug. 1969.

Carmen, J. *Sheridan County Star* [Rushville, NE]. 15 April 1954.

Cash, Marcella. Personal interview. Feb. 1999.

Cedar Face, Reggie. Telephone interview. 6 June 2000.

Cheyenne Daily Leader. 18 Sept. 1877.

Chicago Times. 6 Sept. 1877.

Chicago Tribune. 11 Sept. 1877.

Clark, W. P. Letter to Carl Schurz to Department of the Interior. 7 Nov. 1877. Fort Robinson Archives. Fort Robinson, SD.

Coats, Gary. Personal interview. 15 Sept. 1998.

Comes Killing, Charles. Personal interview. 30 July 1998.

Crow Dog, Dinah. Personal interview. 4 Aug. 1999.

Crow Dog, Leonard. *Crow Dog.* New York: Harper Perennial Publishing, 1995.

Colorado Springs Gazette. 16 Jan. 1955.

De Barthe, Joseph. *Life and Adventures of Frank Grouard.* Norman: U of Oklahoma Press, 1958.

DeMallie, Raymond, and Douglas R. Parks. *Sioux Indian Religion.* Norman: U of Oklahoma Press, 1987.

Deresa, Mitchell. Personal interview. 30 July 1998.

Dickson, Ephriam D. III. "Crazy Horse: Who Really Wielded Bayonet that Killed the Oglala Leader?" *Greasy Grass.* May 1996.

Dillon, Gene. Letter to author. Sept. 1999.

Dog, He. Interview with Eleanor Hinman. 7 July 1930. Nebraska State Historical Society.

Douville, Victor. Personal interviews. Feb. 1999. April 1999.

Ellenbecker, Raymond. Personal interviews. 1975-1995.

Fire, John. Telephone interview. 20 Feb. 2001.

Fire Thunder, Anna. Personal interview. 29 July 1998.

Fire Thunder, Lillian and Mark. Personal interviews. 1 March 1999. July 2000.

Frazier, Ian. *On the Rez*. New York: Farra, Strauss and Giroux, 2000.

Friswold, Carroll. Ed. Robert A. Clark. *The Killing of Crazy Horse*. Lincoln: U of Nebraska Press, 1988.

Freedman, Russell. *The Life and Death of Crazy Horse*. New York: Holiday House Publishing, 1996.

Gonzalez, Mario. Personal interview. 25 April 1999.

Gonzalez, Mario, and Elizabeth Cook-Lynn. *The Politics of Hallowed Ground*. Chicago: U of Illinois Press, 1998.

Goodman, Ron. *Lakota Star Knowledge*. Mission, SD: Sinte Gleska University, 1992.

Gray, Terry. Personal interviews. 18 Sept. 1998. Feb. 1999. Aug. 1999. Nov. 1999.

Guttmacher, Peter. *Crazy Horse*. New York: Chelsea House Publishers, 1994.

Guise, Byron and Eulalia. *An Affair with the Past*. Manhattan, KS: Hawley Publishing, 1983.

Hajny, David. Personal interview. Aug. 1998.

Hal, Lucy. Personal interview. 28 July 1998.

Hamilton, Henry W., and Jean Tyree. *The Sioux of the Rosebud*. Norman: U of Oklahoma Press, 1971.

Hammond, Jean. Personal interview. 11 Nov. 1999.

Hanson, James. Telephone interview. July 1998.

_____. *Famous Indians of Northwest Nebraska*. Henderson, NE: Service Press, 1983.

Hardoff, Richard G. *The Surrender and Death of Crazy Horse*. Spokane, WA: The Arthur C. Clark Company, 1998.

_____. *Lakota Recollections: New Sources of Indian Military History*. Lincoln: U of Nebraska Press, 1997.

_____. *The Oglala Lakota Crazy Horse: A Preliminary Genealogical Study and Annotated Listing of Primary Sources*. Mattituck, NY: J.M. Carroll and Company, 1985.

Hassrick, Royal B. *The Sioux*. Norman: U of Oklahoma Press, 1964.

Havlovick, Pat. Telephone interview. 4 June 1998.

Hayden, Sally. Personal interview. 12 Aug. 1998.

Herman, Jake. "Sioux Writer Says Crazy Horse is Buried North of Pine Ridge Agency." *Sheridan County Star*. 15 April 1954.

Hinman, Eleanor. Letters to Mari Sandoz. n.d. Sandoz Collection. Nebraska State Historical Society.

Hollow Horn Bear, Duane. Personal interview. 4 Feb. 1998.

Holmes, Karol Ann. Personal interview. July 1998.

Holst, Don. Personal interview. July 1998.

Hook, Jason. *American Indian Warrior Chiefs*. New York: Firebird Books, 1990.

Howard, H.P. *Crazy Horse*. N.p.: n.p., 1975.

References

Howard, James. *The Ponca Tribe*. U.S. Government Printing Office: Washington, D.C., 1965.

Hyde, George E. *Red Cloud's Folk*. Norman: U of Oklahoma Press, 1937.

_____. *Spotted Tail's Folk*. Norman: U of Oklahoma Press, 1961.

"Ideal Pow Wow." *Omaha World-Herald*. 27 Aug. 1961.

Indian Country Today. 9 June 1993.

Indian Country Today. 2 July 1996.

Indian Country Today. 22 June 1999.

Indian Country Today. 5 July 1999.

Indian Country Today. 2 Dec. 1999.

Jensen, Ben. Personal interview. 2 April 1999.

Johnson, E.P. Letter to Doane Robinson. 1902. Fort Robinson Archives. Fort Robinson, SD.

Kadlecek, David. Personal interview. 28 July 1998.

Kadlecek, Mabell. Personal interview. 28 July 1998.

Kadlecek, Edward and Mabel. Personal interview. 28 July 1998.

Kadlecek, Edward and Mabel. *To Kill an Eagle: Indian Views on the Last Days of Crazy Horse*. Johnson Publishing Company, 1983.

Kills in Sight, George. Interview with Joseph H. Cash. 1967. Fort Robinson Files. Fort Robinson, SD.

King, James T. *Indian Fights and Fighters*. Lincoln: U of Nebraska Press, 1971.

Lakota, Julie. Personal interview. July 1998.

Lee, Jesse M. Diary entry. 1877. Fort Robinson Archives. Fort Robinson, SD.

Leslie, Frank. *Illustrated*. 20 Oct. 1877.

Levin, Alan. *USA Today*. 22 Mar. 1999.

Liska, Danny. *The Ponca Curse*. Niobrara, NE: Big Foot Publishing, 1990.

_____. *River Rat Town*. Niobrara, NE: Big Foot Publishing, 1990.

Little Thunder, Jake. Personal interview. 9 June 1999.

Mails, Thomas E. *Fool's Crow*. Lincoln: U of Nebraska Press, 1990.

_____. *The Mystic Warrior of the Plains*. New York: Barnes & Noble, 1972.

Matthiessen, Peter. *In the Spirit of Crazy Horse*. New York: Viking Press, 1980.

Medansky, Oleta. Personal interview. 9 June 1999.

Mentz, Tim. Personal interview. 6 June 2000.

Milk, Bernice and Jasper. Personal interview. 9 June 1999.

Mitchell, Edgar. Dowsers Convention. Danville, Vermont. Sept. 1987.

Monroe, Cynthia. Personal interview. 17 Oct. 1999.

Moves Camp, Richard. Personal interview. 10 June 1999.

Mulhair, Charles. *Ponca Agency*. Niobrara, NE: n.p., 1992.

_____. Personal interview. 26 Nov. 1998.

Musil, Marjorie. Personal interview. April 2000.

Neihardt, John G. *Black Elk Speaks.* Lincoln: U of Nebraska Press, 1932.

New York Sun. 14 Sept. 1977.

New York Times. 28 Sept. 1877.

Niobrara Tribune. 27 Aug. 1998.

Noguchi, Thomas T., M.D. *Coroner at Large.* New York: Simon and Schuster, 1985.

Omaha Daily Bee. 3 Dec. 1877.

Omaha World-Herald. 21 Jan. 1906.

Omaha World-Herald. 15 Nov. 1998.

One Star, Lloyd. Personal interview. 4 Aug. 1999.

Paul, Eli. Personal interview. 11 Mar. 1999.

Paul, R. Eli. *The Nebraska Indian Wars Reader 1865-1877.* Lincoln: U of Nebraska Press, 1998.

Paulson, T. Emogene. Sioux Collection. "George Kills in Sight." Vermillion: U of South Dakota, 1982.

Paulson, Emogene, and Lloyd Moses. *Who's Who Among the Sioux.* Vermillion: State Publishing, 1988.

Pfeifer, Caroline Sandoz. Personal interview. 23 Feb. 1995.

Potter, Gale deBuse. Personal interview. 28 July 1998.

Pourier, Bat. Interview with Eli Ricker. 6 May 1907. Nebraska State Historical Society.

Pourier, Bat and Pat. Personal interview. July 1995.

Potter, Jim. Personal interview. 11 Mar. 1999.

Rambow, Charles. Personal interview. 8 Aug. 1999.

Rapid City Journal. 24 April 1992.

Red Bear, Christine. Personal interview. 4 Aug. 1999.

Red Fox, Chief William. *The Memoirs of Chief Red Fox.* New York: McGraw-Hill, 1971.

Red Owl, Ambrose. Letter to author. March 1991.

_____. Personal interview. 28 Dec. 1998.

Respects Nothing, Woodrow. Personal interview. 5 Aug. 1999.

Ricker, Eli. Ricker Collection. 20 Nov. 1907. Nebraska State Historical Society.

Rosane, Darlene. Personal interview. 30 July 1998.

Ruetti, Oretha. *Marysville Advocate.* 3 Nov. 1977. 30 Mar. 2000.

Runnels Brothers. Personal interview. 17 Oct. 1999.

Rybolt, Robert. Personal interview. 28 July 1998.

Sandoz, Mari. *Hostiles and Friendlies.* Lincoln: U of Nebraska Press, 1959.

_____. Collection: 1942. Lincoln: U of Nebraska.

References

_____. *Old Jules*. Lincoln: U of Nebraska Press, 1935.

Scott, Douglas. Personal interview. March 1988.

Scott, Douglas, and Richard A. Fox. *Archaeological Insights into the Custer Battle*. Norman, OK: University of Oklahoma Press, 1984.

Scott, Douglas, contributors Richard A. Fox, Melissa A. Conner, and Dick Harmon. *Archaeological Perspectives on the Battle of the Little Bighorn*. Norman: U of Oklahoma Press, 1989.

Shaw, Amberson. Interview with Eli Ricker. 1 Sept. 1907. Nebraska State Historical Society.

Shaw, Larry and Richard. Personal interview. March 1998.

Shaw, A.G. Shaw Family Adventure Collection. Property of Larry Shaw, Lincoln.

Shumway, Grant L. *History of Western Nebraska and Its People*. Lincoln: The Western Publishing Company, 1921.

Sidney Telegraph [Sidney, NE]. 15 Sept. 1877.

Simonds, Fr. Thomas. Personal interview. 29 July 1998.

Smith, Gary. "Shadow of a Nation." *Sports Illustrated*. 18 Feb. 1991.

Sneve, Virginia Driving Hawk. *They Led a Nation*. Sioux Falls, SD: Brevet Press, 1928.

Standing Bear, Luther. *My People the Sioux of the Missouri*. Lincoln: U of Nebraska Press, 1975.

Strayhorn, Robert. "Northern Indians." *Denver Daily Tribune*. 20 May 1877.

Turner, Fredrick. "Searching for Crazy Horse." *Men's*. June-July 1998.

Valandra, Suzy. Personal interview. 15 Sept. 1998.

Walker, Stanley. State Highway Sign on US Highway 18. Seven miles south of Wounded Knee, SD.

Walstrom, Veryl Armor, Sr. *My Search for the Burial Sites of Sioux Nation Chiefs*. Lincoln, NE: Dageforde Publishing, 1995.

Welch, Don. "The Hawk."

"When Legends Die and Dreams End" *Indian Country Today*. 18 June 1996.

Young, J. Charmayne Valandra. Personal interview. 29 July 2000.

Personal Contacts

Barbara Adams
Lakota College Archivist.

Kelly Jo Albers
Introduced me to Darlene Rosane. Kelly was a friendly receptionist at Cedar Pass Lodge in the Badlands of South Dakota who guided me through the mirages of the wasteland.

Joe American Horse
Chief American Horse's grandson.

Tony Arkeketa
Provided knowledge of Ponca and Otoe history.

Laveda Bark
Of Holy Rosary Mission. She told me some good stories and was a warm person to visit with.

Mary Belt
Worked at the tribal census in Pine Ridge. She shared an article with me about the search for Crazy Horse.

Seth Big Crow
Descendant of Crazy Horse's mother. Thanks for the insight.

Johanna Bordeaux
Showed me the way to Salt Users Camps on the Rosebud.

Shawn Bordeaux
Raised on the Rosebud Reservation and manages a casino.

William Bravebird
Lives on the Rosebud Reservation.

Bob Buchan
> Curator of the Sheridan County Historical Society. Researched Camp Sheridan and possible site of Crazy Horse death scaffold.

Buechel Memorial Lakota Museum.
> Provided help in my research.

Tom Buecker
> In charge of the Fort Robinson Museum. His kindness and direction led to much of the information in this book. He shared the files on Crazy Horse that he had collected and loaned them to me. Without that information this book would not have been written. Tom wrote a book on the Surrender Ledger of Crazy People. He has written articles in search of the elusive photo of the famous Oglala chief, Crazy Horse. He recently published his book, *Fort Robinson and the American West*. My monthly questions were answered with complete detail and kindness. The discussions were fun especially when we intertwined his son's eight man football playoff games and basketball tournament action.

Marcella Cash
> Archivist at the Rosebud Reservation who took the time to answer my many questions.

Reggie Cedarface
> Pine Ridge anthropologist.

Gary Coats
> Clinical psychologist who served the Pine Ridge and had an understanding of the Lakota people because he is a descendant. Chief Red Cloud was his sixth cousin.

Steve Cohorst and staff
> Construction of Crazy Horse genealogy tree.

Charles Comes Killing
> Lakota buffalo hide man. Provided knowledge of Manderson.

Dinah Crow Dog
> Lives in Crazy Horse Canyon.

Denver Art Museum. Archives.
> Provided help in my research.

Mitchell Desersa and her mother Esther
> Members of the Black Elk family.

Gene Dillon
> Descendant of Sioux Chief Standing Bear and Crazy Horse's father, Worm.

Victor Douville
> Lakota cultural teacher at Sinte Gleska University.

Raymond Ellenbecker
> Provided insight into printing, photography, and storytelling. His Oregon Trail and Native American stories through the years were some of the best.

Fremont Fallis
> Provided knowledge of Rosebud history.

John Fire
> Provided knowledge of John Fire Lame Deer.

Anna Fire Thunder
> Retired teacher and principal in Manderson who provided knowledge about local history.

Lillian and Mark Fire Thunder
> Provided knowledge about Crazy Horse. We burned sage together.

Fort Robinson Archives. Crawford, NE.
> Research.

Mario Gonzalez
> Kickapoo Attorney General who knows the genealogy of Lakota people.

Terry Gray
> His help and guidance from the archives at the Rosebud Reservation guided me to places I never dreamed of. He worked for the Smithsonian Institute in the field of archeology and is currently in charge of repatriation of graves for Native Americans.

Dave Hajny
> Railroader who had made Crazy Horse and Indian wars his pastime. Shared his Bear Butte experiences.

Lucy Hal
> Helped me locate people who may have stories about Crazy Horse.

Jean Hammond
> Soft voice of the Conroy and Standing Bear family.

Jim Hanson
> Past director of the Museum of the Fur Trade in Chadron. He is a local historian.

Pat Havlovick
> Librarian in Harden, Montana. Helped me relocate an old article on the crow basketball players my father gave to Ambrose Red Owl.

Sally Hayden
> Former Marysville librarian who now works at Kansas University. Helped me research Crazy Horse's picture.

Duane Hollow Horn Bear
> Descendant of Chief Iron Shell and Chief Hollow Horn Bear.

Personal Contacts

Karol Ann Holmes
> Funeral home operator in Valentine who serves the Rosebud Reservation. The reservation people are quite taken with her sympathy and understanding of Lakota ways.

Don Holst
> Professor and former track coach at Chadron State College. He has a cabin on Chadron Creek not far from where the Red Cloud Camp was in 1876. He introduced me to many knowledgeable people on Lakota culture.

Johnson Holy Rock
> Knew Coffee.

Jayne Jacobitz
> Provided knowledge of Niobrara history.

David Kadlecek
> His parents wrote the book *To Kill an Eagle: Indian Views on the Last Days of Crazy Horse*, which tells many stories of Sioux Indian accounts of Crazy Horse's funeral ceremony. David was a project engineer on the Oahe Dam in South Dakota and now ranches in northern Nebraska.

Mabell Kadlecek
> David's mother and a retired Pine Ridge Reservation teacher.

Cecila Kitto
> Provided knowledge of Ponca and Santee Sioux.

Milos Koskan
> Provided knowledge of South Central South Dakota Cemetery.

Robert Kuzelka
> University of Nebraska.

Julie Lakota
> Lakota College Archivist.

Lakota College Archives. Kyle, SD.
> Research.

David Laravie
> Provided knowledge of Ponca history.

Jake Little Thunder
> Tribal elder and descendant of Chief Little Thunder.

Oleta Mednansky
> Mellette County rancher.

Tim Mentz
> Historic preservation authoritarian.

David Mignery
> Provided family story of Logan Fontenelle who was wounded on the Mignery Ranch in Wheeler County, Nebraska, where young Crazy Horse was.

Jasper and Berncie Milk
> Descendants of Chief Lame Deer and Chief Milk.

Cynthia Monroe
> Of the Nebraska Historical Society. Formerly worked in the state brand inspecting office. She was able to coral many clues I had running wild on the Great Plains.

Richard Moves Camp
> Medicine man and grandson of Chips.

Charles Mulhair
> Ponca historian of the Missouri and Niobrara region.

Marjorie Musil
> Provided knowledge of Otoe Indians.

National Archives Military Records. Commission of Indian Affairs. Washington, D.C.
> Research.

Nebraska Historical Society. Lincoln, NE.
> Research.

Lloyd One Star
> Chief on the Rosebud Reservation and descendant of Chief Iron Tail, Baptiste Good and Brown Hat.

Eli Paul
> Truly a technical researcher and historian. His suggestion on research opened doors that I could not find the knob to.

Pershing Center Archives. United States Military Academy, West Point.
> Provided help in my research.

Caroline Sandoz Pfeifer
> Rancher woman of the Sandhills who got me started by introducing me to the Kadlecek family. Her sister, Mari, wrote the book *Crazy Horse Strange Man of the Oglala Sioux.*

Gale DeBuse Potter
> Historian who is an authoritarian on the Shirt Wearers of Crazy Horse. She works at the Fur Trade Museum in Chadron.

Jim Potter
> Shared written resource material. He works at the Nebraska Archives.

Bar and Pat Pourier
> Their gas station on the Pine Ridge always has Sunny Delight!

Charles Rambow
>   Provided knowledge on Mato Paha (Bear Butte).

Christine Red Bear
>   Lives in Crazy Horse Canyon near Crow Dogs Paradise.

Ambrose Red Owl
>   Always said, "I can beat you further at my race than you can beat me at yours." He was Niobrara's great distance runner of the 1960s.

Woodrow Respects Nothing
>   Father was born during the Massacre at Wounded Knee in 1890.

Darlene Rosane
>   Possesses a remarkable memory of Lakota oral history. Her stories were a great find.

Oretha Ruetti
>   Marshall County historian.

Jack and Victor Runnels
>   Descendants of Chief Standing Bear, the Conroy family, and Crazy Horse's father, Worm.

Robert Rybolt
>   Little Bats trading post and history buff in Crawford, Nebraska.

Dr. Douglas Scott
>   Archaeological researcher at the Midwest Archaeological Institute in Lincoln, and world-renowned expert on the Little Bighorn Battle site. Through Doug's suggestion I conducted experiments in dowsing.

Larry and Richard Shaw
>   Amberson Shaw's grandsons.

Father Thomas Simonds
>   Pastor at Holy Rosary School north of Pine Ridge.

Sinte Gleska University Archives. Mission and Rosebud, SD.
>   Research.

South Dakota State Historical Society Archives. Pierre, SD.
>   Research.

Helen Stauffer
>   Mari Sandoz historian.

Tara Tucker
>   Provided knowledge of Blackpipe Creek and Rosebud Reservation.

Suzy Valandra
>   Directions and history of colors told the Lakota way.

Chad Wall
> Nebraska Archives photo department authoritarian who helped me locate most of the old-time Native American photos I thought would be interesting.

Steve and Jack Warner
> Human behavioralists.

Don Welch
> Professor at University of Nebraska at Kearney and noted wildlife poet.

Albert Whitehat
> Rosebud Reservation drummer and teacher.

J. Charmayne Valandra Young
> One of the great spirits behind the Buechel Memorial Lakota Museum in St. Francis, South Dakota.

Readers with suggestions:
> Tom Buecker, Victor Douville, Rosemary Walstrom, Woody Walstrom, Wally Walstrom, Dr. Jerry Stubben, Rev. Marilyn Wullschleger, Peg Slusarski, Jean Walstrom, Dr. Julie Walstrom

Index

A

Aberdeen, South Dakota 7
Adams, Alex 139
Adams, Barbara 50, 72, 116 - 117, 233, 254
Ambrose Red Owl 23, 25 - 26, 83, 99, 256
Ambrose, Stephen 33, 52
American Dowsers Association 41
American Horse 47 - 49, 60, 64 - 65, 72, 74, 86, 120, 137
American Horse, Joe 49, 229
American Horse, Thomas 123
American Indian Movement 114, 116
Anderson, Eunice 147
Anderson, Thomas 159, 186
Arapaho 29
Arkeketa, Tony 193, 195, 197 - 198
Arkeketah, George 193
Armed Forces Institute of Pathology 42
Atkinson, Jack 132
Austin Good Voice Flute 122

B

Bad Cob, George 218
Bad Faces at Soldiers' Town 31
          see also Red Cloud
Bad Heart Bull, Amos 69, 196
Bad Road 56
Badlands 141
Bald Eagle, Felix 14
Bark, Laveda 84

Battle Medicine Feather   164
Battle of Little Bighorn   6 - 7, 12, 15, 27, 45, 49 - 53, 55, 57, 71, 126, 188, 224, 253
Battle of Rosebud 48
Bazile Mills Creek 27
Bear Butte 53, 127, 227, 231 - 235
Bear Butte Creek 232
Bear Butte Creek Valley 232
Bear Coat 49
Bear Creek 146
Bear Lodge Butte 235
Bear-in-the-Lodge Creek 224
Beaver Creek 8, 15, 23, 55, 64, 120, 122 - 129, 131 - 133, 135, 137 - 138, 147, 162, 179, 207, 231
Beaver Creek Valley 127
Beaver Mountain 122, 126 - 127, 137
Beaver Valley 106, 120, 122 - 126, 136
Ben Black Elk 109
Benton, Thomas 238
Bertels, George 117
Bettelyoun, Susan 129, 167, 169 - 170
Big Blue River 103, 240
Big Brulé Village camp 21
Big Crow, Seth 243
Big Crow, SuAnne 196
Big Foot 13, 104
Big Piney Creek 35
Big White River 189
Bingham Creek 203
Black Buffalo Woman 33 - 34, 131, 166, 211
Black Elk 26, 28 - 29, 31 - 32, 50, 54, 89, 109 - 111, 117, 139 - 140, 143 - 144, 146, 155 - 156, 227, 232 - 233, 235, 237
Black Elk, Ben 14, 26, 109, 122
Black Feet 2
        see also Sihasapa
Black Hills 15, 28, 38 - 39, 52 - 53, 66, 83, 88, 104, 136, 143, 180, 196, 220, 232 - 233, 244
Black Pipe Creek 222 - 224
Black Shawl 7, 15, 37, 131, 151, 207
Blackfeet 47
Blue Eagle 141 - 142

Blue Eyes, Nancy 186
Blue River 193
Blue Water Creek 151
Bordeaux, Brian 173 - 176, 243
Bordeaux, James 122, 162, 167
Bordeaux, Johnna 169, 173 - 174
Bordeaux, Johnny 134
Bordeaux, Lionel 169, 173
Bordeaux, Louis 122, 162, 167
Bordeaux, Shawn 173 - 174
Bordeaux, William 162 - 163, 167, 229, 231
Bourke, Captain John 55, 66, 128, 136
Bradley, Luther P. 15, 66, 85, 88, 104, 132 - 133
Brazile Creek 102
Brininstool, E.A. 6, 66, 75, 86, 104, 131 - 132
Brown, Fred 231
Brulé 2, 14 - 15, 20 - 21, 30, 65, 122, 130 - 131, 136, 152, 159, 163, 167, 179,
        181 - 182, 186, 202, 210
Buchan, Bob 135, 255
Buechel, Father 164
Buecker, Thomas R. 69 - 70
Buffalo Soldiers 45
Bureau of Indian Affairs 114,. 116
Burned Thighs 2
        see also Brule
Burnette, Robert 222
Burroughs, Major 133

C

California Trail 193
Camp Robinson 1 - 2, 4, 6, 53, 55 - 57, 59 - 60, 62, 64, 66, 68, 71, 73 - 74, 77,
        84, 86, 104, 106, 117, 120, 128 - 131, 133, 136, 146, 150, 154 - 155, 166
Camp Sheridan 15, 128 - 131, 133 - 138, 162 - 163, 187 - 188, 237
Camp Sidney 73
Carlisle Indian School 212
Cedarface, Reggie 229
Chadron State College 135, 229
Chase, Joseph 198
Chekpa 118
        see also Lakota Sioux
Cheyenne 47, 54, 231 - 232

Cheyenne Indian Reservation 41
Cheyenne River 232
Cheyenne River Agency 146
Cheyenne River Reservation 12, 154, 162
Cheyenne River Sioux 12
Chief Big Elk 218
Chief Gall 54
Chief Iron Shell 168 - 169, 171
Chief of the Reservation 57
Chief White Thunder 162
Chimney Butte 114, 118 - 119, 142
Chimney Butte 113
Chimney Rock 17
Chipps, Charles 148 - 149
Chips 129, 139, 147 - 151, 153, 216, 231 - 232
Civil War 33, 43
Clark, William Philo 57, 132, 177, 179 - 180, 187
Coats, Gary 158, 190 - 191
Coffee 155, 222
Colonel Forsythe 12
Comanche 6
Comes Killing, Charles 140 - 141, 153
Conquering Bear 19 - 21
Conroy, Frank 212
Conroy, Harry 211
Conroy, John 50
Conroy, Victoria 188, 207 - 208, 211 - 212, 224
Court of Indian Offenses 62
Crazy Horse Butte 138 - 139, 141, 146
Crook, General George 15, 48, 54, 56 - 60, 64, 104, 133, 136, 183
Crow Agency 195
Crow Creek 47
Crow Dog, Chief 172, 201 - 202
Crow Dog's Paradise 164, 171
Crow Reservation 24
Crows 27, 38
Curd, Rollin 113
Curly 21
Custer Battlefield 41 - 42, 44 - 46
Custer massacre 48, 65, 70
Custer State Park 157

Custer, George A. 5, 7, 13, 15, 22, 27, 35, 39, 41 - 43, 45, 49, 51 - 52, 218, 237
Custer, Tom 43
Custer, Tom   43, 45

D

Dakota Sioux   2
Dakota Territory 182
Dakotas 188
Dale Spotted 24
Darren Big Medicine 24
Desera, Mitchell 26
Desersa, Aaron 109
Desersa, Mitchell 28 - 29, 31, 109, 111, 255
Devils Tower 39, 234 - 235
Dillon, Gene 222 - 224
Dillon, Robert 222 - 223
Dismal River 1, 99 - 100, 117, 148, 163, 244
Doc Middleton 203
Douville, Victor 4, 234, 255
dowsing 4, 39 - 46, 199 - 200, 204, 237 - 239, 241 - 242

E

Eagle Hawk 187
Eagle, Jimmy 116
Eagles Nest Butte 149, 171 - 173, 187, 224, 246
Edmunds, Governor 183
Elkhorn River 201
Ellenbecker, Ray 238

F

Falen, Delmar 6
Fallis, Fremont 220
Falls Down, Tim 24
Farrell, George 241
Fast Thunder 117, 152 - 153
Fat Crane 191
Feldhausen, Alan 193
Fetterman, J. William 35
Fire Thunder, Anna 102
Fire Thunder, Lillian 192, 242

Fire Thunder, Lillian 153
Fontenelle, Chief Logan 30 - 31, 258
Fools Crow 232 - 233
Fort Laramie 14 - 15, 20, 50
Fort Phil Kearny 14, 34 - 35
Fort Robinson 7, 15, 22 - 23, 48, 59 - 60, 62, 65 - 66, 69 - 70, 72, 75, 79 - 80, 82 - 84, 120, 132, 142, 152 - 154, 158 - 159, 179, 187, 207, 237, 243
Fort Robinson Museum 95
Four Laws 232
Fourteenth United States Infantry 70
Frayer, Sam 239 - 240
Friswold, Carroll 177, 186 - 187

G

Galligo, John 122
Garnett, William 48, 66, 72
Gausphol, Harry 236
Gentles, Private William 15, 66, 68 - 70, 73 - 74
George Kills in Sight 153, 155
George Respects Nothing 118
Ghost Dog, Nellie 118
Golden Eagle Casino 50
Gonzalez, Mario 7 - 8, 50, 148, 216, 220, 222, 224, 256
Good Weasel 36
Grass Dance 195 - 196
Gratten, John L. 21
Gray, Terry 218 - 219, 227, 243
Great Sioux Reservation 143
Great Spirit 29, 32, 56, 82, 102, 110, 123, 127, 146, 149, 191, 233
Great White Bluffs 29
Great White Father 107, 184, 201
Gregg, Lawson 125
Grouard, Frank 15, 37, 58 - 61, 77 - 78, 132

H

Hajny, David 231
Hammond, Jean 209 - 212
Happy Hunting Grounds 131, 187
Hardorff, Richard 72, 131, 207
Harney, General William 151
Haskell Indian College. 23

Hayden, Sally 6
Hayes, President Rutherford 137, 159
He Dog 6, 34 - 36, 49, 55 - 56, 62, 64, 69, 72, 74, 166, 177, 186 - 187
Herman, Jake 138 - 139, 146, 153
High Forehead 20 - 21
Hinman, Eleanor 6, 33, 49, 55, 60, 136, 155
Hole-in-the-Wall battle 54 - 55
Hollow Horn Bear, Julia 122
Hollow Horn Bear, Julia   120
Holy Butte 187
holy men 14, 31
Holy Rock, Johnson 115
Holy Rosary Mission 84
Home Stake Gold Mines   111
Hook, Jason 33
Horseshoe Butte 225
Howard, H.P. 33
Howard, James 183
Hump 14, 21, 35 - 36
Hunkpapas 54
Hunkpatilia Crescent Moon 2
Hyde, George 158, 177, 179, 184

I

Ice 55
Ideal Creek 215
Itazichipo 2
          see also Without Bows

J

Jake Little Thunder 151
Janis, Antoine 71
Janis, Tom 71, 195, 197
Janovec, Bob 182
Jensen, Ben 116
Jensen, Jack 200
Jordan, Charles P. 177
Jumping Bull ranch 116

K

Kadlecek, David 120, 123, 125 - 126, 137, 231, 257

Kadlecek, Edward 120, 122
Kadlecek, Mabell 120
Kearney, Nebraska 26
Kelley, Edward 71
Kelly, John 71
Kelly, William F. 68 - 71
Kennington, Captain 70, 75 - 76
Kickapoo Nation 7
Kickapoo Reservation 148
Kid Wade 201, 203 - 204
Kopp, Dr. 220
Kotrous, James 200
Kuzelka, Robert 219

L

L. Frank Baum 7
Lake Creek 212
Lakota194, 210 - 212, 222, 231
Lakota Museum 163
Lakota Sioux 1 - 5, 7, 32 - 33, 37, 50 - 51, 56, 59, 81 - 83, 92, 102 - 103, 107 -
        109, 117 - 118, 122 - 123, 126 - 127, 129, 138, 141, 143, 146, 148 - 149,
        154, 158, 163 - 164, 167 - 172, 182, 186, 190, 194 - 197, 216, 218 - 219,
        222 - 224, 227, 229, 231, 232 - 235, 237, 242 - 244, 246
Lakota Standing Bear 212
Lakota, Julie 29
Lame Deer, Chief 215 - 216
Laramie River 229
Laravie 131
Larson, Daniel 41 - 42, 44, 46
Larvie, Nellie 226
Leader Charge, Louie Sr. 167
Leaper 64
Lee, Jesse M. 74, 131 - 132, 134, 138, 162, 180
Left Hand Nose 231
Lemly, Lieutenant 76
Leslie, Frank 134 - 135
Liska, Danny 101, 199, 201, 203 - 204
Little Beaver Creek 142
Little Big Man 56 - 57, 60, 64, 66, 70, 72, 74, 137, 148
Little Bighorn 37, 39, 41 - 43, 45, 47 - 48, 50 - 51, 192, 218, 237
Little Bighorn River 39, 45, 51

Little Hawk 16, 36
Little White River 163, 166, 170, 189
Little Wolf 55
Lodgepole Creek 55
Lone Bear 14, 35 - 36
Lone Eagle 141 - 143
Loup River 30
Lower Brulé, South Dakota 50
Loyal Brulés 64
Lucien, Auguste 21

M

MacDonald, Corporal 69 - 71
Maheo 232
Mails, Thomas 217, 232
Maine, Floyd 142
Maka Sica 146
Making Coffee 222
Man Afraid of His Horse 54
Mandan 47
McDonald, George 71
McGillycuddy, Dr. V.T. 6, 15, 56, 74 - 76
Means, Theodore 118
Medicine Man of the Oglala Sioux 28
Medicine Root Creek 151 - 152
Mentz, Tim 227
Merriville, Joe 72
Midwest Archeological Center 41 - 42
Mignery, David 30
Miles, General Nelson A. 49
Military Road 193
Milk, Bernice 216
Minneconjou 2, 12, 130, 135, 179
Mission, South Dakota 4, 158, 166, 173, 209, 225, 243
Mitchell, Edgar 44
Mlinar, Jerry 225
Moeser, Chancellor James 219
Monroe, Cynthia 69, 258
Moon, Glen 3
Mormon Campaign 70
Mormon Canal Bridge 91

Mormon Trail 193
Morreau River 162
Moves Camp, Richard 148 - 150, 246, 258
Moves Camp, Samuel 150
Mud Water River 189
Mulhair, Charles 182, 184, 192, 258
Murphy, Jon 71
Murphy, Michael 71
Musil, George 40
Musil, Marjorie 198, 258

N

Neihardt, John 50, 109 - 111, 143 - 144, 146
Nester, Kent 241
Nez Percé 58
Niobrara River 20, 22, 28, 35, 90 - 91, 136, 182, 189, 192 - 195, 199 - 201, 203, 222
Niobrara Valley 199, 201
No Flesh Creek 151
No Water 34, 54, 57, 60, 131, 146 - 148, 159 - 160, 166, 211
North Platte River 118

O

Oak Creek 235 - 236
Oglala 2, 7, 12 - 16, 19, 29, 32, 36, 54, 56, 72, 77, 84, 106, 109, 114, 136, 142 - 143, 146 - 148, 150, 155 - 156, 159, 163, 179, 186 - 188, 192, 207, 231
Oketo 193
Okute 227
         see also Teton Sioux
Old Bear 122
Old Hawk 56
Omaha Creek 167 - 168, 171
Omaha tribe camp 30
Omahas 30
One Star, Lloyd 164, 171, 258
Ooenunpa 2
Oregon Trail 20, 193, 238
Otoe 193
Ottah 132
Overland Stage route 193

P

Padden, Jon 3
Pahaska 153
        see also White Butte
Pahaska Butte 153
Palmer Horse Shoe   146
Pass Creek 217 - 218
Paul, Eli 69, 258
Pehin Hunska 65
Peltier, Leonard 114, 116 - 117, 238
Pennington, John 239
Pepper Creek 143 - 144, 146
Pepper Creek Valley 144
Pfeifer, Caroline 19 - 20, 22 - 23, 68, 258
Pichelville Bridge 90
Pine Ridge Agency 12, 151
Pine Ridge Indians 114, 154
Pine Ridge Reservation 6, 11, 23, 25, 47, 49, 62, 66, 71, 84, 95, 106 - 108, 113 - 114, 116, 138, 143 - 144, 146 - 148, 153 - 156, 158 - 159, 162, 190, 195, 197, 207, 209, 220, 222, 229
Pine Ridge Tribe 50
Pine Ridge, South Dakota 8, 106, 127, 142, 196 - 197, 207, 229
Piney Creek 35
Piyawiconi Oglala Lakota College   50
Plant Beside the Stream 2
        see also Minneconjou
Platte River 17, 20, 51, 100, 119, 151, 162
Ponca Agency 136, 170, 177, 179 - 180, 182, 187, 189, 192, 194, 207, 215, 237
Ponca Creek 163, 179, 201
Ponca Indians 91
Ponca Reservation 180, 182 - 183, 201
Ponca River 204
Ponca Valley 187
Pony Express route 193
Poppleton, Andrew 183
Porcupine Butte 12, 139, 208
Porcupine Creek 142, 208
Pourier, Batiste 14 - 15, 23 - 25, 74, 76, 106, 108, 138 - 139
Pourier, Little Bat 22 - 23
Pourier, Louise 142

Powder River 53, 55
Pretty Paint, Jo Jo 24
Pretty Voice Hawk 50
Provost, John 76

Q

Quick Bear Quiver, Ellen 8
Quiver, Harry 225

R

Rambow, Chuck 231 - 233
Rattle Blanket Woman 7 - 8, 243
Rattle Stone Woman 207, 213
Red Cloud 12, 33 - 34, 37, 49, 53 - 57, 60, 64 - 65, 69, 71, 84, 148, 158 - 159, 177, 180, 188 - 189, 191, 213
Red Cloud Agency 53, 55, 64, 71, 129, 136, 143, 152, 159, 180, 186, 189
Red Cloud Band 15 - 16, 62
Red Cloud Camp 14, 33, 49, 112
Red Feather 7, 58, 60, 148
Red Tail Hawk 223
Reiter, Sheila 241 - 242
Republican River 212
Respects Nothing, Woodrow 117 - 119, 142
Rock Bear, Sophie 84
Rock Creek 14
Roper, Max 3
Roper's Mortuary 3
Rosane, Darlene 47, 53, 75, 86, 155, 222, 234 - 235, 254, 259
Rosebud 48, 152 - 153, 162, 170, 174, 177, 191, 193, 207, 222, 234
Rosebud Agency 186, 189, 202
Rosebud Casino 116, 166 - 167, 169 - 170, 173, 220
Rosebud Creek 15, 122, 167, 170, 177, 179, 192, 201, 216
Rosebud Indians 152
Rosebud Reservation 6, 116, 120, 141, 143, 155, 158, 162 - 164, 167, 169, 170, 173, 175, 191, 193, 209, 215 - 216, 218, 222, 227, 237
Rosebud Sioux 187
Rosebud Timber Reserve 169
Rosebud, SD 163
Runnels, Jack 51, 150, 208 - 209, 259
Runnels, Victor 50 - 51, 150, 208 - 209, 259
Running Bear 191

Running Over Water 195
Russel, Jake 139
Russell, Dick 238

S

San Arcs 78
Sandhills 1, 21, 79, 99 - 100, 150, 163, 182, 209, 212, 244, 246
Sandoz, Mari 19, 33, 68 - 70, 72, 136, 141 - 143, 155, 167, 215, 250
Santee Reservation 2
Santee Sioux 4, 83, 99, 101
Santee Sioux Reservation 3, 24 - 25, 101 - 102
Scabby Creek 142, 163, 166 - 167
Scattering of the Ashes 2
        see also Oglala
Shaw, Amberson G. 6, 45, 59 - 60, 67, 201, 209
Shaw, Larry 209
Shaw, Ralph 209
Sheridan County Historical Society 135
Shirt Wearer 6, 34, 60, 166, 186
Short Buffalo 6 - 7, 49, 55
Shoshone 14, 36, 54, 231
Shumway, Grant 70 - 71
Shurz, Carl 179
Sichangu 2, 222
        see also Brule
Sihasapa 2
Simon Eagle 195
Sinte Gleska University 4, 173, 218, 234, 250, 255, 259
Sitting Bull 12 - 14, 36 - 37, 53 - 54, 59, 76 - 77, 188, 215
Slusarski, Mitch 210
Soldier Creek 166 - 167
South Dakota, Custer 87
Spencer, Dick 142 - 143
Spirit of the World 111
Spotted Horse Woman 212
Spotted Tail 53 - 54, 57, 60, 62, 129, 131, 136, 142, 158 - 159, 177, 179, 181 - 182, 184, 187, 201 - 202
Spotted Tail Agency 15, 74 - 75, 128 - 133, 136 - 137, 152, 159, 162, 180, 185, 188 - 189, 220, 237
Sprague, Donavan 35
Spring Creek 216, 222, 240

St. Joe Road 193
Standing Bear Bridge 182
Standing Bear, Chief Henry 51, 88, 183 - 184, 187 - 188, 208, 224
Standing Bear, Ellis 224
Standing Bear, Emily 222
Standing Bear, Luther 56, 142, 177, 187 - 192, 207 - 208, 224
Standing Bear, Willard 188
Standing Elk 191
Standing Rock 123, 209
Standing Rock Reservation 227
Standing Soldier 152
Star Not Afraid 24
State Brand Inspection Agency 70
Stetter, Johnnie 71
Stinking Bear 123 - 125, 127, 129
Stoney Butte 192 - 194
Stunz, Joe 116
Sun Dance 55, 66, 126, 140 - 141, 164, 170 - 171, 179, 195, 210 - 211, 233 - 234
Sweet Water 232
Swift Bear 131, 162 - 163, 167
Swift Bird, Joe 8, 229

T

Teton Sioux 141, 227
They Are Afraid Of Her 37
Three Stars 64
Thunder Cult 229
Thunder Hawk 120
tiyospaye 2, 156
Tongue River 54
Touch the Clouds 15, 76, 78, 131, 159
Treaty of Fort Laramie 183
Tree Grizzly Bears 72
Turner, Fredrick 156 - 157
Turning Bear 64 - 65, 67
Turtle Ribs 216
Two Boiling Kettles 2
        see also Ooenunpa
Two Moon 55

U

Union Pacific   30, 73, 209

V

Verdigre Creek 181, 199 - 200, 203, 245
Verdigre, Nebraska 17, 103, 109, 244
Vogelsburg, Raymond 175 - 176

W

Wagon Wheel Breakfast Club 193, 197
Walks, Everette 24
Wankan Tanka 191, 234
Warner, Jack 190
Warner, Steve 17, 190
Wasichus 31, 143
Water, Alex 164
West Beaver Creek 159
White Buffalo Calf Pipe 233 - 234
White Butte 64, 110 - 111, 139 - 141, 153
White Clay Creek 147, 158 - 160
White Deer 166
White Face, Thomas 122, 124
White Faun 142
White Ghost 5
White Hat 55, 62, 64 - 65
White Horse Creek 13 - 14, 106 - 107, 111 - 112, 118, 138 - 139, 141, 143 - 144,
      146 - 147, 150 - 152
White Horse Creek Valley 139
White Man 50
        see also John Conroy
White Rabbit 211
White River 15, 56, 129, 132, 138, 158 - 160, 177, 202, 215, 225 - 226, 236 -
      237
White River Valley 226
White Squirrel 151
White Woman One Butte 122
Wilson, Dick 114
Wind River 29
Without Bows 2
        see also Itazichipo

Wolf Creek 8
Woman Dress 60 - 61
Wooden Leg 166
Wooden Sword 64
Woodlock, Wallace 218
Workers Project Administration 193
Worm 8, 150, 211, 216, 222, 232
Wounded Horse, Jenny 117 - 118
Wounded Knee 1, 7, 11 - 13, 104, 106, 109, 112, 114, 116, 118, 147 - 148, 152,
    156, 159, 162, 187, 215, 222
Wounded Knee Creek 12 - 14, 16, 104, 106 - 107, 109, 112, 138 - 139, 141 - 142,
    159, 179, 207 - 208
Wounded Knee Creek Valley 28, 118
Wounded Knee Massacre 11, 106, 141, 156
Wounded Knee Valley 28 - 29, 31, 110

Y

Yankton Agency 189
Yankton Reservation 2
Yellow Hair 157
Yellow Medicine Creek 136, 177
Yellow Tail 47
Yellowstone 59
Yellowstone River 37, 53
Young Man Afraid 60, 72, 180
Young, Charmayne 164, 166 - 167, 260

Z

Ziolkowski, Korczak 88